The Sound of Tomorrow

The Sound of Tomorrow

How Electronic Music was Smuggled into the Mainstream

MARK BREND

B L O O M S B U R Y

NEW YORK • LONDON • NEW DELHI • SYDNEY

Bloomsbury Academic

An imprint of Bloomsbury Publishing Plc

175 Fifth Avenue	50 Bedford Square
New York	London
NY 10010	WC1B 3DP
USA	UK

www.bloomsbury.com

First published 2012

© Mark Brend, 2012

Library of Congress Cataloging-in-Publication Data

A catalog record for this book is available from the Library of Congress

ISBN: PB: 978-0-8264-2452-5

Typeset by Fakenham Prepress Solutions, Fakenham, Norfolk NR21 8NN
Printed and bound in the United States of America

Contents

Introduction vii

1   More music than they ever had before 1
2   I like music that explodes into space 29
3   The privilege of ignoring conventions 51
4   Out of the ordinary 73
5   Manhattan researchers 103
6   Because a fire was in my head 123
7   Moog men 151
8   White noise 173
9   It rhymes with vogue 195

Epilogue 213
Notes 225
Watch and listen 233
Sources 251
Acknowledgements 255
Index 257

Introduction

Some time in 1966 Paul McCartney knocked on the door of a house in Deodar Road, Putney, south London. He was there to meet Peter Zinovieff, who owned the house, and two colleagues, Delia Derbyshire and Brian Hodgson, both moonlighting from the BBC Radiophonic Workshop. Collectively Zinovieff, Derbyshire and Hodgson were Unit Delta Plus, a short-lived group dedicated to the promotion and creation of electronic music – not really a band or an organization, but somewhere in between.

During the meeting Zinovieff led McCartney through the house into the back garden, which stretched right down to the River Thames. On the left hand side of the garden, about halfway between the house and the river, a garden building, a large shed, was sunk about four feet into the ground. Zinovieff led McCartney across the garden and down a few steps, opening a door into a secret futuristic kingdom: the best-equipped electronic music studio in the country. The room was packed full of tape recorders, audio oscillators, mixers and, uniquely for a recording studio in Britain at the time, computers.

Not much came of this meeting. Despite later rumours that McCartney was considering an electronic backing for a new version of 'Yesterday', there would be no collaboration between him and Unit Delta Plus. What elevates this brief and apparently fruitless encounter above the status of historical footnote is its symbolic significance. It is a marker of something that was just starting to happen in rock music. At the time, The Beatles were at their commercial and creative peak, leaving behind live performance and Merseybeat for a more sophisticated, studio-bound rock music. A part of that transition involved exploring new directions, and a part of that exploration was investigating electronic and tape music. What McCartney was doing on that far-off day was taking part in a small but clearly identifiable trend in rock in general. A handful of musicians, from established performers to the barely known, were getting interested in integrating electronic music, or electronic sound in music, into rock.

Unit Delta Plus didn't last much more than a year and did little of note. It was broken apart by disagreements between Zinovieff on the one hand and Hodgson and Derbyshire on the other. Zinovieff was an independent inventor, composer and visionary technologist. He was interested in using computers to advance serious *avant-garde* electronic music. Hodgson and Derbyshire were different. Both had knowledge of and an interest in the serious end of electronic music, but much of their work for the BBC was by definition populist. They spent a lot of their time making music and sound for popular television and radio. That difference between Zinovieff and Hodgson and Derbyshire was a microcosm of a tension in electronic music at the time between the serious and the popular. McCartney might not have known it, but in approaching Unit Delta Plus he was approaching something that itself represented two parallel branches in the evolution of electronic music.

When McCartney reflected on this event three decades later in Barry Miles' biography *Paul McCartney: Many Years from Now* he remembered it as a meeting at the BBC Radiophonic Workshop. He recalled getting a number from the phone book and calling Delia Derbyshire. This slight confusion is understandable, and not just because of memory's imprecision. At the time the Radiophonic Workshop was the public face of British electronic music and Derbyshire its most visible member. What the episode demonstrates is that McCartney's awareness of electronic music at the time was shaped, in part at least, by the outpouring of themes, jingles, sound effects and incidental music from the Radiophonic Workshop. But he was also interested in serious electronic music, and in February 1966 had gone to hear the Italian composer Luciano Berio lecture on the subject.

There is a version of history that says that electronic music filtered down from the arid, imposing mountains of serious academic culture into the gentle foothills of pop music. This is the story of Pierre Schaeffer and Karlheinz Stockhausen, of the Paris and Cologne studios, of *musique concrète* and *Elektronische Musik* of Vladimir Ussachevsky and Otto Luening and the Columbia-Princeton Electronic Music Center. That McCartney, a pop musician, knew something about that sort of electronic music validates that version of history. But it is not the whole story. The contention of this book is that there is another history running alongside the emergence of serious electronic music. Right from the start of the twentieth century and the first performing electronic instruments there were people trying to make electronic music for the masses. When McCartney opened the phone book to look for the number of the BBC Radiophonic Workshop he was also validating that second history.

The distinction between serious and popular electronic music tends to get very blurred with even the most casual examination. Indeed, many advances in early electronic music came from the energy created by an overlap between the two. Even so, it seems self-evident that there is a difference in intent as you travel further in each direction from the dividing line. Pierre Schaeffer and Jean-Jacques Perrey, for example, were clearly not doing the same sort of thing, even if they were sometimes using similar means. There are two stories. The one about serious electronic music and its leading figures has been told well and often before. This book touches on it only briefly when it intersects with the second story. That second story is the story of popular electronic music, and that's the subject of this book. It's the story of Samuel Hoffman and Eric Siday; of the BBC Radiophonic Workshop and Manhattan Research; of television commercials and movie scores; of the Ondioline, the Clavioline, the Novachord; of electronics hobbyists and inspired amateurs.

We become acclimatized gradually to new sounds. Even in 1976 The Ramones' distillation of rock 'n' roll was too much for many, yet had Johnny Ramone fallen through a crack in time and come out Mosrite blazing in 1956 he most likely would have been locked up for life. As it was, by 1976 the distortion levels had been creeping up for years, creating a state of readiness for the great slab chords. So it was with electronic music. Early adopters encountered a strongly felt but vaguely defined technophobia from many quarters. The sounds of electronic music had never been heard before and they were met often with bewilderment, anxiety, even fear. As Bob Moog once said: 'Back then, anything that didn't come out of wood or a brass instrument or a string was considered somehow suspect at least ... people were very suspicious of electronic instruments producing musical sounds.'¹ Things have changed. These days a vast slice of popular music is electronic or partly electronic. It hardly makes sense to talk of electronic music as a genre, but rather of many types of music made electronically. The war is over, yet it was not won in a single battle, but rather through many skirmishes, land grabs and creeping advances. There was no tipping point, no dominant figure, no Waterloo, no Wellington. There was no revolution, but rather a gradual colonization. Or if it was a revolution it happened slowly, a succession of Trojan horses edging forward imperceptibly over years. This book argues that hundreds of science fiction movie soundtracks, washing machine adverts, children's television themes and radio jingles made electronic music palatable. Some of that music was entirely electronic, some of it partly electronic. The distinction isn't that important. The point is that all of it helped create the conditions for where we are now.

Another part of the story is that electronic music depends more on its equipment than most other forms of music. The art needs an apparatus; there is a symbiotic relationship. The development of the music cannot be separated from the emergence of new technologies and the invention of new instruments and techniques. But at this point there is the danger of a subtle deceit creeping in. A whole industry is predicated on the idea that acquiring the latest piece of electronic equipment will make you a more creative musician. It becomes tempting to ascribe an almost mystical power to the machines themselves, but without people to use them they are just electrical components, wires, circuits and switches. During the writing of this book Daphne Oram's Oramics system was displayed in a glass case at the Science Museum in London. If you just looked into that glass case it was like staring at a reliquary. There were fragments of a vision, but the spirit had left. You had to listen to the music, and look at the pictures and read the information about Oram herself for the machine to make sense, for the dried bones to come to life. Technological advance can suggest possibilities to musicians who are open to suggestion, but it is the musicians who do the creating. So, the story must be about how musicians interact with technology, and by extension the inventors of the technology as well. Nobody made everything possible with the flick of a switch. Rather, there was a series of technical brainstorms, pioneering musical experiments and commercial opportunism spread over decades, the combined efforts of musicians and composers, inventors and investors.

In the first six or so decades of the twentieth century electronic music often came couched in visionary terms. It was the music of the future, music without tradition, the soundtrack to a coming age where we'd all zip to work in jet cars. Nothing dates more rapidly than that sort of speculative fancy. Thaddeus Cahill's Telharmonium soon looked like a lumbering dinosaur. A theremin science fiction soundtrack of the 1950s became a kitsch period signifier by the 1960s. The revolutionary technique of tape splicing was dismissed as laborious and time wasting once synthesizers appeared. Yet now, decades on, hindsight reveals how all of these phases fitted together. They weren't freak events anchored in time, but steps into the future.

Mark Brend
Devon, England
March 2012

1

More music than
they ever had before

Electric dreams: 1900–50

'**B**e it known that I … have invented a new and useful Art of and Apparatus for Distributing Music Electrically.' So began an application submitted by Thaddeus Cahill to the United States Patent Office in April 1897. Cahill, born in Iowa in 1867, had graduated from the Columbian Law School in 1892 and was admitted to the bar in 1894, but his true love was electronics. Through the 1890s he worked on several schemes, producing an electric typewritor and nurturing a dream of making and distributing music electrically. The 1897 patent application was actually the second he submitted for his electric music, coming nearly two years after the first. The apparatus both applications describe would, when constructed, become known as the Telharmonium, the first publicly performing electronic musical instrument. 'The apparatus', Cahill said 'is wholly electrical and bears little, if any, real likeness to the instruments now known as … pianofortes and organs.' It was a fair claim. Although the Telharmonium was controlled by an organ-style multiple manual keyboard, any resemblance ended there. Rather, Cahill's invention realized a new concept in music, harnessing the power of electrical circuits to generate and distribute a type of musical sound that had never been heard before.

By the time Cahill submitted his patent applications, electricity was a part of life in the great urban centres of America. The first street mains were installed in New York in 1881, the same year that the world's first public electricity supply lit the streets of Godalming, Surrey, in England. The following year September Thomas Edison's Edison Electric Company opened a generating station in Pearl Street, Lower Manhattan, and within a year had more than 500 customers. In May 1883 the Brooklyn Bridge opened, illuminated by 70 arc lamps operated by the United States Illuminating Company, one of many new traders in power springing up in New York. By 1900, there were over 30 companies generating and distributing electricity throughout the boroughs of New York City and in Westchester County.

Running parallel to the emergence of electricity as a force to power not just light, but also transport, domestic conveniences and industry, was the introduction of the telephone. The first telephone exchange opened in Hartford, Connecticut in 1877. The first exchange outside of the United States was built in London in 1879. The history of the telephone is complex and much disputed, with several inventors – Antonio Meucci, Philip Reis, Elisha Gray and Alexander Graham Bell – having what appear to be legitimate grounds for claiming the idea as their own. What happened is what often happens, which is that several people had similar ideas at more or less the same time. It is a phenomenon that surfaces often throughout the history of electronic music. Another is the creative use of technological advances to push forward the music. Indeed, the Telharmonium, the first major event in electronic music, the first performing electronic instrument, fused the then-novel power of electricity *and* the voice of the telephone.

Cahill's technology started with the observation that dynamos generating alternating current create a steady pitch. He imagined a whole series of dynamos, each creating different notes, that could be switched on and off in selected orders, thus creating predetermined combinations of pitches – or in other words, music. There was another aspect to Cahill's prescient dream. The sounds, he found, could be transmitted down a telephone line and heard through the receiver at the other end, wherever it was. Not only would the notes be created by electrical means, but they would be broadcast down the telephone lines. This is where the commercial possibilities became apparent. If you wanted to avail yourself of this miraculous new service you would have to become a paying subscriber. Cahill planned to stream live electronic music into restaurants, theatres and private homes.

After his patent was granted in 1898, Cahill spent three years creating a prototype instrument. Then, with the support of a backer, Oscar T. Crosby, he set about raising further funds by demonstrating this to potential supporters. At the first demonstration, in Baltimore, assembled businessmen and notables gathered around large cones attached to telephone receivers and heard a fluting, whistling rendition of Handel's 'Largo', brought to them by telephone lines from the prototype Telharmonium many miles away in Cahill's Washington workshop. Crosby formed the New England Electric Music Company, raising sufficient funds to construct a more complex and much larger version of the instrument, which weighed in at 200 tons.[2]

In 1906 the Telharmonium was dismantled, packed into crates and transported to New York City. It was installed in the Broadway building at Broadway and 39th Street, the control console at ground level, and the monstrous machinery hidden in the basement. The New York Telephone Company laid special lines throughout the city – a network of underground channels to spread the machine's voice – while speakers were installed in the building itself. On 26 September 1906 the first Telharmonium concert took place. Immediately, it was clear that Cahill was aiming at a mass market. The Telharmonium concerts combined popular orchestral and opera selections with ragtime. This was, above all else, a commercial venture. Many up-market restaurants and hotels of the time employed small orchestras to serenade diners, made up of sometimes twenty or more well-paid musicians. To such as these, the Telharmonium was a direct challenge.

Very soon, the magic music of the Telharmonium was the talk of New York. In December that year *The New York Times* ran an illustrated feature, the first of several, describing Cahill's invention in some detail. Telharmonium music was being broadcast to select subscribers – at that stage, a few local restaurants – at the 'luncheon hour' (12.30pm to 2pm) and at dinner (6pm to 8pm). Within a month private customers would have special telephone lines installed that would be a conduit for electronic music at 20 cents an hour, opened or closed with a flick of a switch – as simple as turning on electric light.[3]

For public spaces several strategically placed receivers with speaker cones were used to generate sufficient volume to be heard above the chatter of diners and the clink of cutlery and glasses. Alternatively, listeners could go to the Telharmonium music room at Broadway House, decked out like a hotel lounge with chairs and potted plants, to hear the music at source. Here you could see performers seated at what looked like a massive organ console, depressing keys that gave off a faint click and the occasional blue spark, while from an artfully arranged flower display the sound itself emerged from a concealed horn. Beneath that public space, buried in the basement, was the Telharmonium's beating heart – 200 hundred tons of cables and dynamos. These inner workings had to be kept apart from the performance room not only on account of their size, but also because they made as much noise as the machine room of a factory, and would have drowned out the music they were generating.

Among the visitors was an aged Mark Twain. He was bewitched, declaring that he would have to postpone his death until he had the chance to hear the new wonder again and again. Twain was a technology enthusiast, an 'early adopter' in today's language, who had a telephone installed in 1877 when he lived in Hartford. Within days he became the first domestic Telharmonium subscriber. As 1906 drew to a close he greeted the New Year with a few friends at his home, grouped around a cone speaker attached to a telephone receiver. The assembly listened to what Twain called his 'electric music factory', the Telharmonium, play 'Auld Lang Syne'. One account reported that:

> the first thing he did in 1907 was to glory in the fact that he should be able to rejoice over other dead people when he died in having been the first man to have Telharmonium music turned on in his house – 'like gas'.[4]

News of this episode crossed the Atlantic, with *The Guardian* reporting a day later that 'the room vibrated with chiming bells'.[5]

In January 1907 another *New York Times* story contained what might well be the first printed expression of an enduring prejudice about electronic music. In this story – which does not have the ring of strictly factual reporting – a pair of Sicilian buskers with a hurdy gurdy pitched their stall near the Broadway home of the Telharmonium, only to be drowned out by the rumblings of what sounded like 'a great cathedral organ'. The buskers realized that they had no hope of competing with this music, 'although theirs had the merit of being real'. The piece goes on to describe listeners' 'wonderment' at the 'electric music' conveyed by the 'air itself'. It also remarks on the instrument's ability to replicate flute, piccolo, bassoon, clarinet and saxophone sounds, combining them into a 'melodious organ effect'.[6] This echoed another report published earlier that same year, which breathlessly announced that:

> in the new art of telharmony we have the latest gift of electricity to civilization, an art which, while abolishing every musical instrument, from the jew's-harp to the 'cello, gives everybody cheaply, and everywhere, more music than they ever had before.[7]

These claims have a familiar ring. Indeed, many recurring themes of electronic music history start with the Telharmonium story. The idea that electronics could replace traditional instruments is a refrain that repeats to this day, and one we will encounter throughout this book. It marks a divide between conservatives who think this is a bad thing – that electronic music isn't real music, and real musicians will be out of their jobs – and enthusiasts, often of a radical bent, who relish the overturning of old orthodoxies and see in electronic music the possibility of democratization of the artistic process. The phrase 'gives everybody cheaply, and everywhere, more music than they ever had before' has something of the socialist rallying cry about it. There are also, in many of these early reports, strains of a sort of quasi-mysticism. This is curious and paradoxical, the juxtaposition of the music of technological advance with the otherworldly and the unknown. All the talk of wonderment, of gifts to civilization and of sounds being conjured out of thin air is redolent of the language of spiritualism, then at a peak of popularity and attempting to shape itself as a formal religion. This sort of language is often heard in the early decades of electronic music, not only from commentators, but inventors, composers and musicians too. Indeed, many figures in early electronic music, inventors and performers, had occult leanings.

And then, going right back to Cahill's patent application, there is the symbiotic relationship between creativity and technology – the *art* and the *apparatus*. Electronic music is only a dream or a theory until the apparatus exists to make it real. It evolves through inter-action between technology and creativity, to the extent that any understanding of it must include the contributions not only of composers and performers, but also of inventors and technicians. This was particularly true in the first half of the twentieth century and explains why many of the most influential figures in early electronic music – Leon Theremin and Maurice Martenot, for example – were both musicians and inventors. Inventors made instruments that created entirely novel sounds, which then suggested possibilities to composers and musicians. Meanwhile, composers and musicians influenced the inventors to make instruments both practical and useful.

There is a tantalizing poignancy about the accounts of the Telharmonium, because they describe something irretrievably lost. We can never hear this electric music, never share the wonderment. The great Telharmonium experiment failed to transcended novelty status and was beset by difficulties. The broadcasts from Broadway House stopped in February 1908, and although Cahill pressed on, building a third Telharmonium that played from another building for a short while in 1910, the venture was soon mired in debt. The visionary scheme was years ahead of the available technology. Cahill's monster was greedy for electricity, and when it played there were power surges and interference on the telephone network, with telephone conversations interrupted by the beast's incongru-ously sweet and ghostly murmurs. Cahill's company was bankrupt by the end of 1914, and eventually his instruments were broken up and sold for scrap. Today, all that is left of the Telharmonium are a few grainy photos and those contemporaneous accounts. After the Telharmonium failed Cahill drifted into obscurity. He died suddenly of a heart attack in 1934 at the age of 66.

If Cahill's venture was populist and commercial, much of the early impetus for electronic music came from the *avant-garde* intellectual fringes. In 1907, a year after the Telharmonium started broadcasting, Italian composer, writer, teacher and conductor Ferruccio Busoni published his *Sketch of a New Esthetic of Music*, which aligned electrical sound sources with the future of music by referencing Cahill's Telharmonium. Then, just as the Telharmonium was in its death throes, the Italian Futurist painter and composer Luigi Russolo was writing his manifesto *The Art of Noises* (1913). In it he proposed that the industrial urban environment had brought with it a new sound world that required a musical response. Traditional forms of music making had too limited a sonic palette, and composers must open themselves up to using the infinite possibilities of sound, and as technology advanced, machines would be created to make these new noises in the musical context.

These were prophetic texts, which would influence a number of later composers and theorists who helped shaped early electronic music, including Edgard Varèse and Pierre Schaeffer. But the Telharmonium aside, there was no way of making electronic music at the time. And it, that great dinosaur of electronic music, would soon be extinct. The art needed the apparatus, and an invention that coincided with the Telharmonium's debut would bring closer the possibility of making that apparatus more widely available. In 1906 Lee de Forest invented the audion electronic amplifying vacuum tube, a forerunner of the triode. Tubes (valves) allowed for the processing, amplification or creation of electronic signals in compact form, revolutionizing the development of electronics, and, by extension, electronic music.

Even if the problem of interference on telephone lines had been solved, the Telharmonium would have failed. It was too big and too expensive: figures of 200 tons and $200,000 feature in early descriptions. It was not an instrument that lent itself to duplication, let alone commercial production. If electronic music were to develop there had to be instruments that were affordable, portable and easily reproducible. The first of these came a few years after the demise of the Telharmonium.

Invented around 1919, the theremin was compact and simple and could be run off a domestic electric supply. Of all the early twentieth-century electronic instruments it is the only one to remain in production. Indeed, over the past two decades it has enjoyed a renewed surge of popularity that shows no sign of abating. At first glance, though, it didn't look like a good bet for long-term survival. A monophonic tone generator with no recognizable controlling mechanism and no features to relate it to any other instrument (no keyboard, no pedals, no valves, no fingerboard, no strings, no reeds), it is devilishly hard to play. Yet its very strangeness has proved to be its strength. It has an elusive, hard-to-pin-down quality, its wobbly tones resisting the geometric structure of neat tonal steps, its relationship to conventional Western music something like that of glossolalia to ordinary speech. It conforms to the tendency amongst early electronic music pioneers to see their endeavours in a mystical light. It sounds like a sound from somewhere else, and it is no surprise that it would be later taken up to soundtrack the imagined other worlds of science fiction.

Lev Sergeyevich Termen was an electrical engineer, cellist and astronomer, born in St Petersburg in 1896. In his remarkable life he lived through the twentieth century's great convulsions, from the Russian revolution through two World Wars to the falling of the Iron Curtain. He also designed the theremin, initially called either the thereminvox or ethervox or etherphone, which derives its name from an anglicization of his: Leon Theremin. He invented the instrument almost by accident.

In 1919, after the turmoil of the Russian revolution, Theremin found himself, along with many other Russian scientists, working in a State-sponsored laboratory. He was fascinated by the human body's capacitance – its ability to store a small electric charge – and how that could exert an influence on an electrical circuit if a person was standing close to it. From this observation he developed an electrical burglar alarm, a 'radio watchman', which was triggered when a body moved into a field around an electrical device. He then adapted this radio watchman for use in another project for measuring changes in gases under varying temperatures and pressures. During this he noticed that hand movements in the proximity of the circuitry changed the pitch of a sound generated by an oscillator, and from this the idea of the theremin, or etherphone as Theremin first called it, was born. Theremin spent some months developing and perfecting the concept. To increase the instrument's range he adopted the heterodyning (beating together) principle, in which two inaudible sound waves at different frequencies combine to create another audible frequency. He experimented with the idea of a foot pedal to control volume, and switches too, before alighting on the now-familiar two antennae system. With this, the instrument is played by hand movements in the proximity of the antennae, changing the electro-magnetic fields around them, which in turn controls the oscillators that produce the sound waves. The right-hand antenna is usually a straight vertical aerial controlling pitch, while the left a horizontal loop controlling volume.

It is this, the manner in which it is played, that gives the theremin much of its enduring power to entrance. To coax sound from what looks like a radio, the performer must not touch it at all, but rather move his or her hands around it, as if speaking to it in some obscure sign language. To anyone unfamiliar with the technology it appears miraculous and strange. The performer is a conjuror creating sound from thin air, or a musical spiritualist summoning ghostly voices from the other side. Film exists of Theremin himself demonstrating the instrument in London in 1927. We see his left hand hovering over the volume hoop like a puppet master's pulling at invisible strings, his right held up in a controlled trembling to make vibrato, like a man struggling to hold back a force he can barely control.

Paradoxically, this entrancing, intriguing aspect of the theremin was also an obstacle to its success. They are limited instruments – monophonic, and generally with a range of up to five octaves – and although in skilled hands the still electronic tone can approximate a bowed stringed instrument like a violin, or a soprano voice, this is a hard skill to attain. In unskilled hands the theremin sounds like malfunctioning radio equipment or the aural squiggles of a child randomly turning the pitch control dial of a test oscillator. All other instruments require some degree of physical sensitivity in a combination of the performer's hands, mouth and feet, an acquired knowledge of how minute bodily movements affect the sound coming from your instrument. For thereminists, minute bodily movements do affect your sound, but you have to do without the tactile and visual cues common to other instruments. Indeed, the reason why thereminists stand rigid before their instruments when performing is because unintentional body movements could change the pitch or volume. Playing the simplest of tunes is a great challenge. Moving your hand to and from the pitch aerial produces a continuous rising or falling portamento. To play a melody line of distinct notes, each with a beginning and end, the volume must be cut or reduced with the left hand at the end of one note, while the right hand is moved to the next note, at which point the volume is increased again. And that's only half the story. To ensure that the notes are pitched correctly requires ongoing judgement, combining listening to the pitch of the note you are making, and remembering how close your hand needs to be to the aerial to produce, say, a C note. To master this technique, perfect pitch and highly developed fine motor skills are necessary.

In 1922 Theremin was summoned to the Kremlin to demonstrate his invention to Lenin. The Soviet leader, who had in 1920 declared that 'Communism is Soviet power plus the electrification of the entire country', was impressed, and saw in the theremin a propaganda tool for his drive for progress. From 1925 onwards Theremin promoted the new wonder instrument internationally, as an example of Soviet ingenuity. He made high-profile appearances in Berlin, Paris and London, and by the time the liner he was travelling on docked at Ellis Island in December 1927 he was famous enough to warrant the attentions of many journalists, eager to meet the man who could conjure sounds out of thin air. A planned three-month stay extended to eleven years, until his abrupt and mysterious departure in 1938.

Theremin applied for a US patent for his invention in 1925, which was granted in 1928. The very first paragraph of the patent establishes a factor that would help ensure the instrument's survival: it is described as simple and inexpensive. The possibility existed for mass production, and in 1929 RCA Victor secured a licence to produce theremins commercially. This led to a production run of about 500, actually manufactured by General Electric and Westinghouse, but branded as RCA instruments. These were tube (valve) instruments with the electronics housed in a large, dark wood cabinet set on legs, which looked, appropriately, something like a radio of the period. In 1929 they were demonstrated in department stores in several major cities across America and attracted interest, but the time was not right. Although the technology inside them was simple, RCA theremins ended up expensive luxury items priced at about $230, and they went on sale around the time of the Wall Street crash of 1929 that precipitated the Great Depression. No more were built after that initial 500, but even so, the RCA theremin marks an important point in history as the first time an electronic musical instrument was available for sale to the general public. Theremin the man and theremin the musical instrument were acclaimed throughout the thirties, bolstered by the tireless proselytizing of

Clara Rockmore, the theremin's greatest virtuoso. She had given advice from a performer's perspective when Theremin was developing the instrument for commercial production, and through the decade toured a classical theremin repertoire, often sharing a bill with Paul Robeson.

Born Clara Reisenberg in what is now Lithuania in 1911, Rockmore was a violin child prodigy. She moved to New York in the 1920s, to continue her study of the instrument, but after a few years she began to have muscular and joint problems, probably caused by childhood malnutrition, which ended her career prematurely. At about this time she met Theremin, who had arrived in New York in 1927. Fascinated by his invention, Rockmore became his student and friend, and an important person in the theremin's early life. She developed a technique for playing the instrument, based on a fingering system, which enabled her to avoid the tendency towards portamento common to all lesser players.

Theremin shared with many subsequent electronic instrument inventors the hope that his instrument would be taken up by the classical music establishment. For a while it looked like it would be. The first composition to use the instrument was Pashchenko's *Symphonic Mystery, For Theremin and Orchestra* (1924), and others followed, written by composers such as Percy Grainger and Bohuslav Martinu. But the revolution never happened, and as the 1930s wore on you were as likely to hear a theremin in a music hall novelty act as at a concert. In Britain, for example, a performer named Joseph Whiteley toured the halls for many years under the name of Musaire, billing himself, inaccurately, as Europe's only thereminist.

In 1928, the year that Theremin patented his instrument in New York, a Frenchman named Maurice Martenot unveiled his own electronic instrument in Paris. Born in 1898, Martenot was a polymath, not only an inventor, but also a cellist, an educationalist and an author. During World War I he had served as a radio operator in the French Army and had observed that electrical equipment could sometimes create audible tones of varying pitch. When the war was over he set about finding a way to harness this phenomenon for musical purposes, a quest which culminated in the launch of what was first called the Ondes Musicales (musical waves) and later the Ondes Martenot (Martenot's waves).

Martenot commissioned Dimitri Levindis to compose a work for his new invention, *Symphonic Poem for Solo Ondes Musicales and Orchestra*. This was the vehicle he used to launch the Ondes Martenot at a concert in Paris, though that early version of the instrument was quite different from the one that later went into limited production, as was another prototype he took on a demonstration tour of America in late 1930 and early 1931. Both, though, had mechanisms that pre-empted the mature instrument's most prominent feature, which allowed the performer to produce theremin-like portamentos, but with more control. The first production model, which dates from 1932, featured two ways of pitching notes: a ribbon controller for portamentos and a conventional piano-style keyboard. A newsreel film from 1934 features Martenot himself demonstrating both 'a real musical instrument without string or wind … it's not necessary to touch the keyboard [demonstrates ribbon controller] but if you like you can play on the key [plays keyboard]'.[8]

Martenot's arrival in America on 4 December 1930, disembarking from the liner *Paris* after a stormy end to his journey, attracted a wave of newspaper coverage that continued as his tour proceeded into the following year. A few weeks into the visit, on 6 January 1931, WABC made the first radio broadcast of a concert featuring Martenot performing with an orchestra. The programme included a rendition of 'Anita's Dance' from *Peer Gynt Suite No. 1* (Grieg). A *New York Times* preview of the event used language that could have been lifted straight from its coverage of the Telharmonium 25 years earlier. Here was 'the musical instrument of the future' with the ability to 'mimic almost every known instrument in an orchestra'.[9] But Martenot himself reported in another story in the same newspaper '… that his primary aim is not to imitate the sounds of other instruments, but to provide new resources of expression for composers and novel color effects to enrich the orchestral palette'.[10]

The press also compared Martenot's instrument with the theremin. In 1928 *The Guardian* considered that Martenot had 'decidedly improved upon the invention which Professor Leo Theremin introduced here last December'.[11] Although the heterodyne sound production technology Martenot used is the same as in the theremin, and both instruments excel at sweeping portamentos, they have little in common beyond that. The Ondes Martenot has a host of expression controls and up to four different speakers, which combine to give a much broader sonic palette and greater interaction between the player and instrument. It is these features that set the Martenot apart from other early electronic instruments of the time, and which continue to attract composers and performers even now.

An Ondist, as Martenot performers are known, has two options for sounding notes. First is the conventional piano-style keyboard, which is usually seven octaves, although as instruments were hand-built to order this can vary. This is fixed by adjustable screws which, when loosened, allow the keyboard itself some lateral movement. The Ondist can then produce vibrato by moving their finger from side to side while depressing a key. The other way to pitch notes is a ribbon in front of the keyboard. The Ondist operates this by inserting his or her index finger into a metal ring in the middle of the ribbon and sliding up and down the octaves. A row of indentations (for white notes) and small brass protrusions (for black notes) between the ribbon and keyboard mark out semitones, giving a tactile reference point for the performer. This feature allows for the range of swoops, inflexions, portamento and microtones so characteristic of the theremin, but with more accurate pitching

As the Martenot is a monophonic instrument the performer uses his or her right hand only to select notes, regardless of whether he or she is using the keyboard or the ribbon. This leaves the left free to control dynamics and timbre using a selection of controls to the left of the keyboard, which are housed in a tray that slides in and out of the body of the instrument. These include a peculiar spongy touch-sensitive carbon filled bag – called a 'lozenge' – that controls timbre. There is also a knee lever to control volume and two foot-controlled pedals (mute and intensity) which give further dynamic control.

The Martenot keyboard unit, which houses the sound producing electronics, is connected to as many as four speakers, or diffusers, selected using buttons on the left-hand control panel. One of these is an ordinary loud speaker. The other three are unique to Martenot's instrument, their distinct sound characteristics combining the electronic tone with acoustic treatments. The *metallique* is a standard speaker with the cone replaced with something resembling a cymbal, which produces a crash like a gong. The most visually striking is the *palme*, which looks something like a psaltery or zither.

Its body is a sound box fitted with a total of 24 guitar-like strings, 12 on each side. These resonate in sympathy when an electronic signal is sent to the speaker. The *resonance,* a reverb chamber, is not always fitted.

If Martenot considered his instrument a new voice for the orchestra, he went some small way to achieving this aim. Many symphonic works, operas and ballets were composed for the Ondes Martenot in the middle decades of the twentieth century, the most famous being Olivier Messiaen's *Turangalîla Symphony* (1948). But Martenot's high aspirations would ultimately limit the appeal of what remains a remarkable instrument. Production continued into the 1980s and Martenot updated the instrument in the 1960s to embrace solid-state technology, but it was always a specialist instrument, made to order by hand. They were intended as instruments for the musical elite, and by and large that is what they still are. Even so, Martenot himself wasn't above doing what amounted to a novelty turn to promote his invention. At a demonstration for the BBC in 1947 he followed a musical selection with impersonations of 'a day-old chick, a nightingale, a mosquito, a blue-bottle, a gale-wind, a bomber and a machine gun'.[12] Martenots survive in limited numbers, like a rare breed extinct in the wild, living on in the controlled conditions of a zoo.

The instruments are used almost exclusively by orchestras for performances of the limited Ondes Martenot repertoire, though Jonny Greenwood has a very late model that he has used on several Radiohead recordings.

At about the same time that Maurice Martenot was introducing the Ondes Martenot to the world, in Berlin, at the Musikhochschule's music and radio lab, the Rundfunkversuchstelle, Friedrich Trautwein was developing his own instrument. Like Theremin and Martenot before him, he gave his invention a self-referential name – the Trautonium. Like the Ondes Martenot, it is touch-sensitive, played by pressing a resistor wire over a metal plate marked with a chromatic scale. Expressive performance is possible by using small finger movements to create vibrato and by applying different degrees of pressure to the wire to make changes in volume. A foot pedal controls overall volume. Telefunken marketed about 100 Trautoniums from 1932–35 and the instrument attracted the attention of German composer Paul Hindemith, who wrote several short pieces for three Trautoniums. Oskar Sala, who joined Trautwein in the early 1930s, continued to develop the instrument and perform with it until his death in 2002. Sala created the Mixtur-Trautonium, adding various filters and subharmonic oscillators, and a second manual. It was Sala, using a Mixtur-Trautonium, who was responsible for the instrument's one big appearance in popular culture – making the bird-like effects soundtrack that usurps a conventional musical score in Alfred Hitchcock's *The Birds* (1963).

The various electric organs produced by Hammond were only part of the company's contribution to the evolution of electronic musical instruments. In 1939 it introduced the Novachord. Unlike the electro-mechanical organs, the Novachord was purely electronic, marshalling sound from an army of vacuum tubes. The Novachord was famously hard to master, requiring a technique that neither organist nor pianist could readily adapt to. It was also big and heavy, weighing in at 500 pounds. Its wood cabinet, over four feet wide, three feet deep and more than three feet high, housed a full-size piano-type keyboard, four foot pedals and numerous Bakelite controls in a strip inset above the keyboard. It looked like a cross between a grand piano and a harmonium. Polyphonic, with twelve oscillators which gave a six-octave range through the use of frequency-dividing tubes, the Novachord could muster up a range of passable string and organ like sounds, all characteristically indistinct in outline, as if the sound blurs into silence at the edges.

The Novachord was launched at the 1939–40 New York World's Fair, which sprawled over 1,216 acres of Flushing Meadows–Corona Park. The fair was designed to allow visitors a glimpse into 'the world of tomorrow', a world, it seemed, in which the dreamy electronic music of the Novachord would be the soundtrack. A short film called *New Horizons* featured a Novachord score, while on the Ford stand popular composer, conductor and arranger Ferde Grofé performed daily with the New World Ensemble, consisting of one Hammond organ and four Novachords, all white. The World's Fair aside, Hammond put considerable effort into promoting the Novachord. There were many magazine adverts, and an audacious celebrity endorsement coup was pulled off when the company gave the first production model to President Roosevelt for his birthday. Despite this, the instrument was not a big commercial success. Production stopped in 1942, with just over 1,000 made. Most of these were sold in America, but at least one made it across the Atlantic to the BBC. From 1940 the instrument was played by Arthur Young, featuring on many of Vera Lynn's wartime morale boosters, including 'We'll Meet Again'. Difficulties in obtaining parts in wartime was cited as a reason for suspending production, but a cost of somewhere close to $2,000 would have put the Novachord way out of the reach of most people. There was talk of production starting again once war had finished, but this never happened.

History seems uncertain what to do with the Novachord. Often described, with some justification, as the world's first polyphonic synthesizer, it is also dismissed as a failure on account of its limited production run. Actually, it was often used and very widely heard in popular music for decades after production ended, sometimes in very unlikely settings. Paul Beaver, of Beaver and Krause, had assembled a collection of Novachords and other electronic instruments in the 1950s and used them to provide often-uncredited music and effects for movies throughout the 1950s and 1960s. But perhaps its biggest legacy was the technology it bequeathed to another Hammond offering, which in turn influenced a series of small mass-produced electronic instruments from other manufacturers.

One of the designers working on the Novachord project was John Hanert. He was also responsible for another pioneering Hammond product; a smaller, simpler instrument that derived some technology from the Novachord, but which would have a longer life and a lasting legacy.

The Hammond Solovox was the first of several instruments that are sometimes described as piano attachments, which were very popular in light entertainment music through to the 1960s. Although now overlooked, they are significant as the first truly mass-produced electronic instruments, which brought, for the first time, electronic music within reach of the not only jobbing musicians, but also the home, the school, the restaurant, the pub and the church.

The first Solovox, the Model J, appeared in 1940, a year after the launch of the Novachord. Production was suspended a year later when industrial resources were diverted to the war effort, but started again after the war with the revised Model K, produced from

1946 to 1948. A final version, the Model L, was made from 1948 to 1950.[13]

The Solovox used some similar technology to the Novachord, but Hanert always intended it as an entirely new concept: a solo voice for playing melodies, which would be attached to a piano (usually, sometimes an organ). To realize this idea Hanert designed a small monophonic electronic keyboard with its own separate 'tone cabinet', an amplifier and speaker combo. The Solovox keyboard, with its big rocker switches and small keys, looked something like an accordion. This style persisted through all subsequent piano attachments. The keyboard was designed to fit immediately beneath a piano keyboard, using special metal brackets. The idea was that performers would pick out melodies on the Solovox with their right hand, while using their left hand free to play a chordal accompaniment on the piano or organ. The amplifier and speaker, a slim line rectangular wooden cabinet with a curved front designed to stand on the floor, was generally fitted, using small chains and hooks, either to the side or underneath the piano. As the owners' manual put it: 'The beautiful sustained tones of the Solovox blend in thrilling fashion with the percussion tones of your piano, greatly enriching even the simplest music.'[14]

The Solovox's three-octave keyboard housed the sound-generating technology and beneath the keyboard a number of rocker switches selected sounds. In the Model L, for example, there were twelve switches, divided into three groups: the first was called register controls (bass, tenor, contralto, soprano); the second tone controls (deep tone, full tone, first voice, second voice, brilliant); the third was untitled and consisted of mute, fast attack and vibrato off. A knee-operated volume lever and tuning controls were also fitted. One or more of both the register controls and tone controls had to be switched on to get a sound from the Solovox. As with the Novachord, the Solovox was designed to make its own unique noise – what the owner's manual called simply 'interesting combinations' – as well as impersonate existing instruments.

Hammond's Solovox, its electric organs and even its Novachord mark an important point in the development of electronic music making. In contrast to Theremin, Martenot and Trautwein, who imagined that their instruments would revolutionize serious classical music, Hammond was targeting popular music from the start. The company wanted to mass-produce its instruments for home, school and church, for popular radio and cinema.

Frenchman Georges Jenny, working contemporaneously, was aiming at the same market. Jenny (born circa 1900) first conceived of his Ondioline sometime around 1938, having assessed what he considered the Ondes Martenots' strengths and weaknesses. He developed the instrument while recovering from tuberculosis in a sanatorium during the war and put it into production in the late 1940s.

For nearly 30 years, until his death in 1976, Jenny continued to refine the instrument. He never licensed the Ondioline for mass production, preferring instead to produce completed instruments in limited numbers or sell them as kits. Initially he built all instruments himself from scratch, but as demand grew he set up a small factory about 100 miles from Paris, where he employed about 20 wheelchair-using staff members. Jenny had suffered from polio earlier in his life and would later use a wheelchair himself. Jean-Jacques Perrey, who gave up studying medicine to become an Ondioline salesman and who became the public face of the instrument, reckons about 700 in total were produced, sold mainly in France and the USA. It is thought that fewer than two dozen survive today.

In its original form, the Ondioline was a monophonic vacuum tube keyboard instrument housed in wooden cabinets with a dash of art deco styling. Like the Solovox, there were two parts: the keyboard unit and the amplifier/speaker combination. The amplifier/speaker cabinet stood about three feet high and housed a single nine-inch speaker, a small amplifier and the Ondioline's sound controls. The small three-octave keyboard was designed to sit on top of the cabinet or on a stand of its own.

The Ondioline keyboard is mounted on leaf springs, which allows for playing a note and simultaneously moving the key from side to side, which gives vibrato. This is the instrument's most obvious debt to the Ondes Martenot. In front of the keyboard is a flat metal braid mounted on a brass plate, which runs the entire width of the keyboard. This is not a ribbon controller for pitch, like the Martenot's. Rather, it produces percussive noises. The keyboard also has a volume knee lever for expression.

Ondiolines produced a range of sounds far broader than the Solovox and other early electronic keyboards that appeared about the same time, but they were hindered by unreliability. Wanting to keep costs down, Jenny often used poor-quality components, which meant that unless carefully maintained the instruments often failed after a few years. Had this not been the case, the instrument might have been more successful, as the Ondioline's filter controls can be used in many combinations. They produce a wide range of tones unique to the Ondioline, as well as others that mimic conventional instruments rather well. German newsreel footage from 1948 shows Jenny, a thin, bespectacled man, showing off his invention's capacity for mimicry. He sits at the Lilliputian keyboard faced by a saxophonist, a violinist and a banjo player. Each of the musicians starts a tune that Jenny then picks up, the Ondioline's filters set to reproduce the appropriate timbre. The idea was that you wouldn't be able to hear the join, and you almost couldn't. In America in particular Ondiolines would later attract media attention on account of similar stunts performed by Perrey.

The Solovox was popular in America in the 1940s and 1950s, although not widely exported, but it was soon eclipsed in its homeland by other piano attachment instruments, made in Europe, which were both more portable and versatile. The most successful and best remembered of these is the Clavioline, designed by Constant Martin (1910–95) of Versailles, France, in 1947. Trained as an electrical engineer and radio technician, Martin experimented with electronic music in the 1930s, launching the Clavioline at about the same time that Jenny launched the Ondioline.[15]

The Clavioline resembled both the Solovox and the Ondioline, with a monophonic sound-producing keyboard with a separate amplifier/speaker combination and a knee-operated volume control for expression. Its great advantage, though, over both the Ondioline and the Solovox, is that the Clavioline keyboard unit packs into the back of the ten-inch speaker/amp combo, making a single portable unit, a feature attractive to a working musician.

The Clavioline's keyboard unit looks very similar to that of the Solovox and Martin must have referenced the American instrument when designing his: three octaves, monophonic, with rocker switches to select tone options. He did include a new feature,

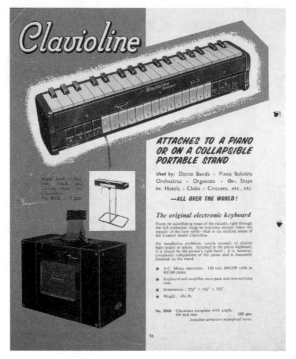

A promotional brochure for the Selmer version of
the Clavioline circa 1955. Credit: Author's collection

though – a sliding switch that could transpose the whole instrument either an octave up or down, making available a total of five octaves, which gave it an advantage over the Solovox. Adverts claimed it could produce 'with amazing fidelity the tonal quality of more than thirty different musical instruments', including various orchestral stringed, brass and woodwind instruments, and, more unusually, musical saw, zither, banjo, bagpipes and Arabian flute.

Martin's decision to license the rights to manufacture Claviolines to Gibson in the USA, Selmer in the UK and to several other smaller manufacturers around the world ensured it would become the most popular electronic instrument of the 1950s. Selmer was the first company to start manufacturing the Clavioline, in about 1950, with Gibson launching its model at the 1952 NAMM (National Association of Music Merchants) show. Both Selmer and Gibson often marketed their Claviolines for home use. Adverts and brochures for the instruments strike a similar tone to those for vacuum cleaners and washing machines from the same period, with ladies in comfortable drawing rooms delighted to find that they now 'have a full orchestra at [their] fingertips'. But the Clavioline, being portable and cheap, offered a great deal to the working musician, and in Britain in particular was embraced by mainstream light orchestral and dance band musicians, and even pub pianists. Once-popular names like Bill McGuffie, Cyril Grantham, Harold Smart and Sandy MacPherson started to use the instrument around the turn of the decade. Suited, genteel light entertainers, they were also accidental revolutionaries, smuggling electronic tones on to the Light Programme and early BBC TV shows. It was adopted, too, by the first generation of rock 'n' roll musicians, with Bill Haley and the Comets, who used one when they first toured Britain in 1957, the first of many.

Hindsight has cast all of these early electronic instruments in a misty, rosy light. Their very names have an incantatory quality and speak a sort of poetry that conjures up nostalgia for a lost image of the future – Novachord, theremin, Clavioline, Solovox. This wistfulness should not obscure their historical importance. They were a means by which, at the end of the 1940s, the idea of electronic music (or music that used some electronic instruments) began to get purchase in popular idioms. If your cultural life encompassed light radio, Hollywood movies and the new medium of television, chances are you would have heard electronic sound in music. It was becoming a recognizable part of the aural landscape. If, on the other hand, your tastes were highbrow, you *might* have come across an Ondes Martenot or a Trautonium, but that was about it. These expensive and rare instruments remained almost exclusively the preserve of a few composers of modern classical music. While others, like the Novachord and the theremin, were rare too, both were reaching audiences of millions through film soundtracks.

Meanwhile, the piano attachments – the Clavioline, the Solovox and the similar Jennings Univox and Maestrovox that followed in the 1950s – were cheap enough and sufficiently plentiful to be within reach of part-time and popular musicians. If you were an enthusiastic amateur musician, or a church organist, or a semi-pro in a dance band, you might actually own one. These gadgets were made in their thousands and could be picked up for the price of a guitar in ordinary music shops.[16] Maybe not much great music was made with them, but they gave many musicians of the time their first experience of the musical potential of electronic sine waves, square waves and saw-tooth waves.

Yet for all their charm, each of this first generation of electronic instruments was limited and flawed. The more sophisticated such as the Ondes Martenot and the Hammond Novachord were hampered by combinations of technical complexity, fragility, high cost and the need to acquire special skills to actually play them. The piano attachments, though easy to play, cheap enough and technically straightforward, were monophonic, with only a modest range of sound colours. The Ondioline fell somewhere in between, but its build quality left much to be desired. Electronic music had reached a plateau in its evolutionary journey. It was like the early days of aviation – the potential was obvious, but the planes could only fly short distances. There just wasn't the apparatus available to make the art.

Then, in 1948, a year after the launch of the most commercially successful early electronic instrument, the Clavioline, three things happened that changed everything. Simultaneous but unconnected, two were technical advances, one creative.

Magnetophon was the model name for the first magnetic tape recorder. It was invented in Germany by the electronics company AEG and the IG Farben chemical company and was unveiled to the public at the 1935 Berlin radio show. AEG sent an example to General Electric in America in 1938. At the time the inventions attracted little international interest as sound quality was poor, but nonetheless the Germans used them throughout the war. German-controlled radio stations often broadcast taped music, and it was this that Jack Mullin, an American serviceman and electronics engineer stationed in England, heard as he tuned in in the middle of the night. He was intrigued, as the sound had none of the scratches and crackles of a 78-rpm record. Maybe German orchestras played live in the early hours? Mullin was not convinced. Towards the end of the war, with the German Army in rapid retreat, he went to Germany and discovered what had really been happening. At a satellite studio of Radio Frankfurt, in Bad Nauheim, Mullin discovered tape machines using a technique called AC biasing to record with a very wide frequency range and low distortion, thus overcoming the technical limitations of the original Magnetophons.

Mullin got permission to send two of the machines back to the USA, as he recognized the potential of the new technology. In the immediate post-war years he demonstrated them to many people in the music and radio worlds, including Bing Crosby, who was impressed. In 1947 Mullin recorded a Bing Crosby radio show on one of his German tape recorders and soon after broadcast a taped Crosby radio show, the first taped show to be broadcast on US radio. By 1948, tape-recording technology was commercially available. The Minitape Corporation (later Stancil Hoffman) introduced a battery-powered device in 1947, and the following year the Ampex Corporation introduced the Model 200 reel-to-reel tape recorder, both based on German Magnetophon technology, thus ushering in a new age of recording.

On 21 June that same year, the Columbia Record Company introduced the 12-inch long play (LP) 33⅓-rpm microgroove vinyl record album. The culmination of research going back more than a decade, the new format offered considerably extended playing time and better sound quality compared to shellac 78-rpm discs. It was also lighter and therefore easily portable, and more durable.

The third event of 1948 wasn't about new technology but was a new vision of how technology could be used in music, and indeed of a new music altogether. On 5 October in Paris, Pierre Schaeffer (1910–95) broadcast his *Concert de Bruits* (Concert of Noises), compositions that included manipulated recorded sounds made by, among other things, trains and saucepan lids, conventional instruments and voices. He called this *musique concrète* (concrete music), the concrete sounds being sounds from real life rather than intentionally musical sounds. With these three simultaneous advances – the tape recorder, the vinyl album and the idea of using manipulated concrete sound as a part of or a basis for music – the conditions were set in place for a new phase in electronic music.

By 1950 large commercial studios were fitting tape recorders and at a stroke greatly improving the quality of their recordings. The new technology had an immediate impact on how musicians worked in studios. In contrast to the wax disc recorders they replaced, reel-to-reel tape machines could be stopped and restarted quickly and easily, which meant that pieces of music no longer had to be recorded in their entirety. If anyone made a mistake, the machines could be stopped and started again, so long as a suitable drop-in point could be found. The practice of tape editing was a natural development of this. Because tape played so fast during recording and playback (recording speeds of 15 inches per second were normal), engineers realized that it was possible to edit different pieces of magnetic tape together by literally sticking one piece to another with adhesive tape – a process called splicing. If the splicing was correctly executed, the physical join between the two pieces of tape would pass over the playback head in a fraction of a second, rendering the join inaudible. So, assuming that the music on separate pieces of tape matched up, the illusion of a live performance could be created by splicing together several sections of music from different performances to make a complete piece.

It was but a short step from this to reimagining the tape recorder, designed to record sound, as a way of creating sound. Other tape manipulation techniques in addition to splicing opened the way not only to recording conventional music in a new way, but to using the recorder as a means to make a previously unheard type of music – tape music, a music that seemed so strange that many people refused to accept it as music at all. If the tape machine was indeed a musical instrument, then mastering these techniques was learning to play it.

Whereas sections of the popular music community had, to this point, embraced electronic musical sound more readily than the world of serious music, it was serious music that first grasped the musical potential of the tape recorder. The most influential figure in the emergence of tape music was Schaeffer. His 1948 concert was actually made using wax disc recording technology, though it wasn't long until Schaeffer embraced tape.

A radio engineer, lecturer, theorist, broadcaster and writer, Schaeffer was not, in the conventional sense of the time, a musician or composer. Yet the repercussions of his experiments with assembling musical collages from snippets of pre-recorded sound echo still in all contemporary sample-based music. The French-born Schaeffer had trained as an engineer and had worked briefly in telecommunications in Strasbourg before moving, in 1936, to Radiodiffusion-Télévision Française (RTF) in Paris. Here he had access to recording and broadcast equipment and a huge library of sound effects recordings on 78-rpm discs. Before long he was experimenting, by speeding up sounds and playing them backwards. In 1949, after the *Concert de Bruits,* Schaeffer and composer Pierre Henry founded the Group de Recherche de Musique Concrète (GRMC), which was recognized by the RTF in 1951. The GRMC was given a new studio, which included a tape recorder, and from this point until the end of the decade Schaeffer pioneered the use of the tape recorder as a musical instrument.

Splicing was the foundation of tape music, the basic skill you had to learn, like practising your scales. Not only could sections of sound be joined together, but the way a piece of tape was cut and spliced to another piece of tape – the actual angle of the join – affected the sound. For example, a diagonal cut created a soft attack or decay that may not have been a feature of the original sound recorded. So, by using different types of diagonal splices, sounds could be altered and musical expression created. Early tape composers often used piano notes with their attack softened by this method. A vertical cut, on the other hand, gave an abrupt attack or finish, again creating a musical dynamic. Tape composers often realized their compositions by sticking together literally hundreds of short pieces of tape.

There were many other techniques. Altering tape speed changed the pitch of sounds and their timbre, so a sped-up bass piano note didn't sound like a higher piano note – it sounded like something else, something that nobody had heard before. Reversing tape played sounds backwards, so a long decay became an ominous build up; tape loops that wound a small section of tape time and again over the playback heads played repetitive patterns and could form the basis of a rhythm; tape echo was achieved by setting up the machine so that sounds recorded on to the tape by the recording head would be played back immediately from the near-adjacent playback head.

While Schaeffer's ideas suggested a new world of unlimited sounds, and the tape recorder became a viable means to capture them, the role of the vinyl album played an important role in the emergence of electronic music. From 1948 onwards, most of the electronic music of the next two decades was realized in part or wholly on tape. This could never be an immediate process; it was always painstaking and involved many stages. So music made in this way could never really be performance music, in the sense of being played in real time to a live audience. Many early electronic music events were billed as lectures or demonstrations and involved practitioners talking about techniques and then playing tapes. So if the music couldn't be performed live, then there needed to be other ways of circulating it if it were ever to attract an audience. Film, radio and television recordings were ways of doing this. The vinyl album – soon to be the dominant commercial format for extended music recordings – was another. The importance of vinyl wasn't immediately apparent, but in time music was made that could not really be performed live, and which wasn't made for film or TV or radio, but which found an audience by virtue of being released on a long-format, high-quality medium.

Karlheinz Stockhausen worked briefly in Schaeffer's studio in 1952. He, along with Werner Meyer-Eppler, Robert Beyer, Herbert Eimert and others, had been experimenting and making plans since 1950, and in 1953 an electronic studio opened at the radio studios of the Northwest German Broadcasting (NWDR) in Cologne. In contrast to Schaeffer's cabal, the German group favoured the use of pure electronic tones as compositional building blocks for their *Elektronische Musik*. For a short while serious electronic music was riven by a doctrinal split between the champions of *Elektronische Musik* and *musique concrète*. Rather like Anglicans agonizing over women priests, this was an issue that aroused powerful passions in a few, but was baffling to outsiders and seems irrelevant now. Even at the time, musicians making more populist electronic music routinely ignored it. Indeed, the process by which revolutionary ideas originate with a small, intellectual elite before gradually filtering down into common use was blurred during this phase of electronic music history. News travelled fast from the elite to the mainstream, and on occasions popular composers were acting almost in parallel with 'serious' composers, while composers with serious intentions who later made popular work appear to have came across similar ideas in advance of, or at the same time, as the two main schools of thought. British film and TV composer Tristram Cary is known to have been experimenting with electronic sound in 1946, while Louis and Bebe

Barron, responsible for the first electronic film score, might well have been manipulating tape as early as 1948. It becomes impossible to tell the story in a simple linear succession of key events initiated by innovators and picked up by others. Rather, people often had similar ideas at similar times, entirely independently of each other. In the case of tape music, popular manifestations of it started to appear in the mid 1950s. Before we explore them, let us go back to the theremin, which enjoyed a resurgence of popularity that began a few years before the emergence of tape music.

2

I like music that explodes into space

Dr Hoffman goes to Hollywood

The theremin enjoyed modest popularity during the 1930s, largely on account of RCA's run of 500 or so production models making the instrument available to a wider group of musicians. Also, its technical simplicity attracted the interest of electronics hobbyists, and 'build-your-own theremin' articles began to appear in magazines from the early 1930s. In America at least its serpentine tones became an occasional feature of the aural landscape, unusual enough to provoke comment, but no longer completely novel. It was featured on the popular syndicated radio show *The Green Hornet* (1936–52), which used Rimsky-Korsakov's 'Flight of the Bumblebee' as its theme song, blended with an appropriately insectoid theremin buzz. That would have distressed Theremin, who saw his creation as a serious expressive musical instrument, but already its proclivity for portamento and vibrato and the eerie drone of the electronic tone itself led to an association with otherness, strangeness, unease and – conversely – humour. British thereminist Musaire (Joseph Whiteley, 1894–1984) picked up on the humour and staged a theremin variety act for years.

Whitelely had bought an RCA instrument for £5 from Selfridges store in Oxford Street, London, in 1930. This he customized, extending

Musaire and his modified RCA theremin, circa 1939. Credit: © The Musical Museum

the range and cutting the case into two parts (the theremin itself and an amplifier/speaker), which he fitted on to a wheeled metal trolley. He painted the two parts of the case pale yellow and decorated them with a scattering of musical notes and lightning flashes.

A balding man who looked older than his years, Whiteley sported evening dress, a carnation buttonhole and a monocle for his Musaire persona. His act comprised popular tunes and theremin impressions of foghorns, seagulls, accelerating cars and so on alongside similar turns on a host of other odd instruments. He was known to invite audience members on stage to look inside the theremin, opening a door in one of the cabinets with a flourish to reveal a painted frieze representing a drinks cabinet apparently mounted inside. A novelty turn it may have been, but Whiteley's theremin technique was advanced and he could hold a tune well. An account of a residency in a department store restaurant in Manchester in 1934 reports Musaire fronting the house orchestra, making a sound that is 'never disagreeable'. Some listeners were so puzzled by the performance that they walked round and round the platform that Musaire was standing on, staring at him and trying to work out how he did it.[17] His act was popular enough to warrant thirty appearances at the Royal Albert Hall and to last well into the post-war television age, when he appeared on children's and variety shows alongside events at hotels, schools and private functions.

Another middle-of-the-road electronic performer of the 1930s was the German-born Martin Taubmann, who played 'Music From the Air' on his Electronde, which he had designed around 1929 after seeing an early Theremin demonstration. Archive film reveals the Electronde to be like a theremin, but with a hand-held cut-off switch and a volume-controlling a foot pedal. This enabled the performer to achieve an attack in the notes, making the instrument sound a little like a Hawaiian steel guitar.

Meanwhile, in 1930s New York, a young thereminist calling himself Hal Hope was fronting an electronic trio playing in clubs and restaurants. Hope was the alter ego of Samuel Hoffman (1903–67), a podiatrist and part-time violinist, who had been given an RCA theremin in payment of a debt. At the time, Hoffman was playing in a dance band led by Jolly Coburn, one of several musicians in the early 1930s who had picked up on the theremin as a novelty turn for popular music. It seems Hoffman encountered Theremin himself, then also living in New York, as years later he referred to becoming 'acquainted with the theremin many years ago through the inventor, a Russian scientist ...'[18]

Hoffman 'made a serious study of the instrument' and in 1936, now trading as Hal Hope, formed his own nine-piece swing orchestra, switching between violin and theremin. With a regular gig at the Casino-in-the-Air, a fashionable New York rooftop restaurant, Hope and his theremin became a talking point. He cashed in by forming Hal Hope's Electronic Trio, in which a Hammond organist and someone playing one of Theremin's fingerboard electric cellos joined Hoffman and his theremin, making the trio surely the first electronic pop band. His fame spread, at least locally. Further New York residencies and radio broadcasts ensued, with Hoffman performing a wide repertoire of popular tunes, inviting members of the audience to try the theremin with predictably comic effect.

In 1941 Hoffman relocated to Los Angeles, where he set up as a podiatrist. During the war years the theremin fell out of vogue, not least because Theremin himself, who had enjoyed considerable celebrity in artistic circles in the 1930s, was no longer around to promote his creation. He had returned, abruptly, to the Soviet Union in 1938, and was for many decades afterwards assumed dead by most in the West, possibly the victim of a political purge. Hoffman was by now in full-time medical practice and considered himself a retired musician, with no plans to continue with his musical career on a professional basis or of doing anything with the theremin. Even so, he registered with the local branch of the musicians' union on the off chance that he might pick up the occasional job to keep his hand in and listed the theremin as one of his instruments as an afterthought. This apparently casual decision would open up an unexpected second career for Hoffman. He was one of a handful of key players converging in Hollywood who came together on the Oscar-winning soundtrack to *Spellbound*, which introduced the theremin to a mass audience for the first time.

But even before that, Hammond's Novachord was becoming a staple audio accompaniment to disturbed states of mind, ghostly happenings and other worlds in Hollywood. A Novachord featured in Franz Waxman's Oscar-nominated score to Alfred Hitchcock's *Rebecca* (1940), adapted from Daphne du Maurier's 1938 novel of the same name. It is used to evoke the memory of the titular Rebecca, and appears whenever her widower or the other main characters think or talk of her. A year later it accompanies Humphrey Bogart as he awakes from a stupor in John Huston's adaptation of Dashiell Hammett's *The Maltese Falcon*. Appearances such as this, generally unremarked on at the time, were like advance propaganda for the new sound of electronics – secret leaflet drops into the ears of the popular audience. There were many more Novachord movie appearances in the following decades, often in soundtracks to horror or science fiction films. Synthesizer pioneer Paul Beaver owned five of them and used them from the 1950s in several films. Composer Jerry Goldsmith was still using a Novachord in the 1960s.[10]

By the time Hoffman moved west, composer Miklós Rózsa was beginning to find his way around the studios of Hollywood. Rózsa was born into an affluent family in Budapest in 1907. His mother, a classical pianist who had studied with pupils of Franz Liszt, introduced him to music. From his father, a Tolstoyan idealist, industrialist and landowner, Rózsa was imbued with a love of Hungarian folk song that would influence his compositions. Set on becoming a composer, he studied in Leipzig before moving to Paris in 1932. There he became friends with the Swiss-born composer Arthur Honegger, who supplemented his income as a serious composer by writing film scores. This appealed to Rózsa, and in 1937 he began what he called his double life (the title of his autobiography) as both classical and film composer, writing music for *Knight Without Armour*, produced by fellow Hungarian Alexander Korda. By 1940, after a short spell in the London film industry, Rózsa had made his way to Hollywood and embarked on a scoring career that would earn him three Oscars.

The British film director Alfred Hitchcock had moved to Hollywood from England just before Rózsa, in 1939. In 1945 he and his producer David O. Selznick approached Rózsa about the score for a new movie, *Spellbound*. They had been impressed with the composer's score for Billy Wilder's *Double Indemnity* (1944). *Spellbound* came about because Selznick pressed Hitchcock to make a movie exploring psychoanalysis, to which Selznick had been converted after recent positive experiences. The film ended up reflecting some of Selznick's proselytizing zeal. The plot revolves around Dr Constance Peterson (Ingrid Bergman), a psychoanalyst at a mental hospital, and her new boss, Dr Anthony Edwardes (Gregory Peck). Dr Peterson notices that Dr Edwardes, who we later learn is suffering from amnesia, has a phobia about sets of parallel lines against a white background. It is this phobia that serves as the cue for a theremin theme that introduced the instrument to a mass audience.

Rózsa met Hitchcock and Selznick just two times during work on *Spellbound*. At their first meeting Hitchcock laid out his requirements: a grand, sweeping love theme for scenes involving the two leads, Ingrid Bergman and Gregory Peck, and a 'new colour' for the Peck character's recurring episodes of terror that run through the movie. Rózsa, who had developed an interest in electronic musical instruments, immediately suggested the theremin, and Hitchcock and Selznick, who had never heard of it, agreed to let the composer try, though with some reservations.

Years later Rózsa described how he had attempted to use electronic sound on two previous occasions,[20] first considering the Ondes Martenot, which he had discovered when living in Paris, for the score for *The Thief of Baghdad* (1940). A year or so later director Henry Hathaway asked for an 'eerie, uncanny' sound to evoke a premonition of death in the war film *Sundown* (1941). Rózsa described the theremin, but nobody involved in the picture even wanted to hear it (he resorted to a musical saw instead). The third time he got his way. Sent away by Hitchcock and Selznick to draft a main theme and a 'paranoia' theme, Rózsa duly composed both. Then, at a second and final meeting with Hitchcock and Selznick, he presented his music – singing the theremin theme to piano accompaniment. Director and producer pronounced themselves satisfied with the tunes, but wanted to hear the instrument itself.

By this time Rózsa had made contact with the man who would eventually conjure his theme out of the ether – Dr Samuel Hoffman. His first choice had been the virtuoso thereminist Clara Rockmore, but she declined, concerned that her beloved instrument would be used simply to make spooky noises, of which she disapproved. So Rózsa consulted the musicians' union in Hollywood and found just one other thereminist listed who could read music. Samuel Hoffman, though now considering himself a retired musician, dusted down his theremin and welcomed Rózsa to his house, the composer arriving with a sketch of the *Spellbound* theremin part with which to audition Hoffman. Hoffman sight-read the part perfectly. Rózsa was impressed, hired him on the spot, and at the second meeting with Hitchcock and Selznick suggested that Hoffman could come along and demonstrate the instrument to them. They, however, wanted to know how it would sound in context, and suggested a trial recording of the theme with an orchestra. This was duly made and dispatched to Selznick and Hitchcock.

Shortly afterwards, Rózsa received a memo from one of Selznick's secretaries saying that director and producer approved of the theremin and wanted it to be used in every scene connected with mental disturbance, and also in the title sequence. There followed over the next few weeks a flurry of memos from Selznick proffering advice and instruction about the music, and how the theremin should be used in each scene, which Rózsa ignored. Eventually, the score was recorded, and, after a dispute about the number of violins used (the imperious producer wanted more), approved.

Rózsa's *Spellbound* music won that year's Oscar for Best Score, and it's easy to see why. The love theme is big, openhearted music that embraces the listener – exactly the sort of thing Hollywood romance required. By contrast, the theremin theme signals Dr Edwardes' phobia about parallel lines against a white background, which surfaces when he sees grooves scored on a tablecloth by a fork, pinstripes on a dressing gown, stitching on a bedspread. The theremin also appears during a surreal dream sequence designed by Salvador Dalí. This was originally slated to run for twenty minutes, but in the final cut comprises of just a handful of short episodes interspersed with psychoanalytic interpretations of the dream action, a scene that lasts just a few minutes. By using the theremin in these sections only – the phobia scenes and the dream sequence – and saving conventional orchestration for the love scenes, Rózsa makes a clear link: the theremin represents disturbance, fear, distress, abnormality. It is the music of unhealthiness, of darkness, contrasted with the swooping strings of light and love and health.

After *Spellbound*, Rózsa went to work again for Billy Wilder, on *The Lost Weekend*. Based on a 1944 novel of the same title by Charles R. Jackson, the film follows Don Birnam (played by Ray Milland) as he embarks on an increasingly desperate weekend binge that culminates with delirium tremens and nightmarish hallucinations. In the film, Birnam is driven to drink by the failure of his writing career, though in the book an allegation of homosexuality is the trigger.

Rózsa wrote his score after seeing a preview screening of the film with temporary music so inappropriate that the audience laughed – not really what Wilder wanted from a stark psychological drama about addiction. So disastrous was the preview that there was talk of abandoning the project, but Rózsa managed to persuade the producer Charles Brackett that the music was the problem. He wrote a theme using the theremin and called in Dr Hoffman to provide 'the voice of alcoholic temptation'. A conservative musical director found the music 'too aggressive, too dissonant ... foreground music rather than the usual background noises',[21] but Brackett liked the theremin and wanted music even more turbulent.

The film opens with a panning shot of the New York skyline accompanied by airy, optimistic violins, before homing in on the open windows of an apartment, a hint of suspense in the violins and the briefest theremin siren call. In those few opening seconds, before a word is spoken, we know that there will be darkness in this story.

As in *Spellbound*, the theremin is used as a cue for disturbed mental states. Every time it appears, usually as a six-note theme paired with violins, the madness for drink falls on Birnam. In one particularly memorable sequence a dishevelled Birnam tries to shake drops from two empty whisky bottles into a glass while the theremin drones over stumbling, stabbing brass. It is the sound of defeated compulsion.

With the new score in place, the film was then previewed again, this time to acclaim, acceptance and no laughter. It went on to win four Academy Awards, for Best Picture, Best Director, Best Actor and Best Screenplay. And although the Best Soundtrack Oscar went to *Spellbound*, Rózsa himself thought *The Lost Weekend* a better film and a better score.

Although *Spellbound* and *The Lost Weekend* did not mark the theremin's first appearance in popular culture, the films did introduce it to a much wider audience than it had ever had before. These were the big movies of 1945 and were watched by millions the world over. They stimulated a renewed surge of interest in the theremin, and Hoffman himself became Hollywood's thereminist of choice – 'the only man in Hollywood who operates the mechanism'.[22] He went on to perform on more than twenty other film soundtracks over the next two decades. Many of these were humdrum B-movies (*Earth vs. the Spider* and *Billy the Kid Versus Dracula*), but Hoffman can be heard on big pictures too, such as 1947's *The Road to Rio* (starring Bob Hope and Bing Crosby), *The Ten Commandments* (1956) and *The Day The Earth Stood Still* (1951).

Rózsa used Hoffman and his theremin on just one more soundtrack, *The Red House* (1947), starring Edward G. Robinson alongside a young Julie London in one of her first film roles. Adapted from a novel by George Agnew Chamberlain, the plot of this black-and-white drama is predictable, but the film is elevated by a degree of psychological complexity and a compelling Robinson performance. The wooden-legged Pete Morgan (Robinson), his sister Ellen and their adopted daughter Meg live on an isolated farm. Ellen and Meg convince Pete that he needs help working the farm, and a classmate of Meg's, Nath, is hired. One stormy night, when Nath decides to use a shortcut home through the out-of-bounds woods, Pete becomes hysterical and warns of screams in the night and an abandoned red house. Nath ignores him and walks into the woods to a swirling Rózsa accompaniment, fighting against howling wind, echoing screams and, inevitably, the theremin. This sets the tone for the instrument's use through the rest of the action, it appearing at times of fear, crisis and anticipation of some unseen dread. In contrast to Rózsa's previous two theremin scores, in *The Red House* the instrument is a texture, almost a sound effect; not a featured lead instrument, but one or two trembling notes. After *The Red House* Rózsa abandoned the theremin in his film work, though he did make use of Ondes Martenot in later orchestral compositions.

Spellbound and *The Lost Weekend* planted in the popular imagination an association between the sound of the theremin in particular, and electronic sound in general, and mental disorder. It might not have been what Theremin had in mind, but the veering, quivering tones spoke of minds cut adrift from their moorings, without fixed points. Hoffman's other great film performance would underline the strongest and most enduring of theremin associations – with outer space.

Mentions of unidentified silvery disc-shaped objects in the sky are scattered through history back to antiquity, but it was a report by pilot Kenneth Arnold, on 24 June 1947, that started the flying saucer craze that swept through America and to a lesser extent the rest of the world. While flying near Mt Rainer, Arnold said he saw nine flying objects, which he variously described as being like a 'pie plate that was cut in half', or more simply 'saucer-like'. To this event the media applied the term flying saucer, which endured to the extent of becoming almost synonymous with the term UFO for some time.

Arnold's report was followed immediately by a flurry of sightings and related events in America and around the world. The most famous of these is the incident on 8 July at the Army Air Force base at Roswell, New Mexico, when the military issued a press release saying that it had recovered a flying disc from a nearby ranch. They later issued a correction, saying that it was in fact a weather balloon, which did nothing whatsoever to dampen the feverish, fearful relish with which the public anticipated imminent extra-terrestrial invasion. Or was it the Soviets and their secret weapons? Regardless, in the next few years there were thousands more flying saucer sightings, many accompanied by photos that, on close examination, were obviously fake, though some defy easy explanation even now.

Contemporaneous with the flying saucer craze ran a fascination with emerging rocket technology. American, Russian and British scientists all competed to build on advances in rocketry made by Germany during the Second World War and by the end of the 1940s the idea of manned space flights didn't seem too far off. This was the atmosphere in which a wave of science fiction films, mainly American, were made through the 1950s, a genre that provided a significant popular culture platform for electronic music. Science fiction wasn't new to the cinema, with adaptations of Jules Verne and HG Wells novels being made before, but 1950s science fiction does have its own recurring themes: human encounters with extra-terrestrial life and inter-planetary travel. Often lower-budget films concentrated on extra-terrestrials invading the world, to eliminate the need for creating expensive sets of the surface of Mars, for example, but some films do involve humans travelling to other worlds.

Science fiction of the 1950s is often thought of as a B-movie genre, but some of the films were big-budget main features. The first of the era, *Destination Moon* (1950), was one of these, shot in Technicolor, with science-fiction writer Robert A. Heinlein as technical advisor and script doctor. It featured a conventional orchestral score, but some uncredited electronic loops can be heard when the spacecraft lands on the moon.

The second American science fiction film of the era, *Rocketship X-M* (also 1950), conforms more to the stereotypical view of the genre – black and white (mainly), short, at one hour and seventeen minutes, and with much action confirmed to the claustrophobic cabin of the rocketship itself. Directed by Kurt Neumann and starring Lloyd Bridges, the film recounts the story of the first manned space flight, intended for a moon landing, but blown off course and ending up on Mars, which was shown with a red tint and turns out to be the scene of past nuclear catastrophe. Ferde Grofé, who had demonstrated Hammond Novachords at the 1939 New York World's Fair, scored the film. He might well have used the instrument again in the *Rocketship X-M* as misty, vibraphone-like keyboard tones can be heard. What he definitely used, though, was the theremin, played by Samuel Hoffman. The instrument is heard through much of the score, an ascending tone accompanying the rocket's blast off and various long-drawn-out notes at most other points in the action that involve the rocket or the Martians (though not, notably, in the tentative love scenes). Unlike Miklós Rózsa before him, though, Grofé doesn't use the theremin as a melodic lead voice. Rather, it is a sound texture, blended in with strings and brass instruments to lend them an indistinct, blurred character. Conservative and limited this might have been, it did set the stage for regular use of theremin and other electronics in many subsequent films in the genre. Hoffman himself performs on several, including *Phantom from Space* (1953), *It Came from Outer Space* (1953) and *Project Moon Base* (1953).

Another credit was *The Thing from Another World* (1951), which tells the story of an Air Force crew and scientists on a desolate Arctic research station, fighting a plant-based alien being they find in a crashed UFO. Although the direction is credited to Christian Nyby, Howard Hawks is generally considered as having a hand in the film's making and script. The score, by multi-Oscar winner Dimitri Tiomkin[23] (1894–1979), again makes use of Hoffman's theremin in an orchestral setting, its wild-howling noise an echo of the chill Arctic wind we hear blowing throughout much of the film.

The theremin first appears to accompany a tentative approach to the UFO. By now the language is familiar: the electronic sound tells us that beneath the ice lays something beyond experience, something strange and frightening. As the action progresses, the theremin is a cue to announce the appearance of the Thing itself. Like its aura, its emanation, we hear the sound before the alien form appears.

In September 1951, four months after the release of *The Thing*, Bernard Herrmann (1911–75) joined Grofé, Tiomkin and Rósza in the ranks of film composers experimenting with electronics. Herrmann came from a Russian–Jewish family. He was born and raised in

New York City and after displaying musical talent as a child went on to study music as New York University and the Juilliard School. He had something of a reputation for irascibility. With his score to the 20th Century Fox production *The Day the Earth Stood Still*, his first Hollywood feature, Herrmann rewired the Fox house orchestra to include Hoffman on theremin alongside violinist Paul Shure playing a bass theremin.[24] The string section was electronically amplified, and amidst the many percussion and mallet instruments sat two Hammond organs, oscillators, four pianos, four harps and about thirty brass instruments.[25] Herrmann was pleased with the score and thought it stood up well over the years, with 'some degree of originality while being conventional'.[26]

The black-and-white science fiction effort was directed by Robert Wise and written by Edmund H. North from a short story called *Farewell to the Master*, by Harry Bates. It stars British actor Michael Rennie as Klaatu, a humanoid extra-terrestrial visitor who arrives in Washington in a flying saucer to deliver a warning to the peoples of the world that unless they end their warlike ways mutual destruction is assured. Accompanied by a ten-foot-high silver robot of fearsome power, Gort, Klaatu's expedition, though peaceful in intent, provokes fascination and fear. He is hunted through the streets of Washington and eventually killed before being rescued by Gort and revived. Standing in front of his spaceship he delivers a final warning message to assembled dignitaries before blasting off home, born aloft on a dense slab of electronic noise. *The Day the Earth Stood Still* can be read as a cold war morality tale, but also as a Christian metaphor: Klaatu takes the name Carpenter for his brief sojourn on Earth, and like that other carpenter before him is vilified and killed for his peaceful message before rising from death and ascending.

Hermann's use of electronics in *The Day the Earth Stood Still* was a giant step forward from Grofé, Tiomkin and Rósza's use of theremins in an orchestral setting. There are more electronic sources, and theremins participate as equals with the conventional instruments. In Herman's score we hear theremin duets, oscillators, reversed sound and electric strings. The composer was shown a rough cut of the film and, left alone to do what he wanted, wrote his score in five weeks. He selected his curious hybrid semi-electric ensemble to represent the alien and the otherworldly, stating his intention with a bold descending oscillator swoop to introduce the action. From then on scenes featuring alien action have partially electronic accompaniment. The movie's spaceship, all smooth curves, found an obvious musical counterpart in the theremin. The gliding voice without tonal steps, a liminal sound on the boundary of music, summons the silver disc moving with impossible ease and speed through the sky with no obvious means of propulsion, its control panels responding to gestures, not touch. Gort walks deliberately and remorselessly to a theremin duet, like a futuristic rendering of Frankenstein's monster. By contrast, when Klaatu visits Arlington Cemetery and the Lincoln Memorial, and seems to make his closest connection with humanity, Herrmann accompanies him with soft, patriotic major key horns, the film's most conventional music. The contrast is striking, and that episode aside the musical action is dominated by theremins playing against fast harp and piano arpeggios, urgent brass and the hazy electric strings. This novel mix of instruments resists easy categorization, and in parts of the score, particularly the scenes when Klaatu causes a worldwide electrical shut down as a demonstration of his power, it is hard to place the combinations of sound. Herrmann also contributed to the film's sound effects, and through the film the gap between sound effect and music, though maintained, is not wide on account of similar means being used to generate both. Gort's death ray is a theremin and an oscillator recording played backwards, while on occasions cacophonous surges, montages of simultaneous backward and forward recordings, break through.

In earlier films theremin use was a simple equation: in *Spellbound* the theremin is the sound of fear and distress, in *The Thing* it represents aliens bent on destruction. In *The Day the Earth Stood Still* there is a tension in the story that required a more complex musical symbolism. Klaatu, though possessed of the power to wreak catastrophe, comes in peace but is feared. The theremins and other electronic elements accompany the alien and evoke its otherness, yet the alien mission is essentially benign. So, the electronic sound evokes both the peaceful extra-terrestrial, and the fearful and misguided human response to it. Modestly successful in its time, *The Day the Earth Stood Still* has endured as a classic, though the force of Herrmann's score has become somewhat diminished. A bold statement for its time, it became generic through imitation, the science fiction music from which all science fiction music clichés derive: 20th Century Fox later reused the title theme in the pilot episode for the TV series *Lost in Space* (1965). Titles in a trailer for the film talk of the alien invasion holding the world 'spellbound', an unconscious nod to the earlier theremin classic.

Before all his science fiction scores, when his stock was high in the immediate aftermath of *Spellbound* and *The Lost Weekend*, Hoffman encountered composer and bandleader Les Baxter, now remembered for his association with the loosely defined exotica genre. It was an encounter that led to more fame for the theremin-playing doctor. Between them Hoffman and Baxter, with the help of composers Harry Revel and Billy May, made three big-selling albums, oddities that blend soothing pre-rock 'n' roll light orchestral instrumentation and wordless vocal cooing with the theremin.

The first, *Music Out of the Moon*, was initially released by Capitol in 1947, as an album of three 78-rpm records (it was later reissued as a vinyl 33-rpm album). Written by the British-born songwriter and composer Revel, and arranged and conducted by Baxter, it was, according to the liner notes, 'music that can affect the sensitive mind in a way that is sometimes frightening'. That may have been true in 1947 – though probably not – but it now sounds like typical middle-of-the-road music of the day, bent slightly out of shape, with theremin lead lines seamlessly integrated, the effect occasionally livened up with some jaunty swing rhythms that would have been familiar to Hoffman in his Hal Hope alias. The use of the theremin made the album novel, but it was unthreatening and commercial music, and it forged a link between the theremin and space five years before *The Day the Earth Stood Still*. It became music out of the moon in a literal sense 22 years later, when Neil Armstrong took a cassette of the album on the Apollo 11 moon landing expedition.

After the success of *Music Out of the Moon* Revel, Baxter and Hoffman regrouped in 1948 for another themed album, *Perfume Set to Music*, released on RCA Victor (the company that had made Hoffman's theremin). The Corday perfume company sponsored the project and Revel composed six impressionistic aural representations of different fragrances they marketed at the time. Corday advertised the album heavily, helping it to number one in *Variety*'s chart in mid-December of that year. This second album also features

Hammond Novachord, an early recording combining the era's two most popular electronic instruments.

Hoffman's theremin trilogy was completed back at Capitol when listeners were instructed to 'turn down the lights, relax in an easy chair and listen' by the sleeve notes of *Music for Peace of Mind* (1950), as Hoffman's theremin hummed languorously over the lush strings once again. It was another huge success.

The significance of these three albums lies not just in their commercial impact. Contrary to Hoffman's previous work on film scores, and other uses to date of electronics in popular music in general, the trilogy uses the theremin as a tool for expressing peace, relaxation and happiness. Soothing background sound for a sophisticated dinner party, the music was written to be innocuous, non-confrontational and easy-going, and the theremin – with its sound free of angles and edges – glides comfortably into this intention, enhancing and complementing it.

Hoffman, by now in comfortable middle age, became an unlikely part-time star. Television appearances from the time show a plump-faced man with thinning hair staring in rapt concentration at a wooden chest with protruding antennae, finishing performances with a bashful smile at the camera. On the Johnny Carson show the doctor and the talk show host reprise the old Hal Hope nightclub skit, with Hoffman teaching Carson how to play, with predictably noisy results. There was even a gig with the Hollywood Bowl Orchestra. Hoffman continued playing his 1929 theremin until his death from a heart attack in 1968, though from the late 1950s credits declined.

Hoffman's peak of popularity as a theremin performer was from 1945 until the early 1950s. His performances prompted a renewed surge of interest in theremins, and as there were then none on the market, the only chance you had of getting one was to turn to one of the build-your-own articles in home electronics hobbyist magazines. All of this caught the attention of Robert Moog, a schoolboy from New York.

Moog (1934–2005) was a nerdy boy with a streak of independent self-confidence borne out of a realization of his own intelligence. His mother wanted him to be a pianist, coaxing him to hours of practice in the hope that he'd become a concert performer. He did become a proficient player, but he was more drawn to his father's electronics hobby. In 1949, with the help of his father, he built his own theremin, which he demonstrated at a school assembly. It was the start of a fascination that would endure, and for the rest of his life Moog was drawn in by the instrument's simplicity and expressive range. At 19 he formed a company to manufacture theremins as kits and ready-built instruments, and in January 1954 wrote an article about the instrument in *Radio and Television News*. A straightforward, didactic piece guiding readers through the construction of a theremin with integral speaker/amp, housed in ¼-inch plywood case, it was not the first theremin article the magazine had published. An earlier piece had appeared in 1949, and Moog's was published in response to public demand for another. In it he wrote:

> The Theremin is generally considered a musical novelty and there are very few accomplished masters of the instrument. The writer believes that the scarcity of instruments rather than any great difficulty in learning to play is responsible for this situation.[27]

Moog would do his bit to address that scarcity. Thanks to him, theremins were available for sale for the first time since the RCA model 15 years earlier. The business was a modest success, and over the next ten years Moog made enough from the business to see himself through an extended college career. More significantly for the future of electronic music, he was making some money selling electronic musical instruments. This entrepreneurial bent, combined with electronics acumen and musical sensitivity, made Moog one of the most influential figures in electronic music's popularization a decade or so later.

It wasn't just in the USA that electronic sound was infiltrating popular middle-of-the-road music. In Paris sometime around the turn of the decade, a young medical student called Jean-Jacques Perrey was deeply impressed by a radio broadcast in which Georges Jenny demonstrated the new Ondioline, which he had launched in 1949. Perrey, who was born in 1929, had spent some time studying music just after the war and was not ready yet to abandon musical ambitions. With the audacity of youth he phoned the radio station and requested Georges Jenny's telephone number, which he was duly given. Perrey then phoned Jenny himself, saying he liked the sound of the Ondioline but couldn't afford to buy one. But, he wondered, if Jenny were to give him one and he, Perrey, became a proficient performer, wouldn't it be an asset to Jenny in terms of publicity? Perrey, avuncular in appearance even as a young man and exuding a cheerful good nature, must have made an impression on Jenny. The inventor invited Perrey to his workshop and agreed to loan him an Ondioline.

Perrey took the Ondioline home and over six months taught himself to play with his right hand while accompanying himself on the piano with his left. When sufficiently proficient, he called Jenny again and asked if he could give him a demonstration. Jenny was impressed by the expressiveness of Perrey's performance and the way in which he played Ondioline and piano simultaneously, and offered him a job as salesman and demonstrator when he finished medical school. Gripped with enthusiasm, initially Perrey wanted to abandon his medical career on the spot and start immediately. But then, so close to qualifying as a doctor, he vacillated and decided to try to combine continuing his studies with working for Jenny. This involved mild subterfuge when Jenny announced that Perrey was to go to Sweden on a sales trip. Perrey concocted an imaginary gall bladder ailment that required hospitalization, took leave from school and went to Stockholm to appear on Swedish TV instead. He stayed for two months, playing a residency in a hotel and securing some healthy orders, with commensurate healthy commission. Convinced there was a living to be made in peddling Ondiolines, Perrey returned to Paris and quit medicine for music.

For the rest of the decade Perrey travelled through Europe selling Ondiolines at such a rate that Jenny, who had initially envisaged building them all himself by hand, had to open a small factory. He commissioned Perrey to record a seven-minute demonstration disc showing off the instrument's impressive range of sounds and sent his young charge on demonstration tours across the continent. It was while he was away on a business trip in Hamburg that Jenny's wife called Perrey to say that Charles Trenet was interested in the Ondioline.

Trenet, born in 1913, was already a big star. A singer, songwriter, novelist and poet, he was prolific and popular with a career that would eventually extend over more than 60 years. Stylistically and chronologically, he fits somewhere between the matinee idol Maurice Chevalier and later singer–writers such as George Brassens. Trenet's reputation in France had suffered in the immediate post-war years on account of his decision to perform for the occupying forces throughout the war, and for a while he retreated to America, where he befriended Charlie Chaplin. Returning to Paris in 1951, he was looking for a unique sound for a new song, 'L'âme des Poètes' ('Soul of the Poets'), and had heard of the Ondioline. Perrey and Trenet met and Perrey demonstrated some sounds. Trenet was convinced and invited Perrey to record with him.

The 22-year-old Perrey found himself in a studio not only with Trenet but guitarist Django Reinhardt and was nervous in the presence of older, famous and more accomplished musicians. But he was put at his ease by Reindhardt, who assured him that he, like Perrey, could not read music, and that Perrey should just play what he felt.[28] Four songs were recorded – just one featuring Reinhardt – with musicians and singer performing live with no overdubs. 'L'âme des Poètes' was released as 78-rpm disc in France by Columbia and became a big hit. Trenet sings the song in the 1952 film *Bouquet de Joie*, this time backed by a small orchestra. The single version, though, features just Trenet's voice against piano, with the Ondioline playing lead. A solo in the higher register is an extraordinarily faithful and expressive rendition of a violin, whereas the counter melodies in a lower register sound closer to an oboe. 'Ma Maison', the song featuring Reinhardt, makes more sparing use of Ondioline, but once again the expressiveness of the playing is evident – proof of the innate efficacy of the Ondioline as a performer's instrument and also of Perrey's mastery of it.

Trenet was enamoured of the Ondioline and renamed his band Trio Vigouroux Ondioline. He invited Perrey out on tour with him, and the pair also recorded a radio series. For an established popular singer like Trenet, using an electronic instrument as lead was a radical step. Yet despite his enthusiasm for the Ondioline, Trenet's use of it was actually rather conservative. For the most part, Perrey mimicked other instruments, rather than tease out the Ondioline's unique sounds. Indeed, the demonstration record he'd made with Jenny also concentrates on the mimicking capabilities of the Ondioline rather than its potential originality. This was a tension that had existed since the days of the Telharmonium and which would continue right up to the Moog era. Throughout that period, electronic instruments were often marketed on the basis that they would allow you to create the sounds of other instruments that you couldn't play: 'A full orchestra at your fingertips', as the Clavioline adverts said. But there was a twist in this tale, because although some of the early electronic instruments were indeed impressive mimics – they could never exactly reproduce the sound of acoustic instruments. This is partly attributable to the speakers the sound was broadcast through. What you got instead was something that sounded a little like a violin or a clarinet or a banjo, but not exactly. Eventually, these grainy facsimiles would become valued as sounds in their own right, embodying a kind of naivety and quaintness.

Perrey's spell with Trenet launched him on a new career. Now he wasn't simply a demonstrator and a salesman – he was also a performer. He toured a solo show around Europe in which he used the Ondioline to demonstrate sounds from around the world – bagpipes for Scotland, zither for Hungary and so on. Perrey the performer would find his voice in the 1960s on a series of albums for Vanguard, which we will come to later. First, though, there was *Mr Ondioline*, a persona adopted around 1959/60 for two EPs of jaunty Ondioline pop released on French label Pacific Records. They weren't hits and are of little note musically, but these EPs earn their place in history for anticipating devices that would become common practice a decade later. The first was the use of multi-tracking to build up banks of monophonic electronic instruments.

For the sessions Perrey multi-tracked Ondiolines on top of a small band, bouncing tracks between mono tape recorders in the absence of a multi-track machine. The result was lightweight commercial pop bent into novel shapes. The sleeve of the first EP, titled *Mr Ondioline*, magnified the oddness of it all. Here we see two Ondiolines stacked one on the other, with the top panel of the upper one removed to reveal an electronic maze, rather like a cut-away anatomical drawing showing veins, sinews and vital organs. This visual emphasis of the technological roots of the music became a popular illustrative device on electronic albums of the late 1960s and early 1970s. Sitting in front of them was *Mr Ondioline* (Perrey) himself, portly, suited, with head and shoulders covered in a hood and cape, with slits for eyes. The idea had been to lend some mystery to the *Mr Ondioline* persona – who was this man with his strange instrument? Unfortunately, the result was somewhere between the comic and the sinister, a villainous wrestler and a cult leader.

Shortly before *Mr Ondioline*'s brief career, Perrey had taken the Ondioline to the Expo 58, also known as the Brussels World's Fair, held from April to October 1958. It was one of several occasions when Perrey, a pop musician at heart, brushed up against the more serious side of electronic music.

More than 42 million people flocked to the fair. They marvelled at its visual centrepiece, the Atomium, a 102-metre tall steel model of a unit cell of an iron crystal. Jenny commissioned several composers to write pieces for the Ondioline for the event, and a demonstration LP of a radio broadcast records these works. A narrator introduces the selection in American-accented English that sounds like it was translated from French. He explains that the Ondioline is a simplification of the principles of the 'internationally known' Ondes Martenot, which can be played by the amateur: 'It is solidly built and need not fear the handling of children.'[29] Despite this emphasis on accessibility, Jenny's commissioned works are brief quasi-classical vignettes, often tending towards the melodramatic and suspenseful.

Expo 58 is now recognized as a pivotal moment in the emergence of serious electronic music. Many of the movement's leading figures were there, and British composers Tristram Cary and Daphne Oram turned up to see what was happening. Visitors heard Edgard Varèse's *Poème électronique* sound installation through 400 speakers, as they were shepherded in groups of 500 through a pavilion designed by Le Corbusier and sponsored by Phillips. A year later when the piece was performed in New York a review said that parts of it 'might have been the sound track of a science fiction film'.[30] The French-born Varèse (1883–1965), who spent much of his life in the United States, is sometimes called the father of electronic music. Alongside his grand statement was a more modest electronic piece by one of Jenny's musicians, Darius Cittanova. He played his Ondioline composition, *Chants pour les Eternites Differentes* (*Songs for Different Eternities*), on top of the Atomium itself. What better evocation of an imagined future can there be than Varèse's *Poème* seeping out of

400 speakers, while Cittanova broadcast the Ondioline over Brussels from the top of the Atomium.

A year later Perrey went right to the heart of the electronic *avant-garde* when Pierre Schaeffer took him on as a student. He spent about six weeks under Schaeffer's tutelage, learning tape splicing and other tape manipulation techniques. Musically, though, teacher and pupil had little in common and the relationship didn't endure. But Perrey would take what he learned and put it to use in his pop creations a few years later.

Perrey was a pioneer of electronic pop, but it wasn't until the 1960s that tape manipulation became a part of his repertoire. Two Dutchmen, who made an album of electronic pop three years before *Mr Ondioline* donned his cape and hood, preceded him to the cutting block.

Dick Raaymakers (born 1930) took on the swinging alias of Kid Baltan when he partnered Tom Dissevelt (1921–89) in Electrosonics, a synth pop duo without synthesizers. Instead, they had the considerable resources of the Philips Electronics research studio in Eindhoven at their disposal, which contained a profusion of tone generators and tape recorders. There they made the very first purely electronic pop record, 'Song of the Second Moon', first released in 1957. Perrey and Jenny visited Phillips in 1958 in a failed attempt to persuade the company to manufacture Ondiolines. While there, Perrey met Raaymakers and Dissevelt at their studio and was amazed by the music the Dutch duo were making, later citing them as an inspiration for his own electronic pop.

A Dutch television clip of the duo at work in 1959 shows them tweedy, reflective and studious, writing notes and spinning labyrinthine tape loops. The studio includes a bank of twelve oscillators pitched to different notes, to allow for the build up of chords, and multiple mono tape recorders, which they still referred to by the original German name, Magnetophons.

Though the album title heralded the appearance of another chapter in emerging electronic music's space obsession, 'Song of the Second Moon' has no obvious musical precedent. For the first time, music realized entirely by electronic means displayed a conventional pop sensibility. All of the pieces on the album have layered sounds that correspond to conventional instrumentation, and each has all the tricks of pop music – time changes, 'instruments' dropping in and out, repeated melodies, recognizable chord shapes. A rhythm section of walking bass tones (betraying Dissevelt's former life as a bassist) and percussive loops and squelches underpins melody, counter melody and portamentos, bubbly eruptions and other musical punctuation marks. The title track alone is markedly complex for an electronically realized piece of the time. An electronic rhythm roughly corresponding to a bass and snare drum multiplies in echoes of itself; a shifting melody; the aural space between filled with whirrs and buzzes. Given the exactitude of the various parts, it seems extraordinary that they were created without a keyboard controller, yet they are all just spliced, looped oscillator tones and occasionally manipulated piano notes.

Disregarding the sound sources, and judging them on melody, rhythm and structure alone, the songs show little rock 'n' roll influence. Instead, they have more in common with the jazz-influenced exotica of the time. But what is more important is that they take electronic music firmly into the pop mainstream. These are not the ambient soundscapes of the Barrons or the classical orchestration with electronic elements of Hermann and Rózsa. Rather, it is electronic pop, pure and not so simple, and in 1957 the world wasn't ready for it. The album, despite several subsequent reissues, remains obscure.

3

The privilege of ignoring conventions

Exploring the Forbidden Planet

There are several versions of the story of the unusual wedding present Louis and Bebe Barron were given when they married on 7 December 1947, each slightly different from the next. The most consistently told[31] is that a cousin who worked at 3M Corp gave them a tape recorder and access to a new product the company was developing – magnetic tape.[32] Another version has a friend giving them the tape recorder and the cousin the tape. There are several versions of many of the episodes in Louis and Bebe's subsequent career, as they were not always completely consistent in what they said. What is certain about this story, though, is that in 1947 they had a tape recorder. At the time, commercial tape recording was in its infancy, with the pioneering Ampex 200 model, the development of which was bankrolled by an investment from Bing Crosby, not introduced until 1948. It is likely that the wedding gift was a German Magnetophon, the type of machine Jack Mullin had brought over from Germany after the war, which Ampex had used as a model when developing its own machine. Later comments from Bebe such as 'It was supposedly the same kind that Hitler had used to record his speeches …'[33] bear this out, and in some accounts the friend (or cousin) was German. Later the Barrons acquired more tape recorders, including a Stancil Hoffman machine that seems to have been specially made for them, or at least customized.

Whatever that first tape recorder was, it granted them access into what was then a very exclusive club indeed. For the first few years of their commercial lives, tape recorders were expensive, specialist equipment, located in radio stations and professional recording studios. The Barrons, maybe uniquely at the time, had a tape recorder at home. And although by their own admission they were *avant-garde* bohemians at heart, they were possessed of sufficient business savvy to recognize the commercial opportunity their acquisition offered.

Bebe Barron was born Charlotte Wind in Minneapolis, Minnesota, in 1925, though in later life she often gave 1927 as her birth year. She spent most of her early life in North Dakota but returned to her hometown to study music, piano and composition at Minneapolis University, followed by a Masters in political science. At some point Charlotte became Bebe and was introduced to Louis Barron by his brother, who she was dating. Louis was an electronics enthusiast who had also returned to Minneapolis, where he had been born in 1920, having studied music at the University of Chicago. He hadn't taken the straight road home, though, breaking his journey with a spell in Mexico where he tried to write a play.

After the couple married they moved to Monterey and then San Francisco. During this period they encountered the French–Cuban diarist and eroticist Anaïs Nin, who had moved to the US from France in 1939, just before the outbreak of war. Nin (1903–77) is now remembered for her writings and for her affair with Henry Miller, but much of her work was published posthumously, and when she met the Barrons she was not a well-known figure. Nin's first husband, Hugh Parker Guiler (1898–1985), a banker and artist, went by the name Ian Hugo when he began making experimental films in the late 1940s and he and Nin became involved with some of the Barrons' earliest creative ventures. Nin and Bebe Barron in particular struck up a friendship, with the older woman becoming something of a mentor to her young friend, and, in time, godmother to the Barrons' son, Adam.

The first collaborations between the two couples were straightforward recordings of Nin reading from her work. The Barrons released these as two vinyl audiobooks on their boutique record label Contemporary Classics, the first in 1949. The two Nin releases are part of a series called Sound Portraits, which is known to include two albums each by Aldous Huxley and Henry Miller. It is possible that the series also included releases by Tennessee Williams, as both Barrons later mentioned recording him. The couple also made at least one 78-rpm disc, a recording of Nin reading from her work backed by voodoo chanting. The six known vinyl albums are intriguing curios, each pressed on pink vinyl. They proved hard to sell, though, as neither bookshops nor record shops would stock them. The venture failed, and Contemporary Classics recordings quickly faded into extreme obscurity.[34]

The couple relocated to New York in 1950. Here they set up home in an apartment on West 8th Street in Greenwich Village, building a studio in the living room. Jac Holzman, founder of Elektra and Nonesuch Records, recalls visiting them in the early 1950s, spending an afternoon with them in a 'room ... full of audio frequency oscillators and tape recorders; some primitive mixing equipment',[35] which was their base for more than a decade.

A few surviving photos of the couple in that studio – Bebe, petite and short-haired, alongside a mustachioed Louis – communicate a shared seriousness of purpose. They appear almost crowded out of the room by the banks of electronic equipment bearing down on them. Knowing the hours they spent there, for months on end, cutting tape and overloading their circuits to destruction, you get a sense of the intensity of their artistic life. Those photos tell another story, too. The layout of the studio represents the breakdown in traditional barriers in the music-making process. There were no separate control and live rooms, no vocal booths. Like many electronic musicians of this era the Barron's were composers, engineers, players (in a sense) and producers, and all of those functions were performed in that one room.

By now the Barrons' understanding of themselves as creative people had been formed by two developments in their thought. The first was one they shared with many electronic musicians of their generation: that is, that the tape recorder need not be just a device for recording sound, but could also be a means of manipulating it into new shapes, for creating previously unheard sounds. It was a creative instrument, not just a practical device. Bebe would later say that this realization dawned on them almost as soon as they got hold of their first tape recorder and started experimenting with reversing tapes and varispeed.[36] It isn't possible to put an exact date on this, but it is possible that the Barrons were the very first people to experiment with tape manipulation.

Another perception shift came when Louis read Norbert Wiener's *Cybernetics: Or Control and Communication in the Animal and the Machine* (1948). The idea expressed in Wiener's subtitle seems to have particularly struck the Barrons: both 'animals' (biological systems) and 'machines' (non-biological systems) can operate according to cybernetic principles. Wiener, a former child prodigy who had gained a mathematics degree at the age of 14, wrote about what happened when a system's action (a system could be animal or machine) changes its environment and that change in environment in turn causes the system to adapt. The Barrons applied this idea to sound-producing electronic circuits, made by Louis, which adapted as a result of alterations to their own internal working, thus causing changes in the sound they emitted. Louis and Bebe deliberately overloaded their circuits (the change in environment), which caused the circuits to adapt (make different sounds). The couple applied a certain poetic vision to this process and began to think of their circuits as living-things: 'They would shriek and coo,' Bebe said. 'They would start out and reach a kind of climax, and then they would die and you could never resurrect them.'[37] Or, as Louis put it, 'We can torture these circuits without a guilty conscience – whereas if we did it musically we might have to torture a musician ... we look on these circuits as genuinely suffering, but we don't feel compassion.'[38]

There was more to this than a vivid turn of phrase. The approach had a direct and audible impact on the couple's music, introducing a random element into their compositions at odds with the meticulous, tightly drilled and literally measured approach of much early tape composition. Other comments the pair made in later life indicate that what they were doing was a kind of improvisation. They would let the circuits loose in the world, record their 'lives', and then, from that mass of raw material, process and arrange the sound to suit their purposes. As a working method it wasn't too far away from the jazz approach of recording miles of tape of improvised takes and editing them into finished masters. But the unpredictability that the Barrons found so exciting, and which gave their music a sense of freedom rare in early electronic music, also posed one simple practical problem: they could never get the same sound twice.

The first piece of music the Barron's made in this way, which is also generally credited as the first piece of electronic tape music realized in the US, was called *Heavenly Menagerie.* Depending on which source you consult, it was made between 1950 and 1952. The couple's resumé, undated but written some time in the 1960s, doesn't list this piece at all. It commences instead with a collaboration with John Cage in a 'foundation-sponsored project to investigate further the relationship of music and sound'[39].

Once established in Greenwich Village, then a magnet for a certain brand of bohemian creativity, Louis and Bebe began frequenting the Artists Club, an informal Friday-night gathering of experimental artists and thinkers. It was here they met composer, music theorist, philosopher, poet, artist and *avant-garde* lodestar Cage (1912–92). Shortly after that first meeting he approached them to ask for their help in a collaborative project to make tape music, the Project of Music for Magnetic Tape, which also involved Earle Brown, Morton Feldman, David Tudor and Christian Wolff. Cage had got a grant from an acquaintance, Paul Williams, who had recently inherited a fortune, to fund the project. Cage gave the Barrons enough of this grant to pay their rent for a year, and the pair were tasked with doing the donkey work for what would become a piece named after their patron, the *Williams Mix*. This involved recording hundreds of snatches of sound (samples) in six categories: city sounds, country sounds, electronic sounds, manually produced sounds, wind-produced sounds and small sounds, the last category being sounds that needed amplification to be properly audible. These were then spliced into eight tracks of magnetic tape, with pitch, timbre, rhythm, type of splice and other variables minutely annotated on Cage's 192-page score. The structure for the piece was derived from the *I Ching*, which Cage had begun using as a way of incorporating chance into his compositional methodology.

Work on the *Williams Mix* took place over about nine months in 1952 to 1953, with the piece premiering in March 1953 at the University of Illinois Festival of Contemporary Arts. The product of this intense labour was a disorientating four-and-a-quarter-minute sound collage that, even now, some sixty years later, would still stand well beyond the furthest boundaries of what most people would consider as music. The Project of Music for Magnetic Tape threw up a few more fully realized works, including one credited to the Barrons alone, *For An Electronic Nervous System No. 1*, which also premiered at the Illinois Festival of Contemporary Arts.

The *Williams Mix* in particular pushed tape music technique to its limits, though for Louis and Bebe it was an anomalous piece of work, assembled from concrete sounds, as opposed to the electronically generated textures that were the raw material for all their other compositions. It was anomalous too in being probably the only time they rented out their studio facilities for someone else. An exceptional episode it might have been, but it was a pivotal experience. Louis later remarked that the experience of working with Cage opened up creative possibilities: 'you realize that you don't have to be restricted by the traditions, or the so-called laws, of music. So we began exploring, and I began developing my circuits.'[40]

The Barrons' involvement with Cage placed them firmly, if briefly, in music's radical fringe. Their other activities reinforced this. At around the same time that they were working on the *Williams Mix*, Louis and Bebe collaborated again with Anaïs Nin and her husband, working under the name Ian Hugo. The result was a short film, *Bells of Atlantis*, which combines protean, phantasmagorical images overlaid with Nin reading extracts from her book *House of Incest*. In fact, she is credited as acting and reciting, though the acting is confined to a few brief appearances rendered abstract by Hugo's treatment.

The Barrons' score ebbs and flows throughout the film, which, at about nine minutes long, provided them with the platform for their longest work from this period. The piece offers an insight into the extreme limitations they were operating within. Any sense of structure and rhythm is created using tape loops. A three-note loop runs for several minutes at the beginning of the film. On top of this structural base, texture and melody (or at least, variations in pitch) are built up using a great deal of tape echo (for texture) and varispeed (for pitch changes). There is less evidence of sophisticated tape slicing to affect timbre than in the *Williams Mix*, and it is possible that *Bells of Atlantis* predates the Cage collaboration (dates are uncertain). Yet despite these limitations the music does strike a mood that complements the images and words, achieving a balance between structure and randomness that make it sound semi-improvised, like jazz musicians working around a theme.

The Barrons' association with Cage continued for about a year, a period Bebe would later recall as a kind of idyll – days of intense creativity followed by evenings of feasting, with each participant taking turns to cook up some gourmet delight. Their studio flat became a place of pilgrimage for like-minded composers and their many visitors included Varèse, Stockhausen and Pierre Boulez. And to cap it all, they were being paid. But it couldn't last, and when they drifted away from Cage sometime in 1953 they were left fending for themselves, artistically and financially. The artistic freedom they welcomed, but money became a problem, as it tends to for experimental artists.

Over the following year or so there were several further small commissions and creative collaborations. These included a film called *Miramagic* by Walter Lewisohn and a mime score. There was also another Hugo film, *Jazz of Lights* (1954) in which Nin and blind musician and man of the streets Moondog travel across New York against a backdrop of impressionistic patterns created from the lights of Times Square. This was all interesting work, and there is a sense that it was with such projects as these that the Barrons felt most at home. But experimental art didn't pay the rent.

By 1954 the space exploration genre of American science fiction was well established and with it the use of electronics in both theme music and effects. Many films of this sort were cheap and quick B-movies, but not all. The first, *Destination Moon* (1950), had been a big-budget affair. MGM's entry into the genre, *Forbidden Planet*, was commissioned in 1954, with work beginning early the following year. The movie started out modestly, but as ambitions for it grew so did the budget. Work continued for over a year, with the film eventually released in April 1956.

Fred M. Wilcox, who had previously made Lassie films, directed *Forbidden Planet*. Cyril Hume wrote the screenplay, from a story by Irving Block and Allen Adler. Hume and Wilcox were Hollywood veterans nearing the ends of their respective careers. The film starred Leslie Nielsen, Walter Pidgeon and Anne Francis. Nielsen, later known for comedic roles, was at the start of his film career – this only his second movie appearance. Francis, though a few years younger than Nielsen, had been in several films since the late 1940s. The two died within a month of each other in 2011. Pidgeon was a matinee idol whose career stretched back to the silent era. Alongside the three human stars was another character, perhaps the best remembered: Robby the Robot. Robby was, at the time, the highest form of artificial life Hollywood had generated, with a recognizable personality and a distinct role in the action.

The story is set on the planet Altair IV, in the 23rd century. A spaceship arrives from Earth in search of a lost expedition sent 20 years earlier to establish a colony. The crew finds just one survivor of that expedition, Dr Edward Morbius (Pidgeon), living with his daughter, Altaira (Francis), born on Altair IV to a mother now dead. They are the only human life on the planet, their companions having perished in a disaster that Morbius alludes to mysteriously. Yet they enjoy a comfortable and peaceful existence, in part due to the attentions of guard and factotum, Robby. We learn later that the planet was once inhabited by a race of beings far advanced beyond even this futuristic rendering of humanity, but that this race, the Krell, were wiped out, though items of their self-maintaining machinery remain intact. The apparent utopian innocence of the father and daughter's isolated life is disturbed by the threat of an invisible monster, the emergence of which coincides with Altaira's burgeoning love for the spaceship's commander, John Adams (Nielsen). Comparisons have been made between *Forbidden Planet* and Shakespeare's *The Tempest*, but the resemblance is superficial. Although *The Tempest* does have a stranded father and daughter (Prospero and Miranda), Prospero engineers events to ensure a return to civilization. As the action of *Forbidden Planet* unfolds, we see Morbius apparently trying to do the opposite.

The sequence of events that led the Barrons to a Hollywood office and a commission to score *Forbidden Planet* seems itself like a rather fantastical Hollywood plot. The music they had produced for the various experimental shorts already mentioned had attracted some attention but hadn't made them any money. Louis, the more commercially ambitious, thought he and Bebe should look for an opening in the world of mainstream film making, and when he heard that Dore Schary, then President of MGM, was due in town the pair decided to engineer a meeting. Learning that Schary's wife was opening an art exhibition, the Barrons gatecrashed the launch party and boldly introduced themselves to Schary, who recalled later being approached by an 'eager eyed and intense' young couple with the appearance of an 'unmade bed'.[41] Their explanation of their electronic music piqued his interest to the extent that he invited them, should they ever be in Hollywood, to call him. With a no-doubt transparent show of insouciance, two weeks later the Barrons did just that. It was sometime in the middle of 1955. That call led to one of Hollywood's power-brokers inviting the impecunious, obscure, though by then better-groomed mavericks to come and see him at his office. He wasn't interested at all in the films the Louis and Bebe had been involved in, just the music, and he sat back in his executive's chair, eyes closed, and listened to the tapes they had brought. By his own account it occurred to him during that first meeting that the Barrons' music would be a good match for *Forbidden Planet*, then in production. He proposed the idea of the Barrons making a contribution to the film's producer, Nicholas Nayfack, and MGM's head of music, the four-times Oscar winner Johnny Green. Nayfack and Green were enthusiastic and the Barrons were invited to a screening of an early edit of the film, with dialogue and basic sound effects like footsteps and doors closing.

Negotiations were set in motion, lawyers consulted and contracts were drawn up, and by October of 1955 the Barrons were commissioned to provide electronic music for *Forbidden Planet*. The deal had a sliding scale of payments, allowing for several eventualities with different rates of pay attached to each – for example, a payment if none of the Barrons' music was used, another higher payment if as little as three seconds was used, and so on. There are minor inconsistencies in accounts of how much the contract was worth, but it was a lucrative opportunity. One credible account[42] gives a figure of $25,000 if the Barrons ended up providing the complete score, which they did, at a time when the average annual family income in the United States was $4,400.[43]

At this point a tantalizing detour appears. This sliding scale of payments in the contract no doubt reflected a reserve somewhere in the heart of the MGM machine about the risk of taking on complete unknowns for such a high-profile project. Bebe said much later that the studio was undecided about how to proceed and considered four options: the Barrons, a conventional orchestral score, a score realized by Harry Partch, or some kind of combination of any of these possibilities.[44] There appears to be no other reference to a putative Partch score, but a 1956 MGM single by David Rose and his Orchestra may have been part of a discarded alternative approach. Rose was a British-born songwriter and bandleader, once married to Judy Garland, and later notorious for writing *The Stripper*. Released in 7-inch 45-rpm and 10-inch 78-rpm formats, the single features music that the sleeve describes as 'inspired by the MGM cinemascope film *Forbidden Planet*'. The release was clearly an official MGM product, intended to promote the movie or benefit from the attention it was getting. The music itself is a mutant hybrid – an orchestral theme with a heavy coating of electronic effects and loops that sound very much like the Barrons'. It gives the impression that the electronic sounds were quickly dubbed on to an already-recorded orchestral theme, rather than the two elements being integrated from the start.

If there was reserve in MGM about the Barrons it was brushed aside, the studio ignoring a succession of precedents. Not content with taking a gamble on novitiate composers using techniques unique to them to make an obscure and novel form of music, MGM allowed the Barrons to work from their studio in New York. This, an abrupt departure from Hollywood convention, led to the Barrons being sent a rough cut of the film just before Christmas 1955. Bebe and Louis then locked themselves away in Greenwich Village for about three months of composing, recording and placing their music into the rough cut of the film. The result was aired at a test screening, with the music not yet properly integrated but playing on a manually synchronized tape recorder. The audience responded warmly, and at this point MGM finally committed itself to using the Barrons' music for the entire score, but not before one final show of corporate reserve. MGM attorney Rudy Monte circulated a tentative memo about possible complications with the score given that it didn't feature, in the conventional sense, any performing musicians. 'Do you suppose that perhaps the musicians union will say that they have jurisdiction over this if we call it electronic music?' he wondered.[45] Not wanting to open that particular can of worms, the studio attempted a neat tactical move to avoid confrontation: the Barrons' score would be termed 'electronic tonalities' and music would not be mentioned. The ruse worked and there never was any union complaint. By April 1956 *Forbidden Planet* was on general release in America.

Much has been made of the revolutionary nature of the *Forbidden Planet* score, but it was not completely without precedent. It was the first full-length commercial movie to feature an all-electronic score, and that score would still sound daring in a Hollywood film even now. But by 1956 electronic sound and space were already indissolubly linked in the popular mind. One review of the film observed:

> The soundtrack, instead of being filled with inappropriate music, is full of new sounds – the bleats, burps, whirs, whines, throbs, hums and screeches which our ears are learning to distinguish as we become ever more familiar with the electronic, and sub-electronic, universe.[46]

Films like the *The Day the Earth Stood Still* had created an expectation that a certain type of film would include electronic sound. *Forbidden Planet*, with its outer-space setting, its robots and rockets, its threatening alien life forms, was that type of film. One way of understanding the soundtrack is to place it as an end point in a remarkably brief period of musical evolution. In the space of six years, electronic sound in science fiction movie music moved through four distinct stages. First there were the quiet, uncredited loops of *Destination Moon*, followed by the theremin in orchestral settings in films like *The Thing* and *Rocketship XM*. Then, in *The Day The Earth Stood Still*, an adapted orchestra including electric strings and organs accompanies two theremins-provided theme music, alongside some electronically generated sound effects made with oscillators, theremins and backwards recordings. This is a transitional work, a half-electronic score that prepares the ears for *Forbidden Planet*, with its entirely electronic score.

The approach the Barrons applied to the *Forbidden Planet* score was the same that they used throughout their creative partnership. Although both were trained musicians they evolved distinct but complimentary roles. Louis was more technically minded and built the circuits that generated the raw sounds. The couple would then activate these circuits and record whatever happened. The language they used to describe the circuits reflects their personification of them, blurring the boundary between animal and machine life. There was much talk of death, of climaxes and breakdowns, of relaxation and tension. This type of language, ascribing to the circuits the characteristics of organic life, is at odds with the tendency toward vague mysticism adopted by many other electronic music pioneers, but it springs from the same source. The sounds were new, and there was no accepted vernacular with which to address them or discuss them. For the Barrons, the circuits were life-like in their inherent unpredictability. This, Louis was later to say, set his and Bebe's approach apart from the most other electronic music of the time, which, he argued, used equipment 'made to be very precise and definite, and people aren't. Art isn't.'[47]

Once the raw sound was captured on tape it fell to Bebe to listen to it all and select what might be suitable for further use. In the context of *Forbidden Planet* this meant choosing sound that could be applied to particular characters or scenes. Once this winnowing process had taken place both Louis and Bebe would process the sounds until satisfied that what they were hearing represented what they wanted to convey. This processing involved all the standard tape techniques – speeding up, slowing down and reversing tape, tape echo, feedback and looping. Then, finally, the assorted sounds would be edited and multi-tracked by bouncing between tape recorders until pieces were deemed finished.

It is this approach, a kind of curating of serendipity, that imbued the Barrons' music with its free-flowing, liquid character. It was as if they were bandleaders and the circuits themselves musicians who they allowed to improvise. Or, as Bebe once put it, the circuits were the actors and she and Louis the directors. The excitement was in waiting to see what these improvisations would throw up and what could be done with them.

'We took upon ourselves the privilege of ignoring conventions'[48] said Louis thirty years after the film's release. Yet though the *Forbidden Planet* score was a radical innovation, it was not anarchic. There are two senses in which it actually conforms to convention.

Many science fiction films made since 1950 tended to use electronic sound and music with electronic elements to evoke alien life, space travel and distant planets. This wasn't a strict rule by any means, but there is a pattern. Schary must have been aware of it when he decided that the Barrons' music would be suitable for the film. In *Forbidden Planet* almost all the action is set on Altair IV and the little that isn't is set on the space ship. This gave the Barrons freedom to approach the entire film as ripe for their attention, without departing completely from audience expectations.

Another aspect of their approach that conformed even more closely to the conventions of film scoring in general, not just science fiction film scoring, was their decision to use leitmotifs to represent various characters and recurring scenarios. This was a planned and deliberate process. Bebe said later: 'We set down a list of characters and approached it like a director would, directing the actors. We would build a circuit for each character ...'[19]

Most film composers that had used theremins or other electronic sources up to that point had found them effective for suspense, fear, distress, other-worldliness or, conversely, comedy. Electronic music in general had not yet learned the musical language of love, and nor had the Barrons. And here the leitmotif approach revealed the limits of the expressive range of their methodology and technology.

Robby is employed as a comic foil at intervals throughout the film, particularly in a sub-plot where he makes 60 gallons of bourbon for the spaceship's cook. Robby's appearances are often accompanied by a skittering, tumbling echo trail of notes, and the scene in which the cook finds the whiskey features a staggering drunk of a theme.

Similarly effective are the cues used for the invisible monster. When it first impinges on the action, entering the spaceship at night, plodding, spongy blobs of sound conjure up images of a menacing, remorseless, ponderous creature. When it approaches the spaceship a second time those plodding sounds are synchronized exactly with the appearance of footsteps in the sand and stairs bowing under a great unseen weight. By the time of the monster's third attack its musical theme is sufficiently established to serve as advance warning of the impending terror before any physical traces become apparent. For the climactic scene when an electric force field reveals the monster's outline the Barrons reserved some of their most exquisitely tortured circuits, howling in a furious rage. We learn that the monster is the primitive, untamed nature of Morbius himself, the Id, and the agonized electronic cries the Barrons give it bridge the gap between personal and impersonal, the human and the monstrous.

Although the raw sound material itself is unusual, this leitmotif approach is established scoring technique. Yet it falls short when it comes to romance. When mild flirtation begins between some of the spaceship's crew and Altaira, the Barrons cue it with subdued, slightly unsettling bleeping that doesn't fit the gentle, coy, mildly suggestive humour the scene requires. The first kiss between Altaira and Commander Adams is accompanied by dreamy washes of sound that might be a choir of Cupid's angels, yet the music's summoning of romance is erratic.

Despite these limitations, the score was a speculative marvelling at what film music might become. From the first second it grabs the attention. The electronic tonalities swoop boldly over the opening title credits and a scene-setting narration that follows. Where in earlier films there might have been a strident orchestral theme resolving into subdued theremin background notes, we hear instead molten, rolling cascades of electronic noise. From thereon, roughly half of the 90 or so minutes of the film feature sonic material that blurs the traditional boundary between sound effects and musical score to irrelevance. Although there are conventional literal sound effects from time to time, often it is left to the Barrons to provide the actual sound of futuristic technology. When the spaceship lands on Altair IV to multi-layered tones timed to cut out when the machine comes to rest, a scene that provoked spontaneous audience applause in a test screening, we understand those tones not as a musical evocation of the spaceship, but the actual noise that the spaceship makes. Similarly, much later in the film, the subterranean Krell machinery makes a grinding industrial sound, again electronically generated. Yet these uses of electronic sound as literal sound effects sit alongside much more electronic sound obviously from the same source, and with similar textures, that serves as music in the conventional sense, cueing the arrival of certain characters or creating atmosphere. So the entire sound world of the film, sound effect and music, is rendered as a whole: one sort of sound coming from one source.

Although the audience of 1956 was accustomed to, even expecting, electronic sound in a science fiction film, they had until this point experienced it in two ways: either electronic instruments cradled in conventional orchestrations or straightforward sound effects made electronically. In *The Day the Earth Stood Still*, until this point the most advanced score in terms of its use of electronics, the theremins are placed with conventional instrumentation and the electronically generated sound effects are clearly that – sounds, not music. In *Forbidden Planet* not only is this distinction between sound and music disregarded; the actual aural textures have few connections with anything familiar. There is melody and harmony and rhythm of sorts, but the effect is impressionistic and abstract. There is a floating, indefinite quality that speaks of eternal drifting through space. Notes disappear down corridors of echo and various contrasting sonorities are multi-tracked to build densely complex abstractions. In the context of the times perhaps the decision to call this sound 'electronic tonalities' was correct after all. If the people sitting in cinemas in 1956 had been asked the question 'Is this music?' most would have answered no. Another answer is suggested when Morbius plays what he describes as a recording by Krell musicians. The extinct Krell were evolved way beyond even the 23rd century human race, possessors of powers of intellect beyond imagining. And what is their music like? It is a brief fragment of sound from the softer end of the Barrons' spectrum.

Forbidden Planet was released to some fanfare, with posters proclaiming 'it's out of this world' and 'nothing like it ever', but it was only a modest commercial hit. *Variety* placed it at number 62 in the year's best grossing films. Its impact wasn't sufficient to prompt a succession of big-budget science fiction movies from other studios and the genre spent the rest of the decade on the b-list. Like *The Day the Earth Stood Still* before it, it is a film that has grown in stature as time passes. Although it has come to be thought of as typifying 1950s science fiction, the combination of Shakespearean allusions, spaceships and Freud with a big studio and big-budget production values sets *Forbidden Planet* apart. Its electronic score set it apart too, and the Barrons, in the immediate wake of the film's release, must have imagined a very different career path stretching ahead of them from the one they eventually took.

At first it seemed that Louis and Bebe had done well out of the film. They received a generous fee and were allowed to keep the record rights to the score, which they exploited periodically over the years. Meanwhile, their music was attracting attention. But within a year things turned sour. *Forbidden Planet* was nominated for just one award in the 1957 Oscars, in the Special Effects category, which from 1939 to 1962 combined visual and sound effects. When the nominations were announced the name of the head of MGM's sound department was mentioned and the Barrons were not. They were incensed, *Variety* reporting that 'a strong complaint has been registered with both Academy of Motion Picture Arts & Sciences and Metro execs by Louis and Bebe Barron'.[50]

The couple commenced legal action, demanding that if the film won that the award should be given to them. It didn't win, but the damage was done. It seems like a headstrong course to pursue. Even if the Barrons were being deliberately marginalized, perhaps their strong reaction was an indicator of other simmering frustrations with the studio or the Hollywood system. Whatever the motives for the lawsuit were, the action failed and was abandoned, but not before the couple had spent a significant portion of their earnings for the film in legal fees.

Considered pragmatically, the lawsuit was a disastrous career move. As novices and outsiders in Hollywood the Barrons would have come up against prejudice anyway when looking for further work. With the lawsuit they must have looked like troublemakers and were probably considered suspect by the Hollywood community. They thought so, anyway, and in interviews over the ensuing years talked in tones of resigned bitterness of blacklists. At first glance events seem to bear that out, as they were never again hired to soundtrack a commercial film. It is possible, though, that in their disappointment the Barrons came to personalize what was actually an impersonal process driven by many competing commercial forces. In the history of electronic music their score has come to be seen as a milestone, and rightly so. But from the perspective of the movie industry at the time it might not have sounded like the future, but just an unusual score to a modestly successful film, and little more. Although it did provoke some comment at the time, many reviewers simply ignored the music or gave it just a cursory mention. *The Guardian's* reviewer didn't notice the Barrons' contribution, but was impressed with the visual effects.[51] The *New York Times* referred briefly to 'the accompaniment of interstellar gulps and burbles – that take the place of a musical score' with no further comment.[52] Far more attention was paid to Robby, who had a little career of his own with a follow-up film and a guest appearance on an episode of TV's *Lost in Space*. Furthermore, the Barrons were physically removed from Hollywood and thus easily overlooked. They did move west eventually, in 1962, but by this time any momentum generated by *Forbidden Planet* had wound down. Their career thereafter has a rather desultory character, though it was not without incident. The undated resumé jumps around from small art house projects to the occasional commercial job, and a few guest university lectures.[53]

The couple's first commercial assignment after *Forbidden Planet* was providing 12 minutes of sound for Gore Vidal's *A Visit to a Small Planet*. Vidal had written the play, a science fiction spoof satirizing cold war fears for television in 1955. He later adapted it for the stage, and it was filmed in 1960 with Jerry Lewis starring. The Barrons were involved only in the stage version of the play. This was a success, running to 388 performances at Booth Theatre, New York City, from February 1957 to January 1958, and earning three Tony nominations. The play's programme credited the electronic sound as 'emotional and rather alarming vibrations electronically created by Louis and Bebe Barron'. The director and star, Cyril Richard, commissioned the Barrons again in 1961, to provide 'electric tonalities' for a musical comedy, *The Happiest Girl in the World*, where their contributions sat uneasily in a light operatic setting. Other work in this period harked back to the couple's *avant-garde* roots, such as the score to a seven-minute experimental film, *Bridges Go Round*, directed by Shirley Clarke in 1958 and shown at Expo 58. There were also occasional short commercial commissions, such as *Quartz Crystal Growing* (1962), which was a Western Electric industrial information short, and an advert for the Ford Fairlane.

A collaboration with the self-styled official witch of Los Angeles, Louise Huebner, was one of the Barrons' odder commissions. This took the form of an album called *Seduction through Witchcraft* (1969), in which Huebner offers occult advice over the Barrons' music. Incredibly, it got a major label release on Warners. Equally curious was a collaboration with the aging Czech actress Florence Marly, once the on-screen wife of Humphrey Bogart. In 1966 a declining Marly appeared in a science fiction horror B-movie called *Queen of Blood*, starring Basil Rathbone in one of his final roles. Marly wrote and recorded a song for the film with the help of Frank Zappa called 'Space Boy', her stern intoning bringing Nico to mind. The song, which wasn't used in the film, was covered in plummeting electronic bubbling that sounded very much like the work of the Barrons, though it is sometimes credited to others. Seven years later Marly wrote a short film of the same name in an attempt to relaunch her career, appearing in it wearing a nude body stocking. This time the credits left no doubt that the electronics were the work of the Barrons. *Space Boy* the film has become a kitsch favourite at science fiction conventions, but was actually nominated for the best short film award at the 1973 Cannes Film Festival, the last time the Barrons brushed up against the establishment film world.

There is no obvious theme to this disparate body of work, but it does reveal much about the predicament the couple found themselves in. The truth is that the Barrons spent the years after *Forbidden Planet* casting around for whatever work they could get. Unable to land any major film commissions, they drifted back into experimental work, where they felt most at home, and picked up the occasional paying job. But regardless of what sort of film or play or ballet or advert they were scoring, the actual music they came up with sounded much the same. Removed from their respective contexts, it would be hard to tell extracts from *Quartz Crystal Growing*, *Forbidden Planet*, *Seduction through Witchcraft* and *Bells of Atlantis* apart. Their approach, though revolutionary in the early 1950s and well suited to the creation of viscous abstractions, was limited and they soon exhausted its possibilities.

A related difficulty the Barrons faced was that by the 1960s they had competitors who could make electronic music with some similar characteristics, yet more conventional structure. In the early 1950s they were virtually alone in America as independent electronic music composers. One reason why they attracted the attention of Cage and Varèse, and later MGM studios, is that they were doing something unique. Yet before long other composers emerged who were making music that, superficially at least, had some of the same features as the Barrons'. Paul Beaver was amassing electronic instruments in Los Angeles and hiring them and himself out to film studios, while in New York Raymond Scott and Eric Siday were building up expensive private electronic music studios and targeting the television advert market. All three made music that, like the Barrons', sounded spacey and weird and futuristic, but in the case of Scott and Siday in particular tended to have more obvious structure, melody and rhythm. Electronic music was still considered with suspicion and even something close to fear in many quarters, and more conservatively minded directors, programmers and commissioners had to get over two hurdles with the Barrons – the concept of electronic music itself and then their distance from conventional metrical structure, rhythm, harmony and melody. With these other composers only the first hurdle had to be negotiated.

Furthermore, the remorseless advance of technology overtook the Barrons. Within the space of ten years they went from being the earliest of adopters to dogmatic idealists for a lost cause. Techniques and equipment that had been advanced in 1951 were dated by the end of the decade, but the Barrons were unable or unwilling to change. When they moved to Los Angeles in 1962 they dismantled their studio and took it with them, reassembling it in a garage and starting again where they left off. They were still using what amounted to the same set-up when Louis died in 1989. Years before the couple moved west Scott and Siday had far more lavishly equipped studios combining electronic instruments, all manner of sound processing gear and better tape recorders than the Barrons. They could work more quickly, and got results that were more cleanly recorded and with more varied sound colours. By 1965 Siday was using a Moog, and Beaver followed suit in early 1967, while Louis Barron was still building his tube-based cybernetic circuits.

The Barrons also struggled with being typecast as space composers. Even as early as 1957 and A Visit to a Small Planet they were effectively parodying their work in Forbidden Planet. And one of the things that upset them most about their decaying relationship with MGM was when the studio licensed their music for use in From The Earth to the Moon, a 1958 filming of the Jules Verne novel of the same name. Their work, unique in 1956, had become generic background space music within a few years.

According to the couple's son, Adam Barron, Louis and Bebe spent the years from 1962 to 1969 in a perpetual sense of frustration about their stalled career, surviving on handouts from their own parents.[54] There were occasional false dawns and dashed hopes. Herb Alpert visited them on one occasion for a discussion, and there was talk of the politician, tycoon and arts benefactor Bart Lytton sponsoring them. Tracing their erratic path through the sixties, there is evidence of pulling in several directions. Theirs was a career uncomfortably balanced between art and science, academia and auto-didactism, the *avant-garde* and the commercial, between music and sound. What the Barrons really wanted to do was make experimental art music, and it was their fate to be caught between a desire to do this and the need to make money. 'We always thought of ourselves as part of the same group as Cage, Ussachevsky and the rest,'[55] said Bebe in 1986, later still declaring that she and Louis were 'never interested in the mainstream'.[56]

Taking those inclinations into account, *Forbidden Planet*, for which the Barrons are remembered, was the biggest anomaly of their career, and the Broadway shows and things like the Ford advert lesser anomalies. But even the art projects were few and far between. Maybe they were victims of inverted snobbery, their brief commercial success marginalizing them from the serious experimental music scene. There is certainly the sense that they never quite found a place in the world of 'Cage, Ussachevsky and the rest'. Ramon Sender recalled going to an event in New York connected with the circle of composers around Elliott Carter and Milton Babbitt sometime in the late 1950s or early 1960s. 'Louis got up there and demonstrated some of his little circuitries and networks. He received what I felt were a lot of very intolerant … looks from the New York composers, who considered his approach very lowbrow.'[57] They were all but ignored in academic circles until the 1980s, by which time it was too late. Even then, much of the attention came from film studies academics rather than musicians.

The move to Los Angeles in 1962 might not have revived the Barrons' career but it marked the beginning of new directions in their lives. Both were politically very liberal and during the decade they joined the Peace and Freedom Party and were involved in anti-Vietnam demonstrations. Louis in particular embraced the hippy movement, and in his late 40s became a sort of uncle figure to younger hippies at love-ins and communes. Bebe later talked about the strain of working together so intensely damaging the marriage and the couple split in 1969 and divorced in 1970. Both remarried.

4

Out of the ordinary

The birth of popular British electronic music

In 1946 the Scottish typographer Ruari McLean, who designed the Puffin imprint for Penguin, sketched a Royal Navy radar operator surrounded by a collection of electronic equipment and a derelict harmonium. The Navy man was Tristram Cary, who was spending a short leave at Oxford University, where he had started studying in 1943 and where he would return when discharged from military service in 1947. The electronic equipment was dubbed 'the machine', a protean collection of odds and ends that Cary was putting together with the intention of making electronic music. It accompanied Cary to London when he moved there in 1948, and would follow him around like a faithful wire-sprouting self-regenerating pet for the rest of his life.[58] At around the same time, a BBC music balancer named Daphne Oram, also based in London, was composing a still-unrecorded and unperformed 30-minute piece called *Still Point* that was to have combined conventional orchestration with pre-recorded instrumental sounds and live electronic treatments using then-standard radio equipment. These were the hidden, modest beginnings of British electronic music.

The country at the time was still in the grip of post-war austerity and rationing remained in place until 1954, and yet at the start of the new decade signs of change were everywhere. The Festival of

Britain (1951) introduced radical modern architecture to bombed-out London, positing a new era of technological progress symbolized by the Skylon, a rocket-like tower that pointed heavenward from the south bank of the Thames; the de Havilland Comet, the world's first jet airliner went into service in 1952; and television was well on its way to ubiquity. Although the BBC had first broadcast television in 1932 and had started again after a wartime break in 1946, it was the live broadcast on BBC of the coronation of Queen Elizabeth II in 1953 that ushered in the television age in Britain. An estimated 20 million crowded around the flickering black-and-white images on 9-inch screens to see the young Queen crowned. On 22 September 1955 The Independent Television Network (ITV) was launched, and on that day the first British television commercial was broadcast.

The early days of British television were governed by a prevailing attitude of improvisation. Everything was new, and programmes were live. There were few established practices to fall back on, so people just tried things out and hoped they'd work, which sometimes they did and often didn't. Electronic music was at a similar stage and the two emerging media became intertwined. By the time the Queen was crowned, affordable tape recorders were on sale, and the county was awash with decommissioned military electronic equipment dating from the war. These were the tools of the budding electronic composer, and as soon as they became readily available a small band of sonic adventurers – including Cary and Oram, F. C. Judd, Desmond Leslie and Barry Gray – began experimenting with electronic music. Within a few years television was the vehicle delivering this electronic music to a mass British audience.

If Britain at this time was changing, reaching out of a constrained present into a bright new future, combining make-do-and-mend necessity with visionary radicalism, Cary and Oram personified this state of flux. Completely unnoticed at the time, their prescient acts set in train a sequence of events that led to the BBC Radiophonic Workshop and EMS Synthesizers, marking them out as the progenitors of a peculiarly British strand of electronic music that smuggled traces of the forbidding high-art aesthetics of the Paris and Cologne electronic music studios of Schaeffer and Stockhausen into the nation's homes through children's television themes, adverts and radio jingles.

Oram and Cary were both born in 1925, Oram in Devizes, Wiltshire and Cary in Oxford. Both attended public schools and both showed some early musical promise. Along with another exact contemporary, Desmond Briscoe, born in Birkenhead, they wrote the blueprint for British electronic music.

Cary's heritage seems best fitted to life as an artistic pioneer. He was raised in a bohemian, artistic milieu, the son of the Irish modernist novelist Joyce Cary. His mother was a keen amateur cellist, and Cary himself made some progress with piano, oboe and horn. An exceptionally bright boy, he won a King's Scholarship to the prestigious Westminster School in 1938, one of only eight a year selected by a competitive entrance examination. This meant his parents paid reduced fees, or no fees at all, which would have been welcome, as money was short in the Cary household. He immersed himself in the life of the school, excelling in swimming, athletics and gymnastic competitions, was active in the school's Scout troop and edited the school magazine, *The Elizabethan*.[59] He left Westminster in December 1942, going up to read Classics at Christ Church, Oxford.

Oram, meanwhile, came from more conventional stock. The daughter of a prosperous businessman, her school records paint a picture of a conventional, hard-working girl. A Girl Guide and a prefect, in 1941 she passed her Royal Schools of Music grade five piano with credit, a good but not spectacular performance for a fifteen year old. She passed her school certificate in 1942 with three 'very goods' (the highest of three pass grades) and four 'credits' (the middle-ranking pass grade), including one for music.[60] She stayed at school until July 1943 before revealing an independent streak by choosing to join the BBC as a junior studio engineer and music balancer, then an unusual career choice for a woman. The following year she read two books, Kurt London's *Film Music* (1936) and Leopold Stowkowski's *Music for All Of Us* (1943), which triggered a fascination with the possibilities of electronic sound. That general interest acquired a much more precise direction when she was sent on a training course, during which the tutor demonstrated a waveform visually represented on the screen of an oscilloscope. Could, Oram wondered, you do it the other way round? That is, draw a waveform that could somehow be turned into actual sound? She would spend the rest of her professional life grappling with the implications of that question.

Meanwhile, Cary's education was interrupted by war. He stayed at Oxford for just two terms before being called up for the Royal Navy. He served from 1943 until 1946 as a radar operator, latterly on the light aircraft carrier HMS *Triumph*. Like many others, Cary found that war service gave him a breadth of experience he wouldn't otherwise have had. The Navy's radar training also gave him a good grounding in electronics that would come in handy later on. During these three years Cary decided he wanted to be a composer and became interested in electronic music. Leaving the Navy at the end of 1946, he returned to Oxford to study Politics, Philosophy and Economics, and then, from 1948, studied music at Trinity College, London, for a year. By this time, the 'machine' incorporated a disc-cutting lathe that Cary had bought with his de-mob pay and a collection of military surplus electronics. It was set up in Cary's flat in Wimpole Street, quite probably the first home studio in the country. As well as his own experiments, Cary sometimes recorded other musicians, including his old school friend Donald Swann, of Flanders and Swann fame. Cary and Oram did not, at the time, know of each other's near-simultaneous electronic epiphanies. It was several years before their paths converged.

In the immediate post-war era pure electronic music barely existed and the use of electronic sound alongside conventional instruments was in its infancy. That changed from 1948, with the appearance of the first commercially available magnetic tape recorders. The earliest models were huge and expensive, but by the early 1950s smaller and cheaper models made the technology more accessible. The device's potential for not only recording sound but also manipulating it and so inventing new sound was quickly realized and led to a surge of creativity around the world. In Britain, that surge swept up Cary, Oram and Desmond Briscoe, though in Cary's case at least his interest in electronic sound pre-dated the tape recorder's commercial introduction.

As news of the experiments in *musique concrète* and *Elektronische Musik* began to filter from Paris and Cologne through to London, Oram in particular could only look on in frustrated envy. Both the Paris and Cologne studios were located in and funded by radio stations. Oram and Cary, on the other hand, were dependent entirely on their own initiative, lone operators without backers, funders or premises. They were boffins on a very tight budget. Oram tried, and failed, to build her own tape recorder, while Cary constructed his own gear from the glut of military surplus equipment then going cheap. But although initial attempts by Oram to interest her employers in the BBC in investing in its own electronic music resource came to nothing, the corporation began making its first tentative incursions in that direction in 1953. In the early 1950s the unknown world of space cast a spell over the popular imagination. As the theremins on American science fiction film soundtracks at the time demonstrated, electronic music seemed the obvious soundtrack for it: futuristic, technological, a little bit frightening.

Journey into Space was a BBC Radio science fiction programme, written by Charles Chilton and first broadcast in September 1953 on the Light Programme, just as radio was beginning to give way to television as the dominant form of family entertainment. Popular in its day, it follows Captain Jet Morgan and his crew of astronauts, who rocket to the Moon (initially, then to Mars in later series) in the distant future of 1965. Electronic sound accompanied the intrepid explorers both in the form of a Clavioline, used by composer Van Phillips in the incidental music, and, more radically, a swooping, echoed oscillator tone that ascended over the main orchestral theme. This was heard at the beginning of each episode, a simple, clear aural picture of a rocket ascending into the forbidding unknown with an announcer declaring in stentorian tones: 'The BBC presents Jet Morgan in *Journey into Space*.'

If it was that imagined future in a popular science fiction fantasy that brought electronic sound to millions of British radio listeners, it was a real and immeasurably more frightening technological development that provided the subject for the BBC's first full electronic score. A radio play, *The Japanese Fishermen*, about a fishing boat caught up in the Pacific H-bomb tests of 1954, was broadcast in 1955. It fell to Cary and the machine to create the tolling percussive hits and ominous drones that make up the soundtrack. Waves of sound wash up a flotsam and jetsam of crackling electronic debris, with varispeed clearly audible. It is music of texture, primarily, with little in the way of conventional melody or rhythm.

By this time Desmond Briscoe, too, was getting interested in electronic sound. A career BBC man, Briscoe spent his entire working life in the corporation, apart from a period of military service during and shortly after World War II with the Grenadier Guards and then the Royal Army Educational Corps. Although his initial involvement was as an engineer and a composer, Briscoe's main contribution to emerging electronic music would be as a manager and administrator. He proved to be skilled at navigating the labyrinthine BBC decision-making process, and was also adept at supporting creative people who came under his charge.

Briscoe inherited from his father, a telephone engineer, an interest in technology. He was also a musician, a teenage drummer and bandleader. After leaving the Army he worked in radio drama at the BBC, encountering Dylan Thomas and Louis MacNeice. His work included balancing musical instruments in live performance and dropping sound effects from 78-rpm discs into drama productions. Like Oram and Cary, he had come across early electronic music from the continent and saw its potential for radio drama. Briscoe and Oram were leading figures in a band of co-conspirators within the BBC who made electronic sound for a number of productions in the years immediately before the formal establishment of the Radiophonic Workshop.

A pivotal work was a Samuel Beckett one-act play *All That Fall,* written in 1956, produced by Donald McWhinnie and broadcast in January 1957 on the Third Programme. McWhinnie, realizing that the sonic complexity the play demanded would be beyond conventional music and sound effects records, enlisted Briscoe to work on sound. The play follows an elderly Irish woman, Maddy Rooney (played by Billie Whitelaw), on what is ostensibly a mundane journey to and from a railway station to meet her husband as he returns from work. The sounds that represent the various events of the journey – footsteps, car engines, a train and so on – are manipulated so that the listener experiences not simply a representational recording of, say, footsteps, but an impressionistic audio cue removed from the purely realistic sphere. *The Disagreeable Oyster,* a surreal comedy by Giles Stannus Cooper, followed *All That Fall* later that year. McWhinnie, too, produced it, with sound by Briscoe. The abrupt switch from serious art to humour in these two pioneering sonic excursions sums up the tension at the heart of the Radiophonic Workshop that was formed in their wake: the serious versus the disposable; art versus entertainment; rarified versus popular.

If electronic music of the time is thought of as a spectrum, at one extreme of which is manipulated sound effects and the other conventional music realized electronically, then these early radio plays that Briscoe was involved in leaned heavily toward the first. On the other hand, even Oram's earliest recorded work displays a much more conventional musicality. Roughly parallel to Briscoe's work, in 1957 she was commissioned by the BBC to write electronic music and effects for a BBC television adaptation of *Amphitryon 38*, a play written in 1929 by French dramatist Jean Giraudoux. Oram responded by gathering rudimentary equipment – oscillators, a tape recorder and some filters – from various BBC studios after they had shut down for the night, taking it all up to an empty room on the sixth floor of Broadcasting House and working from midnight until 4am for several weeks. Broadcast in March the following year, this was the first electronic score heard on British television. The programme itself is lost, but surviving sound tapes demonstrate that Oram was intent on using electronics to make something much closer to conventional music, with her soft, whistling melody over a gently churning loop some distance from Briscoe's electronically manipulated sound effects.

With the success of these early productions, and in the face of persistent lobbying by a small but determined group of BBC staffers, the BBC formalized the experiments in the shape of a new department, the Radiophonic Workshop. There was the sense of the corporation reluctantly bowing to pressure from faintly irritating agitators. Dick Mills, who went on to become the longest-serving Workshop staff member, later said that the unspoken but clearly implied BBC attitude was 'Why don't we give them a room somewhere, fill it with all of this equipment and let them get it out of their systems?'[61]

The BBC opened the Radiophonic Workshop on April Fools' Day 1958, in Room 13 at its studio in Maida Vale, west London, though a press launch didn't happen until May. The first weeks were spent bringing order to the chaotic assembly of equipment that had been liberated from other departments: tape recorders, turntables, oscillators, all the usual tools of the electronic musician, but in this case generally second hand, out of date and sometimes malfunctioning. The mixing desk was an oak-encased pre-war relic that had previously been installed in the Albert Hall. The electronics were gradually augmented by a magpie's nest of bottles to hit, a homemade one-string 'electric guitar' (a single string stretched between two nails in a piece of wood, with a pick up), a melodica, an autoharp, a mijwiz (an Arabian pipe) and other assorted musical toys.

On the door Oram pinned a quote from Francis Bacon's utopian novel *New Atlantis* (1624):

> Wee have also Sound-houses, wher wee practice and demonstrate all sounds and their Generation. Wee have harmonies and lesser slides of sounds. Wee make diverse tremblings and Warblings of Sounds ... Wee have also diverse Strange and Artificiall Eccho's. We have also means to convey Sounds in Trunks and Pipes, in strange Lines and Distances.

Not only was the text strangely prophetic, but Bacon himself – a philosopher, statesman, scientist, lawyer, author, and a Christian with apparent Rosicrucian sympathies – seemed like an apt spirit to invoke: a venturer in thought in the heart of the establishment.

The press launch in May attracted some interest, with journalists from *The Times*, *Telegraph* and *Reuters* rubbing shoulders with specialists from the music, radio and technical press. The term 'radiophonic' was dreamt up to describe what a press release for the event called 'a new sound – suggestive of emotion, sensation, mood, rather than the literal meaning of a wind or the opening of a door. Created by mechanical means from basic sounds which may vary from the rustle of paper to a note from an electronic oscillator ...' This same statement distanced the workshop's output not only from conventional sound effects, but music as well: as far as the BBC was concerned, radiophonics added a new dimension to sound that fell somewhere between the two.

Oram became one of the Radiophonic Workshop's first members of staff, designated Studio Manager. She worked alongside Briscoe, who was given the same designation. Some histories emphasize her skill, competence and experience as a classically trained musician. It is perhaps closer to the truth to say that she was simply the most musical amongst the BBC staffers then interested in electronic sound, most of whom came from a drama and radio production background. Certainly, her school results indicate creditable, but not outstanding, formal musical ability.

Radiophonics quickly took on a peculiar character, where the seriousness of formal electronic music was expressed in popular, middlebrow forms, blurring the distinction almost to the point of irrelevance. One result of this was that the main differences between much of the Radiophonic Workshop's output and the serious *avant-garde* were often ones of length, intent and context. Tonally, rhythmically, melodically, texturally, to a casual listener a brief extract of many Radiophonic compositions wouldn't then have sounded too different from the contemporaneous work of Stockhausen or Henry or Schaeffer, and they wouldn't now. Anyone taking a test involving listening blind to 30-second snatches of late 1950s music by Gene Vincent, Miles Davis and Benjamin Britten would immediately be able to tell that the three extracts were different from each other in some essential, non-negotiable way. The same cannot be said of a similar comparison between much popular British electronic music and serious electronic music of the time. In part, this was down to the extreme limitations imposed on all electronic musicians by the equipment then available. Rather like those mountaineers in the 1920s who tried to climb Everest wearing hob-nailed boots and tweeds, that generation of electronic musicians was striving for something it didn't have the resources to reach. But that aside, the popular and the serious sounded similar because many of the popular composers would rather have been writing serious music, but they didn't have the funding. So instead they channelled their enthusiasms into the theme music, jingles and incidental soundscapes of television and radio.

This tension was particularly painful for Oram and in 1959, craving creative freedom, she cashed in her pension and left the BBC. She moved to Tower Folly, near Fairset, Kent, one of the first oast houses to be converted to a dwelling. There she built her own studio in an octagonal room at the base of the kiln tower and embarked on a freelance career as a composer, inventor, producer, lecturer and writer. Briscoe, meanwhile, remained at the BBC and managed the Radiophonic Workshop until his retirement in 1983. As manager he worked less on composition and more in administering and guiding the department, in which capacity he supported the workshop through its most productive years in the 1960s and 1970s. He did, though, produce electronic sound for *Quatermass and the Pit*, shown on the BBC in late 1958 and early 1959, the third instalment in a compelling and popular series written by Nigel Kneale that ran through much of the decade.

Quatermass was true mass entertainment watched by millions, children and adults. By the time of the third series production values had improved, and Briscoe found himself contributing to a more sophisticated set of programmes. Kneale himself made notes for the sound design, specifying 'electronic vibration with occult noises' and 'droning pulse, into bell, and into deep vibration' amongst other similarly cryptic instructions.[62] Briscoe, assisted by Dick Mills, obliged with recordings of feedback, echoed drums and disconnecting amplifiers to create ominous rumblings, explosive outbursts and hovering oscillations. These sounds were then cut on to discs to be played in the studios during the various episodes, which were broadcast live. The series had conventional incidental music, credited to Trevor Duncan, a pseudonym of Leonard Treblico. The effect of Briscoe's diabolical shards of electronic sound stabbing at Trebilco's tautly orchestrated suspense is powerfully affecting even now.

Cary, meanwhile, was steadily establishing himself as a composer. In 1952, his wife expecting their first child, he moved to a maisonette in a house in Earls Court that had enough space for the growing machine, which at some point was mounted on an old dining room table with holes cut in it to accommodate cables. That same year Cary acquired his first tape recorder, built by Bradmatic, a company in Birmingham that later developed the Mellotron. The year 1955 was pivotal. Not only did Cary land his first electronic commission, *The Japanese Fishermen*, but he also made a breakthrough into films, with (non-electronic) music for the Ealing comedy *The Ladykillers*. From that point on he moved easily between electronic and conventional composition, often combining the two, for concert hall, cinema, television and radio. He was never employed at the Radiophonic Workshop, but by the time it was launched he and Oram knew each other, and he developed and retained connections with many who worked there in the ensuing years. In October 1958 Oram and Cary visited the Brussels World's Fair to attend the *Journées Internationales de Musique Expérimentale*. This was a pivotal moment in the emergence of electronic music. The cream of the European *avant-garde* was present; Edgard Varèse's *Poème électronique* was premiered; and electronic instruments including the Ondioline were demonstrated. No doubt this trip stimulated Oram's imagination, as by January the following year she had left the Workshop and the BBC 'eager to explore wider fields than incidental sounds for plays would allow'.[63]

To some extent, Oram's bid for creative freedom was an exchange of one set of restraints for another. Without a steady income she was obliged to work on a range of commissions at her studio. Some of these – ballet scores and art installations – seem to fit with her serious aesthetic, but there were also television commercials and industrial films, which can't have satisfied her. Yet in different ways much of her music ended up reaching large audiences and through it, and her unceasing round of lectures and demonstrations, she continued to drive the spread of British electronic music. But all of these things – adverts, scores, installations, lectures – were secondary to Oram's true passion. Ever since seeing that waveform on an oscilloscope in 1944 Oram had dreamed of an electronic machine that a composer could use to 'convert graphic information into sound'. Pursuit of that dream gradually took over her musical life.

Cary, meanwhile, remained busy throughout the 1960s, though he too struggled with the freelancers' dilemma, yearning for creative freedom, yet finding that very freedom limited by the need to take on work just to earn a living. His films included a Hammer remake of *Quatermass and the Pit* (1967), which combined orchestral and electronic scoring, and he had the distinction of providing electronic sound to accompany the Daleks when they first glided on to British television in December 1963. He was a driving force in British electronic music throughout the decade, involved in the creation of the first electronic music studio at the Royal College of Music, and in forming, with Peter Zinovieff and David Cockerell, EMS (Electronic Music Studios).

While Cary was pressing on with his creatively nomadic career and Oram was engaged on her great quest that precipitated a drift into musical obscurity, the BBC Radiophonic Workshop was bringing electronic music to the very heart of mainstream culture. When the story of early British electronic music is told the workshop looms large. Maybe sometimes it looms too large, to the extent that it can seem like British electronic music and the Workshop are synonymous. This was not the case. But even so, it was the nearest thing British electronic music had to a recognizable face, a public identity, and a great deal of important music came from it, in spite of being beset with all manner of tensions from the start.

One of these went to the heart of then-current discussions about electronic music. Could you really call it music at all, or was it just noise and sound organized into patterns? Originally, the official BBC line, offered at the press launch, struck a clipped, conservative note that tended toward the latter view: 'By radiophonic effects, we mean something very near to what the French have labelled concrete music. Not music at all, really.'[64] Much later Delia Derbyshire, who would become the workshop's most famous member, expressed a view that would surely have been shared by Oram: 'It was music. It was abstract electronic sound, organized.'[65]

The debate about whether electronic music is in fact music is now redundant, and anyway, in the decades since the Workshop was established, the generally accepted parameters of what constitutes music have grown to encompass far more than they did then. But even so, listening to the Workshop's output with the benefit of decades of hindsight it is quite clear that some of its work was sound effect only ('Major Bloodnok's Stomach' for *The Goons*, for example). Yet from the start it produced relatively conventional music too, even by the standards of the time, with melody, harmony and rhythm. It was the actual sound colours used and way the music was made that made it unconventional.

And it wasn't just that it was created largely without recourse to actual musical instruments. The recording process itself was revolutionary. Recording studios of the time operated an almost feudal system of organization, with a strict hierarchy separating producers, engineers and tape operators, and musical directors, composers and musicians. Everyone knew their place, yet in electronic music these roles melted into each other. Typically, the electronic musician was composer, performer, engineer and producer all at once.

Early on, radiophonics soundtracked both Samuel Beckett and *The Goons*. Later, local radio jingles and children's television themes jostled for attention with Shakespeare, serious documentaries and

OUT OF THE ORDINARY

experimental poets. This constant pulling between high-minded seriousness and the more straightforward need to entertain was another characteristic of the Workshop's early days and an expression of something unresolved that ran through the whole of the BBC. This linked to something else. The Workshop which, after all, was a service department for a large media corporation became a magnet for innovative free spirits. A consistent theme running through its history is of people eager to join what appeared from the outside like a paradise, a furnace of forward-thinking creativity. Early accounts of working practices are enticing: staff allowed to work whenever they felt like it, day or night, closeted in a closed world of gadgets and intriguing devices and given only the vaguest of briefs. Yet all too often creative individuals would find their apparent paradise invaded by a commercial imperative, the mundane need to produce a prosaic piece of work at short notice: a theme, say, for a new regional radio station or a popular television show. Eventually they would leave, burnt out by unrealistic deadlines, disillusioned by bureaucracy. Many of the workshops' most creative members – including Daphne Oram, John Baker and Delia Derbyshire – left because of this, yet it is the very thing that helped create the unique character of British electronic music of the period.

The most famous music to come out of the Radiophonic Workshop is the *Doctor Who* theme. The series also found room for a huge amount of other electronic music, from the Workshop itself and from other composers including Cary, Desmond Leslie and Eric Siday. *Doctor Who* was conceived as a short children's science fiction series for the late Saturday afternoon slot, between the afternoon's sports coverage and the evening's mix of light entertainment. The titular doctor was a lone friend of the universe who, in the Tardis, was free to go wherever he chose, unbound by time and space. There was no thought of it becoming a long-running entertainment institution that would endure into the 21st century. When it started, it was throwaway light entertainment. Workshop staff came to regard it somewhat ambivalently, recognizing the opportunities it offered yet also finding it frustrating that their work became linked to the series at the apparent exclusion of much of their other compositions. Brian Hodgson, responsible for the Tardis' grating take-off sound and the Daleks' voices, says it was known internally as the 'running sore'.[66]

The story of the theme tune is the Workshop's wobbly tightrope walk between artistic innovation and practical necessity cast in miniature. By July of 1963, with transmission of the new series due to start that autumn, the need for a theme tune was pressing. The producer Verity Lambert considered commissioning the French *avant-garde* composers Jacques Lasry and Bernard Baschet, who, under the name Les Structures Sonores, made music with specially built metal and glass sculptures. This idea was soon abandoned as impractical, and Lambert went to Briscoe to discuss whether the Radiophonic Workshop could meet what was becoming an urgent need. The outcome was that Derbyshire was assigned to produce a theme for the new show from a tune written by Ron Grainer, a popular and experienced theme composer of the time. She was to be assisted by Mills, with Hodgson responsible for sound effects. The team had just finished working together on a railway documentary, *Giants Of Steam*. Together they'd created a version of a theme written by Grainer that combined train-like percussive polyrhythm tape loops with live musicians. It was unusual in that the electronic element was fully integrated into Grainer's music, becoming a part of the rhythm track, a drum machine on tape.

Grainer's *Doctor Who* theme was a sparse composition written on a single sheet of manuscript paper. It comprised a bass line, a melody and a few written instructions to convey atmosphere, such as 'wind bubble' and 'cloud'.[67] From this modest text Derbyshire, assisted by Mills, created the original version of the most widely heard piece of British electronic music of the decade in about two weeks in August 1963. The working relationship between the two was a reminder that electronic music and the BBC Radiophonic Workshop hadn't quite eliminated all features of traditional recording studio hierarchy. Mills was a technical assistant, Derbyshire a studio manager, the idea being that the studio manager was responsible for the creative vision and the assistant would help her realize it, lining up the mono the tape machines, plugging in the circuits, assembling the razor blades and chinagraph pencils for tape splicing.

Derbyshire was born in Coventry in 1937 and remained in the city when it was heavily bombed in World War II. Late in life she speculated that the wailing sirens and crashing explosions had shaped something in her in those formative years: 'I was there in the Blitz, and it came to me, relatively recently, that my love for abstract sounds came from the air raid sirens … that was electronic music.'[68] A gifted child from a working-class background (her father was a sheet metal worker), Derbyshire went to Barr's Hill Grammar School in Coventry, then went up to study maths and music at Girton College, Cambridge, from 1956 to 1959. Academically, she didn't do particularly well at Cambridge, gaining an Ordinary degree. Maybe she was distracted from her studies by extra-curricular activity. Records show she was active in many music and drama productions, playing piano, violin and percussion, and singing.[69]

This combination of a feel for music and the capacity to understand the mathematics of sound stood her in good stead at the BBC Radiophonic Workshop, where she arrived in 1962, having worked as a BBC studio manager since 1960. She applied a theoretical approach to her compositions, and was well informed. Hodgson recalls her flicking through the British inventor, writer and musician Fred Judd's first book about electronic music, scrawling pencil notes over the various circuit diagrams, and dismissing it as rubbish.[70]

The original rendition of the *Doctor Who* theme, so imprinted on the collective memory of generations of viewers, was created using the Radiophonic Workshop's quaint collection of sound sources and tape machines. The swooping sounds are test oscillators, the hissing a white noise generator, the twanging bass line the one string guitar. Composer Grainer, on first hearing the realization of his composition, is said to have asked, 'Did I write this?' Derbyshire later said: '[Grainer] expected to hire a band to play it, but when he heard what I had done electronically, he never imagined it would be so good. He offered me half the royalties, but the BBC wouldn't allow it. I was just on an assistant studio manager's salary and that was it … and we got a free [listing magazine] *Radio Times*.'[71]

The public first heard the *Doctor Who* theme on 21 November 1963 at 5.15pm, when the first episode was broadcast. If Derbyshire had looked in her free *Radio Times* that week she would have seen the series described as 'an adventure in space and time' with theme music by 'Ron Grainer and the BBC Radiophonic Workshop'. This realization of Grainer's theme was released as a single. It did not chart, but on the back of the *Doctor Who* series it travelled around the world. The show thrived and grew like some kind of self-generating alien. A series of progressively younger actors took on the central role first held by a grandfather figure, William Hartnell; filming moved from black and white to colour; shaky sets became more substantial. Yet through all of this the theme created in 1963 remained a constant, although updated several times in the ensuing years with additional parts and different mixes. It survived into the age of multi-tracking and synthesizers to touch hands with the synth pop era, eventually replaced by a synthesizer version of Grainer's same theme in 1980. Its longevity in such a widely watched television programme made it one of the most-heard pieces of electronic music of the 1960s and 1970s, and it remains instantly recognizable to millions. Its importance goes beyond its popularity, though. People who might well have run away with their hands over their ears if they heard a bar of experimental modern electronic music were quite happy to sit down in front of the television and listen to music and sound on *Doctor Who* that was created in exactly the same way. It demonstrated that electronic pop music could do all of the things that conventional pop music could – combining a good tune, rhythm and unique sound textures into a memorable, compelling, evocative whole.

Although the *Doctor Who* theme would become the most famous electronic music on British television in the 1960s, it was not the first. Other workshop efforts, including *Quatermass and the Pit*, predated it by years. It was also preceded by an ITV series that featured a complete electronic score. The first episode of *Space Patrol* was broadcast in April 1963, seven months before the launch of *Doctor Who*. A science-fiction puppet series written and produced by Roberta Leigh, *Space Patrol* follows Captain Larry Dart and the crew of Galasphere 347 in the year 2100. Leigh had previously worked with Gerry Anderson, to whom her series betrays an obvious debt, though its puppetry is even more primitive. Yet despite its creaky production values, *Space Patrol* was popular, and was shown in the USA (retitled *Planet Patrol*), Canada and Australia as well as Britain.

The *Space Patrol* credits attribute 'electronics', a mélange of layered tape loops and electronic tones, to F. C. Judd. It was an abstract and challenging soundtrack in any setting, let alone a children's television series.

Even by the standards of British electronic music of the period, when it was normal for composers to work in isolation to some extent,

*Fred Judd playing his home-made keyboard
synthesizer, circa 1965. Credit: © Freda Judd*

Judd was a man alone. He wasn't really a member of any of the few
and occasionally overlapping circles that made up British electronic
music, a part neither of the serious music establishment, the BBC
Radiophonic clique, nor the commercial music business. Although
he did make some relationships with other key figures (he knew
Daphne Oram, and Hodgson recalled him visiting the Radiophonic
Workshop), the autodidact author, editor, composer, inventor and
electronic music evangelist conducted a solitary campaign out of a
modest terrace in Woodford, north-east London.

His natural milieu was the lost world of amateur tape recording
clubs, electronic hobbyist magazines and home movie aficionados.
Editing magazines, writing articles, touring the country giving
demonstrations of electronic music techniques in church halls and

technical colleges, the impact of his proselytizing is impossible to quantify. As a composer and musician his output was modest, though absorbing.

Judd was born in 1914, and like many people of his generation he was fascinated by radio and electronics. This enthusiasm found an outlet during war service in Coastal Command, which brought him into contact with radar. Judd was also a musician, a competent self-taught guitarist and keyboardist, and an inveterate maker of gadgets. These interests converged sometime in the 1950s in an emerging interest in electronic music, and Judd assembled what must have been one of the very first home electronic music studios in the country. His first book on the subject, *Electronic Music and Musique Concrète*, appeared in 1961, one of the very first 'how to' guides for budding electronic experimentalists.

That a whiff of the exotic and weird continued to haunt British electronic music is underscored by the fact that this volume, and a later one called *Electronics In Music*, was published by Neville Spearman Armstrong, a gentlemen publisher whose books reflected his eclectic fringe interests. Judd's informative, plain-speaking texts sat uneasily in a list that included more sensationalist books covering subjects as diverse as flying saucers, the occult and wrestling. There is a metaphor here for Judd's whole career in electronic music: a middle-aged, self-taught man who looked and sounded like the deputy manager of a hardware store or a lecturer at an adult education college, with cigarette in hand and pen in top pocket, trying to interest the masses in a style of music dominated by eccentrics and bohemian intellectuals. A photo of Judd's home studio shows the tape recorders and oscillators in a setting of mundane domesticity: a coffee table, a vase of flowers, a lamp, net curtains. It was electronic music by, and for, the peculiarly British common man – the amateur enthusiast, the do-it-yourself hobbyist. It was also very good: highly competent, in a technical sense, and revealing considerable depths of imagination and compositional skill.

Judd's output divides into two broad categories: freeform, eerie atmospherics, the style employed for *Space Patrol*, and more structured, rhythmic electro-pop that bears some resemblance to the slightly earlier work of Kid Baltan and Tom Dissevelt, with which Judd was familiar. He was particularly skilled at creating electronic approximations of relatively conventional pop arrangements using tape loops to form a rhythm track, on top of which he would build up chord structures and melodies. Although at heart a tape composer, Judd also used electronic keyboards and treated electric guitar. One photo shows a Jennings Univox keyboard in Judd's set-up, and he also designed and built his own synthesizer. Exactly what this was, how it worked and what it could do, we will probably never know, as it is now lost, but it seems that Judd had it operational as early as 1963.

In terms of recognition and audience, *Space Patrol* was the one big event of Judd's recording career. The bulk of the rest of his music appeared on a series of 7-inch records from the early 60s, sold by mail order through *Amateur Tape Recording* magazine, which Judd edited. These were intended to provide sound effects and themes for home cine moviemakers and amateur tape recordists. Much of this material was later retitled and compiled on a Studio G library album *Electronic Age* (1970).

Space Patrol was shown on the commercial television network ITV. When launched in 1955, the channel offered an opportunity for electronic expression not available at the BBC – the advert. The brevity of the format and its need of a memorable sound signature was something which composer and bandleader Barry Gray was quick to notice. He was already an established and experienced professional, with a musical career encompassing composing, arranging, performing and producing. Born John Livesey Eccles (he changed his name in the 1950s) in Blackburn, Lancashire, in the north of England, in 1908, he was the oldest of the British electronic music pioneers. He was different, too, in that he made extensive use of early electronic musical instruments alongside the tape techniques favoured by most of his contemporaries.

Gray cuts a likeable figure – short, bespectacled, avuncular, with a gentle northern speaking voice sounding a little like Alan Bennett's. With wide interests pursued with boyish enthusiasm, he was popular with his musicians and generous to his fans, in the habit of making tapes of his music to send off to enthusiastic children who had written to him. Gray was nearly 50 when the first wave of rock 'n' roll broke, and though he later wrote a few songs attempting something of the style, his roots were already too deep elsewhere.

He was well informed about classical music, liking Bach, Mozart, and Beethoven in particular, and was able to write for an orchestra, but Gray was not a classical musician or composer either. Rather, he was a multi-faceted operator formed in the world of pre-rock popular music and light entertainment. Working freelance, he kept busy in the 1950s writing for publishers, film producers, the BBC (including a popular Terry-Thomas radio series *To Town With Terry*), and working as an arranger and accompanist with artists as varied as Eartha Kitt, Hoagy Carmichael and Vera Lynn. And he began composing and recording jingles for television commercials shortly after the launch of commercial television in Britain.

Gray's interest in electronics in music seems to go back some distance. In an interview he gave toward the end of his life he mentions being interested in electronic music from the 'early days', referring to the Neo-Bechstein, an experimental electronic piano dating from 1929, and the theremin.[72] He took note of the theremins in soundtracks to early 1950s sci-fi films like *Rocketship X-M* and he was an early convert to magnetic tape. But this interest was always in tension with a conservative musical instinct, which favoured conventional orchestral scoring and considered electronic music suitable only for certain situations.

Gray set up a home studio in 1950, and as the decade wore on he became increasingly fascinated with electronic musical instruments and tape recorders, which gave rise to some spectacularly odd music. A commercially successful musician, Gray was financially comfortable. He was able to build up a home studio far better equipped than many commercial studios to explore this new world of electronic sound. In 1958 he installed a four-track Ampex tape machine, one of the first in the country. In this respect he bears some similarity to Raymond Scott and Eric Siday, both popular musicians who turned to electronics in middle age, funded by their earlier success.

Gray's studio was set up in two downstairs rooms of his home in Dollis Hill, north London. It was more like a traditional recording studio than many other electronic studios of the time, with separate control and live rooms and a window between the two. Gray often recorded there with drummers, guitarists and other musicians. Much of his music for television originated in this studio, though as the live room was small, he would move to professional studios when working with larger groups of musicians.

Gray was an adept tape editor and when he first started to write electronic music for television he relied on this approach, often using pianos and electric steel guitars as his original sound sources. But atypically amongst British composers he liked to use electronic instruments and gradually filled his studio with them. He started with a Clavioline, a Hammond organ, an audio sweep test oscillator and a ring modulator that was specially made for him. Later, and more unusually, he added an English-made Miller Spinetta and an Ondes Martenot. Gray was unique among British musicians in using the delicate, complex Martenot for popular music, which he thought of as 'virtually a better variation of the theremin with more pitch control' and useful for generating 'incredibly eerie electronic effects'.[73] He bought his instrument in 1959, visiting the inventor in Paris for a month's instruction and maintaining a correspondence with him for the rest of his life.

The Spinetta was a curiosity from The Miller Organ Company, based in Norwich. Miller specialized in electronic church organs, but also had a subsidiary called Musical Research, concerned with more experimental musical uses for electronics. The Miller Organ Company and Musical Research had the British rights to use electronic music circuits designed by Constant Martin, the inventor of the Clavioline. Musical Research made for the BBC the Multi-Colour Tone organ, a vast white elephant that gathered dust in the Radiophonic Workshop for years, rarely used. The Spinetta was intended for wider commercial production, and Miller sold them through Harrods for a while.

This was an all valve, twin manual instrument shaped like an angular grand piano, with a separate cabinet containing a power supply, amplifier and speaker. The cabinet could fit underneath the main console, or stand separately from it. The main manual was a polyphonic 88-note keyboard with full-sized keys with various controls influencing tone, attack, decay and so on. This could produce constant organ-like tones and decaying tones akin to an electric piano. Above the main manual was the second, solo manual, a three-octave monophonic accordion-style keyboard derived from a Clavioline, with sound options selected using a large rotary dial.

A surviving Spinetta demonstration recording by William Davies, a regular on BBC radio in the 1950s and 1960s, reveals an impressive range of sounds, but the instrument was not a success. Like the Hammond Novachord before it, it was expensive, heavy, big and complex, its ambition outstripping the available technology. It was made in very limited numbers for just a few years in the early 1960s. One did make its way to the BBC Radiophonic Workshop, where it sat next to its unloved big sister, the Multi-Colour Tone organ. It is unlikely that any survive.[74]

Gray made extensive use of both the Ondes Martenot and the Spinetta in a series of adverts for products as diverse as Hoover washing machines, Tide washing powder and Aspro painkillers. Mixing electronic keyboard instruments with tape music, and lurching from electronic sound to jocular small band arrangements, these fragments have a unique identity amongst the mass of electronic music being made for British television at the time.

Although Gray seems to have been most comfortable with a comedic, cartoon-like approach, he was perfectly capable of creating less-structured atmospheres. Sections of his soundtrack to a documentary about the Hoover Keymatic washing machine, recorded circa 1960, would have sat comfortably in a science fiction setting. It is important to recognize, though, that Gray's interest in electronics was not evidence of some kind of subversive *avant-gardism*. His few documented remarks about his electronic experiments seem to betray ambivalence, as if he was both fascinated by what he was doing and dismissive at the same time, not thinking of it as real music. Indeed, late in his life he was still expressing conservative views about electronic music that seem at odds with the work that he did:

> I am not partial to actual melody in electronic music, when it's supposed to be creating weird or astral or spacey effects … generally most of my electronic music has been what I call electronic effects rather than music.[75]

He coined a term to describe the electronic elements in his work, 'musifex', which appears jotted in many of his surviving manuscripts and notes.

In 1956 pop music in Britain was upended by rock 'n' roll and skiffle. Both of these forms had little impact on Gray, but this was a pivotal year for him, too, as he met Gerry Anderson, the creator of the children's 'supermarionation' puppet series including *Thunderbirds*, *Captain Scarlet* and *Joe 90*. Gray was associated with Anderson for the rest of his career, and his best-known work was born out of this relationship, though his adverts were as widely heard.

Roberta Leigh, a songwriter and a prolific and still-active author with well over 100 books published under various names, was the catalyst that brought Gray and Anderson together. She was later responsible for *Space Patrol*, too. Leigh knew Gray through their mutual association with Vera Lynn, who had recorded several of Leigh's songs, which Gray had arranged. When Leigh proposed to Anderson an idea for a children's television series, *The Adventures of Twizzle*, she demanded that Gray be appointed the musical director. Anderson hired both Leigh and Gray, and the composer was set to work transcribing and arranging blueprint tunes hummed into a tape recorder by Leslie Clair, another friend of Leigh's. Anderson was impressed as Gray developed Clair's aural line drawings into fully arranged pieces music and recorded them using a band including Bert Weedon on guitar. When the series was broadcast two EPs of music and songs were extracted for release by HMV in 1958. That same year Gray provided music for a further Anderson/Leigh collaboration, *Torchy the Battery Boy*. This time, Leigh sang her own tunes into the tape recorder for Gray to shape into fully realized themes, which he did making use of the Clavioline. The following year Gray went to Paris to pick up his Martenot, which was pressed into service for his next Gerry Anderson job, the futuristic *Supercar* (1960). From then on the Ondes Martenot was a feature in Gray's sound world. He would return to it many times as a composer, sometimes playing the instrument himself, at other times hiring in the virtuoso French Ondist Sylvette Allart. Gray then contributed to another Anderson series, *Fireball XL5*. In Gray's mind it was science fiction like this that was the proper setting for electronic music: 'Electronic music is mostly suitable only for visuals that are concerned with such things as laboratories, space, very weird and perhaps even strange situations, astral sequences etc.'[76] As the decade wore on he had ample opportunity to put that belief into practice.

A peripheral yet fascinating character on the British electronic music scene of the time was the splendid Desmond Leslie (1921–2001). The youngest son of a baronet, Sir Shane Leslie, and a cousin of Sir Winston Churchill, Leslie was born at Castle Leslie in County Monaghan and educated in England, where he would spend much time in adult life. Leslie lived with ebullient aristocratic vitality. It was the sort of life made possible by the combination of an enquiring intelligence, the in-built self-confidence of the landed gentry and a private income. He was a fighter pilot in the war, and in 1953 co-authored, with George Adamski, the first-ever book about UFOs, *Flying Saucers Have Landed.* A man of many parts, he also wrote the screenplay for the film *Stranger from Venus,* inspired by *The Day the Earth Stood Still.* He was briefly famous, or notorious, for punching critic Bernard Levin on live television, in revenge for a perceived slight on his first wife, actress and singer Agnes Bernauer, who performed as Agnes Bernelle.

The incident happened in 1963, before 10 million watchers of the satirical show *That Was the Week That Was.* Just as Levin is introduced, Leslie walks into view, talking of a bad review Levin had given of a stage show featuring Bernelle. Chivalrously, Leslie asks the owlish and diminutive Levin to stand, before knocking him sprawling with two swinging right hooks. The episode is often credited with prompting the introduction of a time delay in live television.

In the mid-1950s Leslie set up his own studio to assemble what he called sound pictures. These were abstract *musique concrète* pieces drawn from thousands of recorded sounds, the titles of which reflect Leslie's *grand-guignol* style: 'Music of the Voids of Outer Space', 'Death Of Satan', 'Sacrifice BC 5000'. This embrace of the exotic themes and *avant-garde* techniques was set off nicely by Leslie's declaration that one of his pieces was assembled using recordings of a child's humming top from Harrods and the horn of a 1951 Morris Oxford. Futuristic strangeness improvised out of the mundane and quotidian, this is a microcosm of British electronic music of the 1950s. Initially, Leslie circulated this music on private pressings to friends, but by the early 1960s it began to show up on various library records, and from there found its way into early episodes of *Doctor Who.* Leslie's sound can be heard intermittently in the very first series in an episode called *The Brink of*

Disaster, the second part of a two-episode story called *The Edge of Destruction*.[77]

Because of his intriguing story, it is tempting to ascribe significance and merit to Leslie's music where really there is just fascination about his life. Some of it does achieve an eerie power, but it is challenging fare. An often melody-free sound collage of looped bleeps, siren-like tones, layers of fuzzy static and crashing denunciations like pianos being thrown down a staircases, all but the most acclimatized of listeners will probably sympathize with Arthur C. Clarke's description of one of Leslie's books … a farrago of nonsense.

Although many of these British pioneers ended up making commercial music for television, radio and film either because they wanted to (Barry Gray, Fred Judd) or they had to make ends meet (Tristram Cary, Daphne Oram), none of them engaged much with pop music in the rock 'n' roll, hit singles, teen market sense. It was left to the non-singing, non-playing, tone-deaf songwriter and producer Joe Meek to blaze that particular trail. In the world of rock 'n' roll, a world full of careerists posing as rebels, Meek was a true outsider. But there is a sense in which he fits neatly into the story of British electronic music in the late 1950s and early 1960s. Like so many others profiled in this chapter, he too cuts a solitary figure, fashioning a dream world from valves and solder and magnetic tape. The difference was that his dream also included Buddy Holly, electric guitars and number-one singles. He was the first British adventurer to introduce electronic music to the pop single. An uneasy relationship it might have been at first, but Meek was chaperoning it when future members of The Beatles were still playing skiffle.

Born in 1929 in Newent, Gloucestershire, in the rural west of England, Joe Meek was a poorly educated working-class boy. He was hardly literate and could not sing in tune, or read music, or play an instrument. His mother is said to have put him in dresses until he started school, as she had wanted a girl. He was sensitive and volatile, and while his brothers and peers went fishing, shooting and apple scrumping, Meek preferred to retreat to a garden shed that his parents had allowed him to occupy. He was fascinated by electronics, recording technology in particular, and in this refuge he found contentment dismantling old radios and gramophones. He left school at 14, and after several jobs in radio shops and a spell doing national service in the Royal Air Force, he arrived in London. Soon he was working as an engineer at the country's leading independent recording studio, IBC, where he recorded several big hits of the time, including Lonnie Donegan's 'Cumberland Gap' and Frankie Vaughan's 'Green Door'.

Tactless, gauche and ambitious, Meek found the hierarchical structure of the traditional recording studio frustrating. The roles of engineer, producer, songwriter and manager rarely overlapped, but Meek wanted to do everything. He managed three years at IBC before setting up Lansdowne studios with an independent jazz producer, Denis Preston. The partners enticed many IBC clients into Lansdowne and the relationship thrived for a while before Meek once again started to chafe against the perceived obstructiveness of the unimaginative people surrounding him. He walked out of Lansdowne in late 1959. His experiments with the musical possibilities of magnetic tape began in earnest around this time, when he set up his first home studio in Holland Park, west London. He had already experimented with tape manipulation, extreme compression and cavernous reverb in his previous studio jobs, but having rudimentary recording equipment at home gave him the freedom to go further. It wasn't long before Meek, still boyish in his enthusiasms at 30, was hatching a plan for a project that would give free rein to his ideas.

Along with music and electronics, another of Meek's passions was outer space. He was absorbed by the nascent space race, believed in extra-terrestrial life, and had a head full of pre-Apollo images of silver spaceships and little green aliens. This provided the concept for *I Hear a New World*. Birthed over about six weeks in late 1959, most, if not all, of the recording of this curio took place at Meek's home studio. *I Hear a New World* was never released in Meek's lifetime. A sampler EP trickled out in very limited numbers in February 1960, with a second EP and the full album planned for March. Distribution problems with Meek's own new Triumph independent label, on which the EP was released and for which the album was slated, put an end to the project. It survived in a bootleg netherworld until 1991, when British reissue label RPM first finally released it in its entirety. So, in commercial terms, *I Hear a New World* is an irrelevance in Meek's career. Artistically, though, it was the laboratory in which the musically challenged visionary perfected his mysterious alchemy.

I Hear a New World was composed and produced by Meek, but like all of the tone-deaf svengali's creations it needed the contribution of a willing accomplice and interpreter to make communicable musical sense of Meek's tuneless singing. Rod Freeman filled those uncomfortable shoes. He and his Blue Men – a seven-piece rock 'n' roll band with skiffle leanings – are the credited recording artists. Made in a domestic setting, with Meek conjuring up his aural approximations of space that permeate the album by manipulating recordings of running tap water, it really was a kitchen sink production. This was one of the first times the techniques used by serious composers of electronic music were employed in a record that, while not exactly pop, at least wanted to be popular. Apart from the treated sound effects, the album's instrumentation mixed the conventional – electric bass, electric guitar and drums – with a swooping lap steel guitar, Clavioline, and a piano prepared with thumbtacks in the hammers. The whole lot was siphoned through Meek's closely guarded collection of self-built reverb, echo and compressor units, and recorded on to several semi-professional tape recorders he then owned.

The album's twelve songs are about three different species of imagined alien – the Globbots, the Dribcots and the Saroos. It's here that a yawning flaw opens up, with Meek using sped-up voices to represent the speech of the aliens, stamping the project with unfortunate and unintended novelty credentials. Thankfully, there are several instrumental tracks free of this blight. One of these, 'Glob Waterfall', builds tension effectively with a heavily treated ascending run on the bass notes of a piano. This repeats against a background of bubbling water-like noises that, whatever their original source, are most definitely *concrète* rather than traditionally musical. There is a regular pattern to these, indicating a tape loop. Periodically, the music reaches a climactic gong-like crash. It is an incredible creation for a tone-deaf pop producer working in a home studio at the close of 1959. In notes on the sleeve of the EP drawn from *I Hear a New World*, Meek himself, with his limited grasp of written language, struggled to articulate the effect he was reaching for in 'Glob Waterfall'. Reading those words while listening to the music shows that the gap between his imagined lunar landscape and his musical impression of it was not large:

The water rises to form a huge globule on top of a plateau, and when it's reached its maximum size it falls with a terrific crash to the ground below, and flows away into the cracks of the moon; then the whole cycle repeats itself again and again.

Nothing dates more quickly than a vision of the future, and *I Hear a New World* would, had anyone heard it, have seemed quaint within a few years. Now, it's a voice calling from a planet as distant as the ones Meek imagined. It can't be hailed as a lost masterpiece: the material is often poor, the performances variable, and it would not have been a success if properly released. What it is, though, is a prophetic but deeply flawed attempt to make pop records using tape music techniques. Meek held up a mirror, apparently accidentally, to then-current developments in art music – an unknowing appropriation of *avant-garde* techniques for the uneducated pop masses. He liked to work alone late into the night in his home studio, anxious to the point of paranoia about competitors finding out how he did what he did, so many of his sonic secrets went with him to the grave. But enough evidence exists in the form of anecdotes from people who worked with him and the records themselves to conclude that Meek was using the very same techniques as serious composers of electronic music. Meek was interested in inventing sound. Its source quickly became all but irrelevant – it was simply raw material to be pulled this way and that, chopped up and reassembled, stretched, shrunk, digested and spewed out in all but unrecognizable form.

Joe Meek's second home studio, in a rented flat above a leather goods shop in Holloway Road in north London, was the scene of his greatest triumphs. Here he wrote and recorded dozens of songs for dozens of artists, making finished masters that he then hawked around to major labels under the aegis of RGM Productions (named after his own initials). Working in this way he produced many hits and many more flops. 'Telstar' was the greatest hit of them all.

Nothing fired Meek's imagination like space travel and electronic technology. When NASA launched the tiny Telstar 1 satellite from Cape Canaveral on 10 July 1962, Meek was thrilled. Roughly spherical, measuring just 34.5 inches long, and covered in solar panels, the futuristic glitter ball completed its silent orbit on the earth once every 2 hours and 37 minutes. Although just one of many satellites launched since Sputnik 1 in 1957, Telstar 1 was marked out for special things. It was the messenger that would relay the first live transatlantic television broadcast, on July 23. These ghostly, indistinct images captivated Meek, and he heard a tune in his head.

There are several accounts of what happened next, from which a broadly consistent story emerges. Meek began his idiosyncratic and laborious compositional method, singing a very vague approximation of the tune over a pre-existing backing track. An associate, Dave Adams, then deciphered the music encrypted in Meek's cacophonous wailing, a slow process of trial and error. By this painful labour the song was born, and a few days later The Tornados were called in to record it. The band was a part of Meek's stable of artists, an instrumental rock group and also Billy Fury's backing band. At the time Fury was booked for a summer season in Great Yarmouth, and during a Sunday break in performances the band drove the 120 miles or so back to London to start work, under Meek's strict guidance. On that day and for a few hours on the Monday morning the band recorded the backing track to 'Telstar' and the single's b-side. But the melody line had yet to be recorded by Monday lunchtime, when The Tornados had to drive back to Great Yarmouth.

That was the work of Geoff Goddard, another of Meek's collaborators, with whom Meek shared an interest in spiritualism and a belief that the late Buddy Holly communicated with them. It was he who gave Meek's tune, deciphered by Adams, its tremulous, innocent optimism by layering Clavioline and piano parts, with Meek calling instructions from the control room. The result was the most radical British rock 'n' roll record yet recorded, The Shadows in space, held up by the fizzing electronic trickery that begins and ends the single. It's not electronic music in the pure sense. There are vogue-ish twanging guitars and galloping drums. But with a chorus of Claviolines and the tape textures so prominent, 'Telstar' was pop's first big blast into the new electronic world, encapsulating in just over three minutes the faith in technological progress that characterized the early days of the space race. Released on Decca records in the UK and London records in the USA, 'Telstar' became one of 1962's biggest hits, topping the charts in both countries, the first British rock 'n' roll record to do so.

5

Manhattan researchers Raymond Scott and Eric Siday

Louis and Bebe Barron's Greenwich Village studio, with its collection of largely pre-owned or homemade equipment accumulated over time and crammed into their living room, was typical of many home-based electronic music studios in the 1950s. Not far away, in Manhasset, Long Island, New York, was another home-based electronic music facility set up about the same time as the Barrons' that couldn't have been more different. A space age dream factory of gleaming chrome, white walls and a thousand flickering lights occupying eight rooms of a thirty-two-room mansion, it was the private domain of a broad-faced, dark-haired man calling himself Raymond Scott. As home studios go, it was in a class of its own.

Harry Warnow was born in 1908, in Brooklyn, New York to Russian–Jewish immigrant parents. Music was in the Warnow family, and Harry's older brother, Mark, was a conductor, violinist and a musical director for CBS. He encouraged Harry, eight years his junior, to follow in his footsteps. Heart disease was in the family too, with both brother Mark and father Joseph dying young. Harry studied piano, theory and composition at the Juilliard School of Music, graduating in 1931 and finding his way into the CBS Radio house band. He adopted the pseudonym Raymond Scott soon after, maybe to spare his brother accusations of nepotism.

As Raymond Scott he would go on to have a long music career, in two phases. He was a hugely successful pianist, composer and bandleader, and an electronic music pioneer. The two phases were distinct, though there was some overlap. As a composer and bandleader, Scott was mainly active throughout the 1930s and 1940s and on into the late 1950s, when the work gradually tailed off. The Raymond Scott Quintette, actually a six-piece band, served with various line-ups for years from 1936 and notched up many hits penned by the prolific Scott. Carl Stalling arranged a number of his compositions for Bugs Bunny and other cartoons, and through this route tunes like the taut, speedy 'Powerhouse' became etched into the memories of millions. It is this connection that has led to Scott sometimes being described erroneously as a cartoon composer. Despite nominally fronting the Quintette and taking on other leading roles, Scott was a shy man and not a natural performer. In film and television performances he usually ensured that his band mates got the close attention of the cameras, while he remained in the background.

Scott's work from this period is normally termed jazz, but this is a flag of convenience. Although unashamedly populist and popular, the songs are eccentric and odd, full of unexpected tempo switches and risky harmonies. Furthermore, his approach deviated sharply for the jazz tendency toward improvisation and individual musical freedom within loose structures. He was known as a hard taskmaster, marshalling his various bands with military precision. For the Quintette and his other ensembles Scott left few open spaces for self-expression, but rather drilled them to exactitude, controlling every note and beat.

Unusually for a musician of the time he also took keen interest in the electronics of sound. He had his own disc-cutting recording equipment years before tape recorders appeared, and recorded and minutely analyzed band rehearsals. He adopted tape early, and left behind a vast archive of reels and discs accumulated over decades, recordings of everything from musical experiments to telephone conversations. And as soon as he made his way into a recording studio Scott could be found in the control room, on the wrong side of the glass for a musician, checking what the sound was like when it came out of the speakers. In time he would dispense with other musicians altogether, and with the glass that divides the control room from the live room, and spend all his time listening to the speakers. Although he was secretive about it, it appears that he began making electronic music in the late 1940s, and from the 1960s onward it consumed him. For a long time the money he made from the first phase of his career funded the second.

Scott was not a trained electronics engineer, but an intuitive autodidact. Although more a hobbyist on a grand scale than a businessman, he generated a power surge of ideas and patents: the Clavivox, the Electronium, multi-track tape recorders, electronic door bells, rhythm machines, sequencers. Many of these might have become viable commercial products, but for some reason they rarely left Scott's imagination and palatial studio. His failure to actually sell his inventions, despite an apparent intention to do so demonstrated by his forming a succession of companies with catalogues, demo records and price lists, is the mystery of the second phase of his career.

Scott formed his first electronics corporation, Manhattan Research, Inc., in 1946 and was soon patenting electronic musical devices. Always reticent about this aspect of his work, it is impossible to judge how quickly he made progress, but it seems like he invested a lot of time, money and energy from the start. Nine years later, in 1955, Bob Moog and his father visited Scott in the huge studio, as Scott wanted to use the circuitry from a Moog theremin. By that stage Scott had a 30-foot-long wall of electronic equipment, which, Moog speculated later, he must have been accumulating for years.[78] The association between Moog and Scott continued intermittently for the next 15 years, with Scott sometimes asking Moog to build him devices and circuits, though Moog never really knew what they were intended for.

Jean-Jacques Perrey also visited Scott's studio, turning up in 1960 shortly after arriving in New York. He was there to demonstrate the Ondioline, with which Scott was sufficiently impressed to place an order. In modified form, it took its place in Scott's rig alongside an Ondes Martenot and what was by now a vast collection of Scott's own inventions.[79] Although he did manipulate magnetic tape sometimes, his use of tape recorders was generally conventional, as recording devices. This set him apart from many other electronic musicians of the time. It was to his banks of instruments and tone generators that he turned to produce his sounds to realize his compositions. Enough photos of the studio survive to give an idea of the industrial scale of the operation. The cover of a promotional LP advertising Scott's Jingle Workshop (1957 or 1958) shows him lovingly caressing a tape recorder set in a 10-foot-high electronic wall, while his second wife, the singer and actress Dorothy Collins, lounges in the foreground in a director's chair. Salivating articles in electronics magazines reported whole rooms full of spare parts, a lavishly equipped machine room for making the circuitry, and estimates at the studio's worth ranging from $100,000 to $200,000.

Perrey and Moog were lucky: very few people got to see inside Scott's fabulous private kingdom. For a few years from 1960 onwards, though, many started to hear what he was up to in there. By this time television ownership in the United States had rise to about 90 per cent of households, with the medium now the dominant form of home entertainment. Scott had been making television advertising jingles for some time when by his own account, in 1960, he was asked to find a 'distinctive new sound' for a campaign advertising Vicks cough drops and tablets.[80] For Scott there could be only one way to create a distinctive new sound and that was by bringing his formidable electronic armoury to bear. Scott gave this account in a lecture in 1962, but it is possible that it is a simplification of a longer, more gradual process that stretched back many years. A posthumous compilation includes recordings from the 1950s that have some electronic content, even if they aren't completely electronic.[81] But even if there was a more protracted route the end point was the same. For several years through the 1960s Scott made a string of television adverts for Sprite, Nescafé, Baltimore Gas and Electric Company and others, all of them electronic.

Many of the adverts can be grouped in two broad categories that mirror the way electronic music was used by other composers in film and television at the time. The first was as a humorous device, of which that Vicks jingle was typical. A cheery little tune sung by Collins, born along by jaunty percussion, it was a miniature novelty pop song, completely standard advertising fare of the period – commercial and catchy to the brink of inanity. And Collins and a cough aside, it was entirely electronic, percussion and all. An advert for Sprite ('Melonball Bounce', 1963) was similar, rhythmic electronic arpeggios supporting male and female voices, punctuated with a few sound effects, electronic bubbles and squelches. Scott made these pieces in the belief that the general public perception of electronic music was that it sounded like a 'nuclear war', or, in its mildest form, like 'outer space music'. He, however, believed not only that 'electronic music can be used in a light way' but also that he had 'licked the problem of lightness in electronic music'.[82] He could do 'outer space music' too, or at least futuristic music.

Companies that wanted to emphasize the visionary technology of their products also commissioned Scott. Two slots he made in 1963 for engineering company Bendix 'The Tomorrow People' comprise more abstract electronic textures as a vehicle for bracing voiceovers about space travel and holiday resorts under the sea. A 1960 piece promoting Vim detergent tablets was similar. This time the voiceover is a housewife who has 'never had a whiter wash', followed by a stentorian male voice talking of laboratories and 'scientifically measured' detergents. This was a common approach in consumer advertising at the time, with the home reimagined as a techno-paradise packed with labour-saving devices, making life so much easier. Scott's music is the ideal soundtrack: obviously played by a machine, a simple repeated phrase with a fragment of melody.

These recordings were remarkable for their sound quality. So much electronic music of the era was made using multiple tape-dubs and rudimentary sound sources that the resultant grainy vagueness around the edges of the sound as the notes fade into a background of tape hiss has come to be accepted as a signature of the genre. Scott, by contrast, had his wall of dazzle filled with machine-tooled, custom-built modules, multi-track tape recorders and the best electronic instruments of the time. He also had decades of recording and live radio experience, and had learned how to capture and balance sound. His music was beautifully recorded, clear and precise with a tonal depth rare in contemporary electronics. In this respect, and in his ability to draw on novelty pop compositional chops, he resembles British composer Barry Gray, who was making electronic TV adverts at exactly the same time. Gray too dabbled in tape manipulation, but preferred to use electronic instruments. It seems unlikely that Gray and Scott would have been aware of each other, but they ended up exploring similar musical territory, both with multi-track home studios, a fascination with electronics and decades of commercial pop experience to draw on.

Much closer to home there was another musician with a similar background to Scott who was also making electronic music for adverts. Eric Siday was born in 1905 in Ealing, west London. His father, George, worked as an accountant; a younger brother, R. E. Siday, became a noted mathematician. Siday was a musical prodigy, entering the Royal Academy of Music in 1919 at the age of 14, where his first instrument was violin, the second piano. He achieved the certificate (the highest level of attainment) in violin playing in 1923.[83] While studying he worked as an accompanist at silent movie theatres and was recording in dance bands from the 1920s onwards, developing a hot jazz style that he also put to use on BBC radio.

In 1939 Siday moved to New York, first signing up as violinist and arranger for Fred Waring and his Pennsylvanians. Though he did record under his own name, for Victor, he was not really a star or a household name in the way that Scott was, but rather a seasoned, respected accompanist and arranger with some of the era's big names. His violin technique was sophisticated: fast, furious and full of double-stops and even simultaneous sounding of all four strings. He was a 'flash fiddler', as one reviewer put it.[84] Apart from his more commercial work, Siday wrote several longer pieces. He also teamed up with Austen 'Ginger' Croom Johnson, who he had known at the BBC back in London. Johnson and Siday co-authored a successful jingle for Pepsi Cola in 1939, 'Pepsi Cola Hits the Spot', and would go on to create many more. Initially the pair worked with conventional instrumentation and voices. It was while working with Johnson that Siday honed what he later called 'the art of miniaturization',[85] which he would put to profitable use when he turned to electronics.

During the 1950s Siday became interested in electronic music and began introducing electronic elements to some of his collaborations with Johnson. In 1957 the pair produced a series of jingles and indents for the Cincinnati radio station WCKY, using 'a 20-piece orchestra, a nine voice choir and the newest in electronic sound effects'.[86] Johnson died in 1964, but some years before that Siday had started making purely electronic jingles on his own, which were so successful that by the middle of the decade *Time* magazine was hailing him as one of the best-paid and most widely heard composers in the world. He called these jingles 'identitones': brief, memorable sound logos designed to create an immediate association with the given product or corporation. *Time* claimed that approximately 80 per cent of Americans heard Siday's electronic music, in the form of these identitones, at least once every day.[87] Whether such a claim is verifiable or not, there can be no doubt that a lot of people were listening to Siday's music, though hardly any of them would have known anything about him. He created dozens of identitones for television adverts, radio stations and television corporations, which ensured that his music was broadcast to millions daily throughout the 1960s and well beyond his death in 1976.

Siday was an anonymous figure, and though sometimes mentioned in the music, radio and television trade press any public recognition was more likely to be on account of the lingering afterglow of his hot jazz violin days. He didn't seem to mind, though. The few photos of him from this period show a man with the grey hair and waistline of comfortable middle age, ensconced in the home studio where he spent most of his time. Populated by sturdy tape recorders, with two speakers angled down from the wall like staring eyes, compared to Scott's domain it looks cramped and mildly chaotic. Papers, tape boxes and spools are piled up on top of available surfaces. This electronic musician's equivalent of a writer's den occupied two rooms of a ten-room apartment that Siday shared with his wife Edith in New York's prestigious Apthorp building, where neighbours included the Catch 22 author Joseph Heller. Tom Rhea visited him there circa 1970 while researching a PhD on the history of electronic musical instruments. He recalls Siday as charming, interested and courteous. The studio itself included the second-ever Moog synthesizer and an Ondes Martenot, alongside tape recorders and mixers, but it was modestly equipped compared to Scott's.[88] The Moog became a mainstay of Siday's sound after he acquired it in 1965, but before then he depended on the Martenot, alongside the tape manipulation techniques and other electronic tone generators.

Like Scott, Siday was a storied veteran of the commercial end of the music business by the time he became an electronic musician. This experience equipped him to write a catchy tune and also to promote his new endeavour in a way that would overcome resistance and prejudice. Together, these attributes go a long way to accounting for his success. Whereas much electronic music heard through mass media at the time was designed to create a general atmosphere or background accompanying texture, Siday's music was meant to be memorable – and it generally was. His theme for Maxwell House coffee, titled 'The Perking Coffee Pot' (though often known as 'The Singing Coffee Pot'), was so familiar that throughout the 1960s when it was mentioned in various magazine features no further introduction was necessary than something along the lines of 'the famous Maxwell House coffee advert'.[89]

Along with this facility with a tune, Siday knew how to market himself. He repeatedly emphasized electronic music's advantages for advertising, namely a limitless supply of unique sounds and lower production costs compared to booking a band into a conventional studio. He also circulated examples of his wares on numerous demo recordings and library discs. Although Siday's signature style was effervescently melodic, he could evoke darker moods, such as on 'Conflict No. 2', which combined percussive tape loops with a wheezy Martenot melody and portamentos.[90] Much of Siday's music in this vein appeared on various library music albums, and by this means made their way back to Britain. Nearly a quarter of a century after he had left London, Siday's former paymasters at the BBC made much use of his electronic library music on *Doctor Who*. His first appearance was in the first series in a two-part story *The Edge of Destruction*, which also featured contributions from Desmond Leslie. More commonly, though, he offered collections of short tracks with titles that reveal the music's intended use: 'Sports Desk', 'Football Results' and 'News Room'.

The Maxwell House advert, first broadcast in 1959, was used continually for six years and then less frequently for another ten. By Siday's standards it was quite a long piece, in most uses running through adverts of about a minute long, though this was achieved by repetition of one phrase. In its most familiar form it comprises three parts, starting with a percussive, bubble-popping sound that was roughly synchronised with a film of a coffee percolator in action, joined by a similar but lower-pitched part and then a bass sound. Although all three sounds are percussive in character, they sound notes distinct enough to form a melody. Some mystery surrounds the actual sound sources. The strict repetitive phrasing suggests layered tape loops, with tuned percussion a possible raw sound, though the bass part might simply be a bass guitar. However, reference is sometimes made to a one-off Moog percussion sequencer being a sound source for the advert. This raises the possibility that the music was modified or re-recorded at some point during its long active life using the Moog module, while retaining the distinctive character or an earlier recording, which certainly pre-dated any Moog equipment. A more typical Siday advert was the seven-note, eight-second Westinghouse Electric Company theme that accompanied the endorsement 'You can be sure it's Westinghouse.'

A Screen Gems TV identitone used for a decade from 1965 was another of Siday's successes. All of five seconds long and performed on the Martenot, it signed off episodes of many popular series, including *I Dream of Jeannie*, *The Monkees*, *The Partridge Family* and *Bewitched*. Like the Maxwell House advert, the Screen Gems logo (the 'S from Hell', as it was sometimes called) generated a life of its own. For Siday this was the ultimate achievement: a few seconds of music becoming not only forever associated with a particular brand or product, but taking up permanent residence somewhere in the memories of countless millions.

Based in New York and selling electronic music for advertising, Scott and Siday were rivals in a sense, though seemingly friendly ones. Siday considered Scott 'touched with genius'.[91] They had much in common. Of a similar age, both were academically trained musicians, both active and very successful in commercial music from the 1930s to the 1950s. But whereas both too became fascinated by the musical possibilities of electronics and learned to use those tools to great effect, it was Scott alone who possessed an inventive technical streak. For Siday, the electronics were a means to an end, whereas for Scott they were a means to an end and an end in themselves. There is a compelling sense that he loved the process of making electronic musical equipment, and partly because of this his studio was far better equipped than Siday's. The latter took advantage of this superior equipment at least once. Correspondence between the two men dated June and July 1965 confirms that Siday booked Scott's studio for three short sessions, at a $40-an-hour day rate and $50-an-hour evening rate. Scott says that he is 'trying to establish some kind of rate schedule', and asks Siday's opinion, indicating that Scott was considering opening his secret kingdom to commercial clients.[92]

Television adverts were the most visible part of Scott's electronic music career, but in his mind not the most important. Siday was far more successful, which must be partly attributable at least to the way he concentrated on composing and marketing. By contrast, Scott was always more interested in inventing. He poured his energy and money into a spate of electronic inventions that surged out of him throughout the 1950s and 1960s. Many of these seem like the whimsical fancies of a man lost in a world of relay switches and transistors: the Fascination series, a collection of devices that automatically generate themed background textures such as nature or space sounds; an electronic bicycle bell; a vending machine that plays a tune for the selected product. Others are evidence of a far-reaching imagination able to fuse musical and electronic possibilities, and might have become viable commercial products.

The Clavivox was the most readily understandable of Scott's electronic musical instruments. The patent for it was filed in 1956, the application document describing what was in intent another attempt at making controllable portamento, like the Ondes Martenot before it and Paul Tanner's homespun electro-theremin after it. Controlled by a three-octave keyboard, the instrument's main feature was its capacity to 'smoothly and accurately' slide in pitch from one note to another on the keyboard, whether higher or lower, without having to press any intervening keys. Additionally, the Clavivox featured an electro-mechanical vibrato that, Scott claimed, combined the performance benefit of manual operation with the precision of electronics. Various other controls gave a wide range of tone colours.[93] The proposed playing style betrayed an obvious debt to the Ondes Martenot, with which Scott was familiar. The performer would pick out the notes on the monophonic instrument with their right hand, while the left hand would operate a small bank on tone and expression controls. Photos confirm that there were at least two versions of the Clavivox. The first has a dark body, the second, which appears in advertising literature, is in a lighter wood case, with the controls grouped further to the left. It looked neat and stylish, and judging by appearances alone it is possible to imagine it in a tiny commercial niche somewhere close to the one occupied by the Ondioline. Rhea, who took one to Nashville and tried to market it in the studios there for a while without any success at all, soon came to think otherwise, realising that its mechanism would require constant attention.

The most prescient of Scott's inventions, and the one that exerted the greatest influence over his subsequent career, was his sequencer. By his own account he built his first sequencer in 1960, inspired by Wurlitzer's Sideman drum machine of 1959 – 'the uncanny new rhythm instrument', as adverts described it.[94] This was the first mass-produced drum machine, following an earlier Chamberlain effort that drew on taped samples. By contrast the Sideman's sounds are electronically generated, its operation electro-mechanical. An electronic motor drives a wheel, to the rim of which are attached rows of contact points. Each row of contacts triggers a particular drum sound. The points are spread around the wheel and the spacing of the contacts in each row generates a particular rhythm. This prompted Scott to envisage something that would generate sequences of notes, not just rhythm patterns. In time Scott's sequencers found their way into the grandest of his schemes, the Electronium.

As always with Scott it is not possible to verify exact dates, as he was secretive. He did, though, leave behind evidence of what we would now understand as a simple sequencer in an album trilogy called *Soothing Sounds for Baby*. As the title suggests, the trilogy comprised music intended to soothe, calm and lull to sleep babies. The records were originally released on Epic in 1964, in collaboration with the Gesell Institute of Human Development, which provided insert information booklets. Each of the three albums is aimed at a particular age group: 1 to 6 months; 6 to 12 months; 12 to 18 months. The music becomes gradually more complex through the age ranges, but all consists of repetitive rhythmic and melodic patterns, generally overlaid with a lead melody played on some kind of keyboard instrument. These simplistic melodies often tail away in a vapour trail of echo, creating a dreamy, soporific effect. All sound sources are electronic.

The repeated patterns that form the basis of each track sometimes run for well over ten minutes. Electronic musicians of the time did generate repetition using tape loops, but a characteristic of those loops was often-tiny irregularities in timing created by a miniscule unevenness in the lengths of tape, the effect being a slight jerkiness to the rhythm. This became more pronounced if tape loops were synchronised to play together. In *Soothing Sounds for Baby* many tracks have more than one repetitive pattern playing with none of these slight irregularities. Instead, there is an unwavering strictness of timing that also rules out human performance. In 'The Happy Whistler' from Volume 2, for example, an unchanging electronic percussion pattern integrates perfectly with a similarly generated bass line for nearly 11 minutes. The exactitude of those patterns rules out playing by musicians in real time, and they don't have the feel of tape loops, so the assumption must be that they were generated by what would come to be called a sequencer. A machine was playing the notes. Indeed, the music, for all its tweeness, has something of the propulsive, insistent, relentless quality of sequencer-based pop music that began to appear in the 1970s.

These albums would have been created in 1963, or maybe a year earlier, which makes them the first sequencer records and Scott a musical clairvoyant. It is probably a mistake to herald them as influential releases, though, and similarly to declare Scott the founding father of sequencing. The trilogy failed commercially and was all but forgotten until re-released in the 1990s. There is little evidence of intervening generations of electronic musicians being inspired by these albums, even though their combination of stark, repetitive minimalism and hypnotic serenity does prefigure a lot of synthesizer music by artists like Tangerine Dream and Kraftwerk. And although Scott was the first to realise a sequencer, the idea was in the air and very soon after other people were exploring the idea without reference to him. Don Buchla (Buchla's Box) and Peter Zinovieff (EMS) both began climbing the same mountain by other routes shortly after Scott had embarked on his journey, each apparently with no knowledge of what the others were doing. After all, once you accepted that electronic machines could make musical sound, it was only a small step to imagining that they could perform music.

Sequencing aside, the *Soothing Sounds for Baby* series was an early entry in another emerging trend in electronic music, the association with peace, calm and relaxation that would eventually lead to the new-age synthesizer music of the 1980s. Samuel Hoffman's theremin and orchestra album *Music for Peace of Mind* had hinted at this in 1949. In 1957 Jean-Jacques Perrey made another early incursion into this territory with an album of Ondioline and organ music called *Prelude au Sommeil* (*Prelude to Sleep*), which was distributed to hospitals and psychiatric institutions in France, intended to relax the distressed. Whether in practice Scott's music helped babies get to sleep is another matter. The cover artwork of the trilogy's reissue shows a cherubic infant apparently skewered by a sound wave going in one ear and out the other.

Scott's sequencer became a part of his most ambitious invention. Sometime around 1959 he began work on the Electronium, not to be confused with a Hohner electric accordion of the 1950s with the same name. Developing this machine gradually consumed him, at the expense of other projects. But, like Daphne Oram's Oramics system, it was a grand scheme never finished to its inventor's satisfaction. Unlike the Oramics system, though, it looked finished. Photos show an elegantly sculpted three-part console housed in a dark-wood cabinet, adorned with intricate, and ergonomically balanced rows of lights and switches, resting on a vast executive desk. The operator sits in front of the centre part of the console and is embraced by curved extensions that project at angles on either side. This machine survives, though at the time of writing it is in non-functioning condition.[95]

The Electronium, or at least the version of it that survives, is a 12-channel sequencer. Each channel has a tone generator assigned to it, and each tone generator has in turn an array of controls that influence and change the sound created, for example accent, counterpoint, tremolo, reverb and so on. All 12 channels can be played simultaneously. According to Alan Entenman, an engineer who worked for Scott on the Electronium circa 1970, the machine is part analogue and part digital. The tone generators, filters and noise generators are all analogue, but all parameters are controlled digitally. In this way the music could be stored and reproduced digitally, using an integrated digital recorder that saved and played back the Electronium's digital settings.[96]

Scott did not intend the Electronium to be a performing instrument in the conventional sense. Although he was able to use it to perform versions of existing music, it was not designed with that in mind. Rather he imagined it as means to simultaneously compose, record and perform new music. The composer would interact with the Electronium to create new music, which it would be able to perform and record in real time, as it was written. It was to be an 'artistic collaboration between man and machine',[97] wrote Scott in 1970.

Herb Deutsch recalled discussing this with Scott, and Scott saying that he found composing time consuming and hard work and would much rather have a machine do it for him.[98] The Electronium was intended to be that machine, a musical equivalent of the shiny labour-saving appliances filling kitchens in the post-war years that were meant to herald an age of leisure. Scott's aspiration was the ultimate nightmare of the conservative element of the music establishment, which tended to frown gloomily upon any advances in music technology, seeing them as threats to musicians' livelihoods. Had he been able to realise it, not only would Scott's Electronium make music entirely electronically generated – it would co-compose it as well.

The question at the heart of the Electronium story is how the composer and the Electronium interacted. Initially, the machine didn't even have a keyboard. Rhea recalls Scott demonstrating it to him, with little more than a few flicks of a micro-switch apparently enough of an interaction to create a piece of fully formed music.[99] Scott provided a method of operation, but this is opaque: 'A composer "asks" the Electronium to "suggest" an idea – theme – motive – whatever',[100] he writes, before going on to explain that once the composer is happy with one of the Electronium's ideas he or she starts recording, and then takes various steps to modify and develop the idea. In other words, the composer thinks, for example, that he or she would like a particular pattern to play faster, so adjusts the tempo control. Those later steps are easy enough to understand, as the Electronium was laden with controls to influence whatever sound it was generating by changing its key, tempo, the gap between notes, the character of the notes themselves and so on. What isn't clear is how the asking and suggesting happened. Where did the ideas and themes, the sequences of notes, the rhythm patterns, come from in the first place?

Scott's language has contributed to a myth that the Electronium was possessed of some kind of artificial musical intelligence, inviting the conclusion that the machine and man were on an equal footing.[101] The Canadian musician Bruce Haack worked with Scott for a while in 1970 and seems to have embraced this idea:

> Raymond Scott ... has come up with a device that I will be steering, it's a completely new concept, there's no keyboard, and as I think I will be able to create ... it's really communication between man and machine for the first time.[102]

But marvellous visions of wires trailing from Haack's skull into the back of the Electronium, the great benign machine reading his thoughts and entering into creative dialogue, are sadly unfounded. Although it is not possible to say with absolute certainty until the restoration is complete, it seems that the Electronium was not artificially intelligent. The armies of lights and switches and controls might suggest otherwise, but it could not really generate ideas on its own, or act randomly in the true sense of the word. Rather, it operated on a principle built on the observation that most Western music is made up, at some level, of patterns – rhythms, chord progressions, melodic sequences that repeat, interact and vary. If the Electronium came pre-programmed with huge numbers of these patterns, and each of them could be altered in thousands of ways, the basic operational principle is then a vastly more complex version of that used by drum machines of the period. With something like an Ace Tone Rhythm Ace you could select and to some limited extent modify factory pre-set patterns. You would choose a waltz, for example, and adjust its tempo, and mix it with other patterns, and subtract the snare drum sound. The Electronium seems to have worked on the same principle. The difference was that it offered 12 simultaneous sound sources, each with multiple pre-sets and a huge number of controllable variables. This enabled the composer to create music of great complexity, even if the starting point was a collection of pre-sets. Entenman confirms this understanding: 'The Electronium did have lots of pre-sets to choose from and in fact there were millions of permutations.'[103] But even this confirmation must be accepted with a caveat that Scott continued to work on the Electronium for another seven years after Entenman's involvement, and it must have changed in that time.

So how should we think of the Electronium? The place it occupied in Scott's life is similar to that filled by Daphne Oram's Oramics machine. Both were unfinished symphonies, grand masterworks destined to remain incomplete, their creators defeated by time and a lack of money, and perhaps, too, by a quirk in their temperaments, an inwardness that could only become more marked the longer they stayed in their rooms poring over their circuits. Maybe it is best not to fix it in any of its physical manifestations, even the last and most fully realized, but instead to see it as an evolving outworking of Scott's fecund ingenuity, plastic and protean.

As the 1960s progressed Scott's career took a puzzling turn. He was diverting more and more energy to inventing, and as even the advert work tailed off he did very little composing. Many of the inventions appeared to have some commercial potential, yet he failed to make a commercial success of any of them. This might be understandable if he had been a sequestered mad professor, with no sense of the music business in particular and the commercial world in general. Yet here was a man who had made a very comfortable living not only from his talent as a musician, but his ability to navigate the system. For about thirty years Scott thrived as a commercial musician, moving with apparent ease through large entertainment corporations. Even allowing for the different qualities needed to succeed commercially as a musician compared to those required for an inventor, he must have picked up some understanding of how markets worked in a general sense from his music career. It is strange that the first part of his career was so successful commercially, while the second wasn't. So what happened?

Some, Bob Moog included, have spoken of Scott's fear that other people would steal his ideas. Rhea says that before he visited Scott he was obliged to sign a 'document that essentially vouchsafed that I wouldn't reveal anything I might see at his facility' and that Scott 'never wanted me to record anything we discussed (having a fair streak of an independent inventor's paranoia about having his work "stolen")'.[104] In a poignant, unaddressed letter, written toward the end of his life and found among his papers when he died, Scott appears to confirm this explanation: 'I was so secretive … perhaps neurotically so.'[105] Scott wasn't alone in harbouring a tendency toward secrecy and fear of intellectual theft. Daphne Oram became isolated for similar reasons; so did Joe Meek. There is something about locking yourself up in a room and working alone for years that brings this tendency out in people. But it is too simplistic an explanation on its own. It neglects the fact that Scott did attempt to publicize what he was making with catalogues and adverts, and even allowed several magazines to interview him.

Like Thaddeus Cahill with his Telharmonium and Daphne Oram with her Oramics system, Scott was cursed with vision. His ideas were years ahead of the technology he had at his disposal to realize them. Not only that, he was also an autodidact with no formal training in any technical discipline to guide him. This meant that not only did he have trouble communicating what he was trying to do, as his writings about the Electronium demonstrate, but also that he had trouble actually doing it. The Electronium was never finished to his satisfaction. In part, this is attributable to a perfectionist temperament that could never resist one final improvement, but also to the fact that his vision demanded technology that didn't yet exist. Maybe he didn't quite have, on his own, the technical ability he needed. Even the Clavivox, a much simpler prospect, was under-developed. With their beautifully designed cabinets and neat control panels these instruments looked liked products, but they were really prototypes.

Scott might have benefitted from technical and business partners to help him with his inventions, but he was solitary by nature. Not many people could invent things and convert them into commercial products on their own, yet that's what Scott was trying to do. Scott had always been a dictatorial rather than an enabling bandleader, telling people what to do rather than empowering them. Once he'd dispensed with other musicians, collaborating with machines only, maybe he had finally created the world he wanted. The buttons and switches couldn't disagree, or answer back, or turn up late for rehearsal.

Scott didn't always work completely alone on his electronic music inventions, but when other people were involved it seems they were drafted in to perform particular functions. They were contractors, not collaborators. Bob Moog's experience with Scott is typical, commissioned to build this or that circuit from time to time, without ever seeing the full picture. Contrast this with Moog's own approach, always open to suggestions from others, and working collaboratively with musicians to shape his inventions. As the 1960s went on Moog had fostered strong links with both the academic music community and an emerging generation of rock musicians. Scott did neither, and his isolation was deliberate and self-willed. He was happy with his private kingdom, and at one level he probably didn't want to share any part of it, even though he also, conversely, wanted to sell his instruments. More prosaic factors would have been an influence here, too. By the time Scott became immersed in electronic music he was a middle-aged man, not in the best of health, and also wealthy, at least at first. Without the need to make money, all his energy was spent on the inventing, and there was nothing left for manufacturing, marketing and selling.

Scott's son by his first marriage, Stan Warnow, who has made a film about his father believes that he did indeed want to sell his products but that financial naivety and incompetence hampered this. Scott was good at earning money as a musician, but poor at managing it. Or maybe he became poor at managing it, and having earned so much for so long he became casual about it. When his second marriage broke up and the grand house was sold, Scott used his share of the proceeds, a considerable sum, to buy travellers cheques. These he cashed whenever he needed money until there were none left. There was no investment plan.[106]

Deutsch offered another possible explanation to the puzzle. He wondered if Scott harboured a sense of inferiority in the face of the academic music establishment that held considerable influence in electronic music in the late 1950s and early 1960s.[107] Although he was a Juilliard graduate and an inventive composer, Scott was a popular musician, sometimes even a novelty musician. He certainly knew about developments in serious electronic music, but did he feel uncomfortable engaging with that world when his natural milieu was the pop tune? In American electronic music of the period the gap between the serious and the popular was wider than it was in Britain. Whereas British composers like Daphne Oram and Tristram Cary could do serious work and take commercial commissions, their contemporaries in America tended to do one or the other. Warnow describes visiting the studio of composer Morton Subotnick when a graduate film student, and

Raymond Scott in his home studio circa 1957.
Credit: © Stan Warnow

then meeting him in 2011 at a film festival that was showing his film about his father, *Deconstructing Dad*. Warnow explained to Subotnick that he'd visited his studio years earlier, and that his father was the electronic musician Raymond Scott, only to find that Subotnick had never even heard of him, though the two men were active at the same time.[108]

Whatever was going on in Raymond Scott's mind, there was a clear disconnect in his activity. The succession of inventions and patents was matched by a bewildering array of corporate identities: Manhattan Research Inc; The Electronium Corporation; The Jingle Workshop; The World of Sound; Raymond Scott Enterprises. Yet for all that he hardly sold a thing. It's as if there was a constant need to move from one idea to another without bringing any to fruition. Attempts at marketing were made, but they don't ring true. A World of Sound product line brochure is a marvel of disjuncture.[109] It announces an electronic bicycle bell at $7.95, and a top of the range Electronium at $4,950. Who was this price list for, you wonder, and was it ever circulated?

In late 1965, when Scott's second marriage ended, he moved his studio from Manhasset to an industrial complex called Willow

Park Center, Farmingdale, Long Island. There it occupied one huge room. He married for a third time and continued to work on his inventions and a dwindling number of advert commissions. A last big commercial opportunity came his way when the President of Motown, Berry Gordy, enquired about the Electronium.

6

Because a fire was in my head

Do-it-yourself electronic sound in American rock

At the beginning of the 1960s electronic music was in an uncertain position. A primitive technical basis for it was by now readily available. Tape recorders were common, and people had learned how to use them as creative tools in a manner that foresaw sampling. Electronic sound generators like test oscillators were cheap, easily obtainable and simple to operate. Just these two items were enough to set up a rudimentary electronic music studio. There were also several electronic instruments on the market. But there was little evidence of this on record, and your best chance of hearing electronic music was on television or a film soundtrack.

In serious music some saw a way ahead that seemed open and bright with possibility. The tension between the two main branches of electronic music, *Elektronische Musik* and *musique concrète*, had slackened, and many composers were routinely combining pure electronic sound, concrete sources and conventional instrumentation. There were even early developments in computer music, sequencers and programmable synthesizers, though these were largely confined to research facilities. Some anticipated a decisive move away from conventional tonality and instrumentation. But there was a paucity of serious electronic music recordings available. A 1959 *New York Times* article pointed out that as electronic music couldn't really be performed live in the conventional sense the album seemed like an obvious medium for composers, and yet only a handful of records of this type were being released. If there was a market for this type of music, it wasn't being serviced.[110] Clearly, for all the drum beating, the revolution hadn't yet won widespread support in record companies.

And while there was support in some circles for serious electronic music, for every Stockhausen or Ussachevsky there was an Aaron Copland (1900–90). In an assessment of the first sixty years of twentieth century music, *The New Music 1900/60*, the celebrated American composer struck a distinctly ambivalent note:

> What I am saying is that composers are in danger of being put out of their own house. The writing of music has begun to attract a new type of individual, half engineer and half composer.[111]

He goes on to explain that he isn't trying to frighten people with the idea of 'orgrelike figures taken from science fiction who are about to invade the art of music', and yet many of his more conservative colleagues were worried about exactly that.

In popular music there was a similar spread of attitudes. Although electronic composition was accepted, sometimes grudgingly, in film and television music, it certainly hadn't yet got anywhere near rock 'n' roll. Indeed, as the 1960s, an age of cultural upheaval, got underway, rock 'n' roll was mired in a conservative phase. The Elvis who came out of the Army was a very different act from the Elvis that went in. Meanwhile, Little Richard found religion, Eddie Cochran and Buddy Holly were killed, Gene Vincent began a long, alcoholic decline, while Jerry Lee Lewis and Chuck Berry attracted the unwelcome (to them) attention of the authorities, to the detriment of their careers. The sharp edges had been sanded into safe, inoffensive curves. A glance at the American charts of the time shows them dominated by vapid teen idols, musical soundtracks, novelty songs and middle-of-the-road balladeers. With a few notable exceptions – Dion, Roy Orbison, The Everly Brothers – rock 'n' roll was not making good on its early promise, growing weak and flaccid in the comfortable embrace of show business. It wasn't until the middle of the decade that it once again became a radical and challenging force.

Yet soon, in the midst of this conservatism, a handful of musicians in America tried to foment a revolution that ran parallel to events in serious electronic music, experimenting with electronic sound in rock, much in the same manner as Joe Meek in London. These efforts were scattered and unconnected. There was no scene. They were spread across the full spectrum of popular idioms, from the most disposable of novelty tunes to the outer fringes of art rock. In fact, the earlier of these pioneers tended toward the commercial end of the spectrum, with the more experimental musicians coming later. In spite of the range of styles attempted, these musicians were trying to do exactly the same thing. They had all glimpsed the future, but they weren't sure how to get there.

Del Shannon's 'Runaway', which pre-dated 'Telstar' by a year, was the first and biggest of a run of hits that ensured Shannon's commercial survival well after the British invasion had dispatched with most of his peers. It, and many of his other hits, were stamped with an immediately recognizable sonic trademark – a solo that sounded a little like a violin and a little like a flute, but most definitely wasn't either.

The instantly catchy and unusually structured 'Runaway' was written by Shannon with his pianist, Max Crook (born 1936). The trademark Shannon sound leads approximately twenty-five seconds of the single's two or so minutes. It was played by Crook on an instrument he dubbed the Musitron (a contraction of music and electron), actually a modified Clavioline. Crook had been interested in electronic sound since the 1950s, and had considered a Hammond Solovox before settling on a Gibson Clavioline.

When I spoke to him some years before writing this book he talked of 'an intense desire to create something new and different in the sound of music. Electronic principles applied to the field of music seemed to me to be the primary way to accomplish this goal.'[112] Those words could serve as an article of faith for any number of electronic musicians of the time, and you could ascribe them to any of the period's serious composers and get away with it. In Crook's case the urge to 'apply electronic principles to the field of music' led him to cobble together the Musitron. In the 1960s he was secretive about its working, not wanting to lose a perceived advantage over other mere organists or Clavioline players. No doubt, too, he realized that a dash of mystique does a pop career no harm at all. In time it emerged that his modifications were modest, including altering the Clavioline's circuitry to extend its range, and adding a mechanical pitch bender attached to its tuning circuit. He also added a homemade vibrato unit, and a series of similarly sourced reverb units, including one based on a garden gate spring. Shannon himself loved the Musitron and was keen to integrate it into his overall sound. That enthusiasm eventually translated into several big hits with electronic solos, which, at the time attracted a great deal of curiosity that became a part of Shannon's myth. What is that sound?, people asked.

Crook and Shannon weren't making electronic music, but conventional rock and roll with an electronic solo replacing what, convention dictated, ought to have been a guitar or a saxophone. It was a small but significant step, but Crook was unable to sustain a professional musical career. Apart from an appearance on a Liberace album, little more was heard of him after his association with Shannon. He did, though, form an electronic pop duo called The Sounds of Tomorrow, which performed later in the 1960s without releasing any recordings.

Having spent most of the 1950s travelling around Europe giving Ondioline demonstrations, toward the end of the decade Perrey ran into Jean Cocteau, who was much impressed with the instrument and Perrey's act. He advised Perrey that a move to America would further his career and promised to introduce him to someone who could help. A few weeks later Edith Piaf's secretary called Perrey and summoned him to meet the singer. She too was impressed with the Ondioline and invited Perrey to perform on stage with her at the Paris Olympia in 1959. Then she funded studio time to make an Ondioline demo recording, which she sent, with an introductory note, to a friend in New York called Carroll Bratman. After about three weeks Perrey received a letter from Bratman containing an air ticket to New York. Bratman was a percussionist who had played professionally with symphony orchestras and as a pop studio musician. He had a taste for exotic percussion instruments – gongs, bells, tuned drums – and in 1945 he opened Carroll Music Service in New York, hiring out his collection to orchestras and studios. Percussion aside, he liked unusual instruments, and the Ondioline took his fancy.

Perrey flew to New York with his Ondioline in March 1960 and under Bratman's patronage set about composing, recording, performing and promoting the Ondioline. He toured the country giving demonstrations and appeared on several high-profile television shows, including *I've Got a Secret*, a CBS game show that ran for 15 years from 1952. 'Jean-Jacques Perrey, from Paris, France', as he shyly introduced himself, appeared in June 1960, sat chewing gum behind a piano, flanked by a clarinettist. The pair played what appeared to be a brief piano and clarinet duet before whispering to the presenter their secret. This flashed on the screen but was not revealed to a studio panel. That secret was that the clarinettist was miming, and that it had been Perrey who had played the clarinet part on the Ondioline.

The show's entertainment then hinged on the panel making hopelessly inaccurate stabs at the nature of the secret, though in this case the comedic effect was compromised when the panel immediately guessed correctly that the clarinettist was miming and that the 'other gentleman' was making all the sound. As the four panel members talk over each other the word 'electronically' can be heard, before someone else proposes that Perrey was a ventriloquist who had sung the clarinet part. They then decide the sound was made by an 'adjunct' to the piano, at which point the 'little rascal', the Ondioline, is revealed. Perrey then spends five minutes demonstrating the Ondioline's capacity for mimicry, responding to requests from the panel to do French horns, banjos, cellos, bongos and so on. It's an impressive display, and as a variety act bears some similarity, in concept at least, to Musaire's theremin impressions of revving engines two decades earlier.

That the panel knew the secret was electronic is telling. The idea of an electronic instrument that could mimic 'real' instruments wasn't new to them, though presumably the Ondioline itself was. The instrument became more widely known later that year on account of its use by composer Alex North in the Stanley Kubrick film *Spartacus* (1960). With that boost, and thanks to Perrey's efforts, the Ondioline was in vogue for a while. In 1963 it appeared in the American singles charts for the first time, making string-like sounds alongside the trombone of Kai Winding, a one-time musical director at the Playboy club. His instrumental hit 'More', from the movie *Mondo Cane*, was drawn from the album *Soul Surfin'*. On this and a subsequent follow up, *Mondo Cane No. 2*, released to cash in on the single's success, Winding himself is credited with playing the Ondioline, though Perrey is now generally acknowledged as the performer.

Winding produced archetypal smooth, inoffensive, middle-of-the-road instrumental music. Rock music and the Ondioline weren't introduced until sometime Dylan sideman Al Kooper came across the instrument at a private demonstration at Carroll Music. Kooper hired an Ondioline from Carroll for the Gene Pitney album *I Must Be Seeing Things* (1965). The Blues Project's classic single 'No Time Like the Right Time', a minor hit elevated to immortality when it was included on the *Nuggets* compilation, features Kooper's best Ondioline moment, a raga-style solo. '[I liked] the fact that I could play it with the heel of my hand and play Coltrane-ish scales that way,'[113] Kooper said.

Perrey, meanwhile, pressed on with a ceaseless round of Ondioline activity. He appeared on children's TV as *Mr Ondioline*, though without the cape and mask in case he frightened the children. In 1966 he returned to *I've Got a Secret* for what amounted to more or less the same stunt as his first appearance. This time he followed the denouement with a mimed performance with Gershon Kingsley of a track from their just-released Vanguard album *The In Sound from Way Out*. This was the first of a series of four instrumental electronic pop albums for the label, two with Kingsley. *The In Sound from Way Out* was made entirely by combining meticulous tape techniques with the Ondioline, but by then the French instrument was obsolete. The other three Vanguard albums combined it with the Moog synthesizer, which consigned the Ondioline and its generation of electronic instruments to history.

Another electronic pioneer to appear on *I've Got a Secret* was the unclassifiable Bruce Haack (1931–88). The troubled Canadian-born savant ploughed a wildly idiosyncratic furrow through the electronic music field from the mid-1950s until his death. Gifted with the aural/musical equivalent of photographic recall, able to hear a piece of music and play it back immediately from memory, Haack was an autodidactic musical prodigy. He grew up in the isolated mining town of Rocky Mountain House, Alberta, an only child. Unable to enrol on the University of Alberta's music course because of an inability to sight-read, he instead studied psychology while writing and performing music widely in his spare time. These extra-curricular activities brought him to the attention of The Juilliard School and in 1954, supported by a modest scholarship from the Canadian Government, he moved to New York. He soon made friends with another new student, Ted Pandel, who was a supportive presence for the rest of Haack's life.

A mythology has sprung up around Haack that paints him as a troubled man, scarred by a loveless upbringing. He is said to have taken peyote with Native Canadians as a teenager, and throughout his life he struggled with addictions to drugs and alcohol. He appears an archetype of the electronic music outsider, a self-taught eccentric forging a career out of a mashed blend of occult spiritual interests, homemade gadgets, and a fascination with space and the moon landings. His friends and collaborators thought him a genius. Photos show a heavily built man, often with arms folded, seemingly appraising the world with disdain. This was not the sort of personality you'd associate with children's entertainment, and yet that was the realm in which Haack first made a mark.

He lasted about 18 months at the Juilliard before dropping out, but his obvious musical abilities led him into a free-ranging career of pop song writing, classical composition and *musique concrète* creations. None of this made him much money, however, so he started to work as an accompanist with the dance instructor Esther Nelson. This led to the formation, with Nelson and Pandel, of Dimension 5 records, which began to release a series of records for children from 1963. By this time Haack, despite having no electronics training, was making primitive electronic instruments from found objects including disembowelled radios. These included the Electronic Wind Tunnel, the Horn Fuse Plateau and the Sono Vocal Chorus Electronique.[114]

Home recorded at Haack and Pandel's apartment, and with their naive homespun cover art, the Dimension 5 releases flew in well below the mainstream radar. Nelson later spoke of Haack's natural ability to engage with children and his lack of self-consciousness. This is apparent in the music. It reveals a magpie-like imagination, jumping from one glittering fascination to another, combining instruments, sounds and styles. Haack's electronics featured from the start, but by *The Way-Out Record for Children* and *The Electronic*

Record for Children (released in 1968 and 1969 respectively, though each recorded in the year before release) he was fashioning entirely electronic music for kids. Simple, repetitive and rhythmic, it was like kindergarten Kraftwerk, its innocence and playfulness at odds with the opaque theorizing of the adult rock album he was beginning to make at the same time.

Haack's electronic instruments earned him a degree of minor celebrity and he appeared demonstrating them on US TV several times, including *The Tonight Show with Johnny Carson* and *I've Got a Secret* (twice). Of all Haack's gadgets it was the Dermatron (sometimes called the Peopleodeon), which used the heat and conductivity of the human body to trigger variable pitches, which got the most attention in these settings. On a 1966 episode of *I've Got a Secret* the Danish comedian/pianist Victor Borge introduces a buzzing perspex dome trailing wires back behind the stage curtain. The wires, it turns out, are attached to twelve chromatically pitched young women, and the dome is the Peopleodeon. Borge then wires himself into the dome and proceeds with his comedy turn, running up and down the women touching their hands in sequence and playing a tune of electronic tones, which the dome accompanies with a constant background hum of static. The presenter then introduces the machine's inventors, and Pandel and Haack stand in the audience to take their bow.

By 1968 Haack's career direction was a succession of angles like a cannoning pinball. As well as the children's records and light entertainment TV plugs, his friend and business manager Chris Kachulis started to secure TV advert commissions. Products that benefitted from Haack's attentions were Goodyear Tyres, Kraft Cheese and life insurance. In 1968 Haack also started serious work on what he came to call 'head rock', which was his own peculiar brand of electronic rock inspired by the era's psychedelic rock and heavy blues, to which Kachulis had introduced him. He was by then approaching middle age, a little late to start a rock career by most standards, and listening to this head rock there is the unavoidable sense that Haack didn't quite *get* rock music and culture. The records, for all their idiosyncratic fecundity, sound as if they were made by visiting aliens trying to mimic earth's youth culture.

The first and most fully realised of these, *The Electric Lucifer*

(1970), was conceived, written and largely recorded in a period from late 1967 to the end of 1969 during an intermittent road trip on the New Jersey coast that Haack took with Kachulis. During this time Haack was also building up his studio, equipping it with his home-built electronic musical instruments, and tape decks and mixers he modified. Here he recorded most of *Electric Lucifer*, assisted by Kachulis, who sang on several songs.

By turns oblique, playful, dark and ebullient, Haack's head rock is music of many parts, not all of which fit comfortably together. The opening song, 'Electric to Me Turn', is bouncy novelty pop with vocoder vocals. This approach surfaces regularly throughout, alongside a chanting, stagey style reminiscent of pop musicals of the period. Snatches of guitar and heavily treated percussion are heard, but most of the music is comprised of dense layers of electronic sound. Lyrically, the album is a Blakean meditation on the struggle between good and evil and the reconciliation of spiritual extremes, an expression of Haack's personal religious vision. In the liner notes he speaks of a God so gracious that even Satan will be forgiven. In a parallel universe *The Electric Lucifer* might have been taken up as a soundtrack for the post-Utopian mood that prevailed after the end of the sixties dream, but, despite a major label release, it failed to find much of an audience.

The name of thereminist Samuel Hoffman began to appear less in credits as the 1950s rolled on. In part this was attributable to the emergence of a rival inspired by Hoffman himself. The musician, author and academic Dr Paul Tanner was a high-ranking session trombonist on the staff of the American Broadcasting Company who had worked with Glen Miller, Henry Mancini and Frank Sinatra. He also wrote several books, including a best-selling jazz primer, and taught at UCLA. Tanner was playing a film soundtrack session sometime in 1958 (probably *Earth vs. the Spider*). Also amongst the musicians was Hoffman, who, according to Tanner, was having trouble pitching his instrument to the orchestra.

Tanner had at this point no interest in electronic music, but he thought there must be a more practical way of tuning electronic sound, and he set out to find a better way of doing things. With a friend, actor and electronics enthusiast Bob Whitsell, Tanner made an instrument he called the electro-theremin, which wasn't a theremin at all, but simply a test oscillator with a mechanical operating system. An early version of the instrument debuted on a 1958 album called *Music for Heavenly Bodies*, on which Tanner shared billing with Andre Montero and his Orchestra. Replete with a visual pun of a sleeve (naked shapely female flying through space), this was light orchestral mood music blending strings and electronics in a similar vein to Hoffman's trilogy of theremin albums a decade earlier. The album's liner notes declare that the electro-theremin 'provides a sense of the unknown … of falling off into the whistling world of infinite space', reinforcing the space/electronic music interface that was, by then, a cliché. They also point out the differences between a real theremin and Tanner's electro-theremin, but that didn't seem to achieve much. Even now Tanner's instrument is routinely described as a theremin when discussed in the context of its most famous appearance.

So what was the electro-theremin? Simply, a mechanical means of controlling a variable pitch audio oscillator that produced a sine wave tone. The oscillator and the mechanism that controlled it were housed in a simple wooden box. A slot ran along the length of the box, with a hand-operated slide control protruding through it. This control connected to a pulley system that in turn rotated the oscillator's pitch control dial. A drawing of a piano keyboard was mounted along the length of the slot, calibrated so that when the control aligned with a particular note on the dummy keyboard, the oscillator would sound that same note. This meant that Tanner could easily pitch notes, and, because there was no step up between notes, still create the portamento characteristic of a real theremin.

Tanner, a studio veteran with a bulging contacts book, began getting calls as soon as *Music for Heavenly Bodies* was released, and the commissions rolled in. In spite of its primitive nature and rudimentary construction the electro-theremin proved versatile in Tanner's hands. He could hold a tune easily and accurately yet approximate a real theremin's vibrato and portamento. Much of this work conformed to the now-established conventions. There was sci-fi, including *My Favorite Martian*, a CBS TV series that ran from 1963 to 1966, in which Tanner contributes to the theme and provides a sound signature for whenever the titular Martian levitates. In the 1964 B-movie *Strait-Jacket* the electro-theremin accompanies axe-murderer Joan Crawford's mental disintegration. In an NBC comedy show from 1959/60, called either *Ford Startime* or *Lincoln–Mercury Startime*, depending on which division of Ford was running the commercials in the show, Tanner used the electro-theremin as a 'voice', rather like the whistle voices of the later British TV programme *The Clangers*. All of this amounted to a lot of exposure for Tanner's home-made gadget, yet this was eclipsed when Brian Wilson called him.

In 1966 Wilson was assembling The Beach Boys' *Pet Sounds* and a new single of unprecedented sophistication and complexity, 'Good Vibrations'. He wanted electronic sound in both projects and called on Tanner, by then one of the best-known electronic musician on the books in Los Angeles. It remains unclear still whether Wilson, when booking Tanner, thought he was getting a real theremin or not. He still tends to refer to Tanner's instrument as a theremin, and an urban myth has grown up, reinforced by mentions in books and CD liner notes, that it is an antennae-controlled instrument on The Beach Boys recordings. But it was Tanner with his humble box of tricks who took his place alongside some of rock's biggest session players, including Hal Blaine and Glen Campbell, recording the *Pet Sounds* song 'I Just Wasn't Made for These Times' on Valentine's Day 1966. A few days later he was back for the first sessions for 'Good Vibrations'.

Whatever Wilson did or did not understand about the theremin, he was clear about what *sound* he wanted. Speaking later, he said:

> When 'Good Vibrations' was forming itself in my mind I could hear the theremin on the track. It sounds like a woman's voice or like a violin bow on a carpenter's saw. You make it waver, just like a human voice. It's groovy![115]

Bootlegs and later legitimate issues of the sessions show Tanner's playing prominent from the start, but becoming more so as time went on, and by the final take the undulating sine wave was mixed high.

Pet Sounds was released in May 1966. It features a brief Tanner solo just before the slow fade on the classic 'I Just Wasn't Made for These Times'. This demonstrates the electro-theremin's appeal, with precision pitching that only the very best 'real' thereminists could ever achieve; elegiac music in which the electronic sound nestles comfortably, a sound of human warmth for once, not alien, or distressed or comic. Five months later came 'Good Vibrations', now so routinely acclaimed as one of the great pop productions that its impact at the time has been lost. Its greatness lies in Wilson's conjuring of pop magic out of enormous complexity, fitting into its three and a half minutes unparalleled instrument combinations and unexpected structural leaps. Tanner's electro-theremin can be heard most clearly against the juddering rhythm cellos that underpin the 'I'm picking up good vibrations' section. The closing fade reprises this section without vocals, so one of the last things you hear is Tanner's electronic tone.

After 'Good Vibrations' Wilson asked Tanner to perform on stage with The Beach Boys, an offer Tanner declined due to other commitments, and conscious of being a generation older than the band. With Tanner unavailable and The Beach Boys touring, an alternative was urgently needed. The band approached Moog salesman Walter Sear for a solution, and he demonstrated a conventional theremin for them. This, the band immediately dismissed as impractical, bewildered by the instrument's complete lack of visual cues, so Sear passed on the problem to Bob Moog himself.[116] The outcome was an irony several layers thick. Moog, the theremin enthusiast, was commissioned to design and build a special ribbon-controlled device to mimic Tanner's electro-theremin, itself built to mimic a real theremin. This would be played by Mike Love, who had objected to Wilson's sonic adventures in the first place, preferring to splash around in the frothy shallows of the band's surf era. Meanwhile, the success of 'Good Vibrations', featuring what was routinely and incorrectly described as a theremin, prompted a resurgence in sales of Moog theremins. This was a boon as the company was short of cash, but it also gave shape to an idea that had been forming in Moog's mind for a while: that rock musicians, pockets bulging with fat record company advances, were the obvious market for his electronic instruments.

In September 1967 Tanner was called up again to serve with The Beach Boys, contributing a two-note hook to the title track of the *Wild Honey* album. By that time he was at the point of standing down the electro-theremin and exiting the world of electronic sound. He found himself at another session with someone playing a

Moog synthesizer, and recognized at once that the new instrument trumped his homespun device a hundred times over. The electro-theremin was retired to a hospital where it was used to conduct hearing tests until the hospital collapsed in an earthquake and the electro-theremin went with it.

In 1965 a new age in music was quietly ushered in when Moog sold his first modular systems. Most early Moogs – expensive, complicated, bulky pieces of equipment – went to well-heeled academic institutions harbouring experimental composers interested in the new instrument's apparently limitless sonic capabilities. It would be a year or two before Moogs first made their presence felt in the wider world of pop music and several more years again before they became commonplace. At the same time, on the cusp of this new era in electronic music, a handful of American rock bands were taking a different approach, attempting to combine the low-tech ingenuity that characterized electronic music before the synthesizer with (mostly) straightforward rock 'n' roll.

The electronic two-piece Silver Apples took their name from a line in the W. B. Yeats poem 'Song Of Wandering Aengus', from which the title of this chapter is drawn. Coincidentally, an experimental classical electronic album called *Silver Apples of the Moon* (1967) by Morton Subotnick, recorded with a Buchla modular system, also took the same Yeats line for its title. The two are not related. Simeon Coxe, leader of Silver Apples, was a self-professed rock 'n' roller with no background in serious electronic music. He chanced upon a door into the new world when he made friends with someone who had an oscillator that he used to play along with classical music through a record player. Coxe tried the same idea, playing along to a Rolling Stones record, and was hooked.

That was in 1966 or 1967, when Coxe was fronting a succession of straightforward rock bands that were making little headway. The last of these, The Overland Stage Electric Band, was a routine two guitars, bass and drums covers band playing the Greenwich Village coffee house circuit when Coxe joined. By this time he had bought his friend's oscillator for $25 and he started to plug it into a guitar amp at the band's gigs. Coxe noted that this fascinated audiences, but within months of his arrival the line up began shrinking, members driven away one by one by the howling sine and square waves.

Eventually, there was just Coxe and a drummer, Danny Taylor, left. Necessity being the mother of invention, they decided to continue, and Silver Apples came into being. The pair developed a novel approach based on Coxes's electronic sound and Taylor's elaborate drum set up, with both members singing.

As the oscillator was now the band's sole source of melody and harmony, there was an obvious and compelling need to find a route to greater musical complexity. At the very least, Silver Apples needed to be able to change chord. A prerequisite for this was achieved by adding a few more oscillators, and by extension a few more notes. Next came the challenge of fashioning the rig into a performance instrument so that one man could 'play' several oscillators at once. The oscillators Coxe was using were the same sort of laboratory test equipment beloved of the pre-synthesizer generation of electronic composers, with pitch controlled by large rotary dials. Those people, though, tended to use them in controlled studio settings, in conjunction with tape techniques, to create melody and harmony. In such conditions a few minutes of music could take weeks to realize. If Silver Apples wanted to play live they had to find a way to operate the oscillators in sequence in real time. This was achieved by routing each oscillator through a telegraph key, which Coxe 'played' with his hands, feet and forehead, turning pre-tuned oscillators on and off as the music demanded. Finally, Coxe felt a need for more textural sophistication. The pure sine waves generated by the oscillators could sound cold and clinical, so he routed them through fuzz units, phasers, sound filters, radio circuits – anything he could lay his hands on that would allow him to manipulate the character of those piercing waves of sound.

Before long Coxe found himself in the embrace of what drummer Taylor christened The Simeon. It was a changeable beast that rapidly grew to gargantuan proportions, at one stage consisting of nine oscillators (five bass, three rhythm and one lead), an echo unit, two tone controls, a wah wah pedal, a radio, three amplifiers and assorted foot and hand switches. Despite its size, the Simeon was limited. For example, bass parts had to use only whatever five notes the bass oscillators were tuned to at the start of a song, as Coxe could not retune them without stopping playing. Yet despite this, when combined with Taylor's huge set of tuned drums, it offered Silver

Apples a palette of sound colours unlike virtually anything else in rock 'n' roll.

Thus uniquely equipped, Silver Apples set about building a career, funded by a manager named Barry Bryant and assisted by lyricists Stanley Warren and Eileen Llewellen. Bryant offered the band to New York's record labels, attracting the interest of just one, a failing independent named Kapp Records. With no other offers on the table, Silver Apples signed with Kapp, and some time in early 1968 commenced recording of their debut album in the label's tiny four-track studio. The sessions almost ground to a halt when the producer reported sick. Coxe, Taylor and manager Bryant had no studio experience and were left to their own devices. Taking advice where they could find it, they gradually mastered the rudimentary multi-tracking technique often used on four-tracks, recording drums and bass parts on to all four tracks of one machine, which were then mixed down on to a single track on another machine. The remaining three tracks were then filled up with rhythm and lead oscillator parts, vocals and sound effects.

The eponymous Silver Apples debut album, drawn from these sessions, opens with 'Oscillations'. This encapsulates the band's strengths and weaknesses, demonstrating both the limitations of the Simeon and the band's ingenuity in overcoming them. Starting with an ascending tone like a flying saucer taking off, the song settles into a one-chord drone from which it never budges. With Coxe and Taylor chanting in harmony, a measure of variety is found through Taylor's complex drum patterns and carefully planned stops and starts in the oscillator drones. The result is an exercise in mesmeric repetition with just enough of a tune to warrant release as a single. It received some regional airplay, but was hampered by poor distribution, as were all the band's subsequent releases.

By now, the Simeon was a labyrinthine maze of leads linking dozens of components, and dismantling it, transporting it, and reassembling it at a venue took many hours. At one of Silver Apples' first gigs, a free concert in New York Central Park in front of 30,000 people, Coxe and Taylor had to start setting up early in the morning for a show that started at 3pm. Touring was out of the question until Coxe contained the monster's innards within several custom-built cases, which could be transported and plugged into each other with relative ease.

Silver Apples toured and recorded for the rest of the decade, but with little commercial success. There was one tantalizing encounter with the big time when in spring 1969 the band were recording at the Record Plant in New York, occupying the same studio as Jimi Hendrix, with one act packing up its gear each day to make way for the other. On one of those occasions Silver Apples jammed with Hendrix, an event reputedly committed to tape. In 2003 the Hendrix fanzine *Jimpress* published a forensic study of this episode, concluding that recorded evidence of it survives, with the bass notes of the Simeon being audible on Hendrix's version of 'Star Spangled Banner', especially at the end. Regrettably, not even the scantest recorded evidence of another intriguing Silver Apples collaboration, an onstage jam with Tyrannosaurus Rex, survives.

Another band that once jammed with Jimi Hendrix was Lothar and The Hand People, active in New York around the same time as Silver Apples. The five-piece formed in Denver in 1965, relocating to New York in 1966 and going on to record two albums for Capitol, *Presenting ... Lothar & The Hand People* (1968, produced by Robert Margouleff) and *Space Hymn* (1969, produced by Nick Venet). Mixing cheery folk rock with darker psychedelia, the band's material was competent and well performed, while lacking a spark. They were notable, though, for being the only band of the time to put the theremin (called Lothar – the band being The Hand People) at the centre of their sound. The band also used Moog synthesizer.

The title track of Lothar and The Hand People's second album got some radio play and remains their best-known song. A Moog-generated sitar-like drone underpins a lengthy spoken monologue, exhorting the listener to relax, before the track morphs into a typical period acoustic anthem, all quasi-profundity and space symbolism. It's an engaging listen and a choice example of an early attempt to integrate synths into rock. It is, though, pretty conventional rock music of the time, whereas Silver Apples sounded distinctly *other*. As far as Coxe was concerned, there were no other bands doing anything remotely close to what Silver Apples were doing, 'except that a couple of people kept saying that there was this band called The United States of America that were classically trained musicians using lab synths, and they were so amazing, but we never heard them play'.[117]

This is half right: The United States of America weren't using lab synths, but they were classically trained musicians. Their leader, the composer, academic and ethnomusicologist Joseph Byrd, had a background in post-war experimental music. He had spent the late 1950s and early 1960s in education while hovering on the periphery of various *avant-garde* scenes. He even had a spell studying with John Cage, which he says entailed 'throwing the I-Ching for the notation of his *Atlas Eclipticalis*.'[118] Byrd was never a main player in the *avant-garde*, but mixing in such circles shaped his outlook, setting the angle for his brief, tangential foray into rock.

By 1965 Byrd was studying for a doctorate at UCLA but spent most of his energy involving himself in that institution's New Music Workshop. In 1965, with funding from UCLA Associated Students, he took part in a set of concerts and events called *A Steamed Spring Vegetable Pie* (the title chosen, randomly, from *The Alice B. Toklas Cookbook*). The final concert of that series closed with a LaMonte Young's piece in which a giant weather balloon is inflated on stage using a vacuum cleaner. This took about half an hour, and Byrd, concerned that he might lose the attention of his audience, put together a blues band featuring his friend Linda Ronstadt on vocals to provide additional entertainment as the balloon grew. He later reflected that 'the realization that rock was an access to a larger public came out of that concert, and the idea of forming a band began taking shape'.[119]

Byrd left UCLA in 1966. Up until then, the blues band aside, his career had been confined to experiments with *musique concrète* and tape manipulation. Now he wanted to go into the realms of electronic sound generation. For a while he used a primitive tone generator made by Tom Oberheim, who later manufactured Oberheim synthesizers. When Oberheim wanted his gadget back Byrd came upon an aerospace engineer who was working in Orange County, one Richard Durrett. Under Byrd's direction, Durrett built a small, hand-held configuration of oscillators, controlled by a potentiometer for each oscillator and a selector that changed the interaction between them. Byrd says:

Only one waveform could serve as tone generator and one to modulate its pitch. So you could have a saw-tooth wave modifying a square wave tone ... I guess the art, if there was any in such a primal kind of thing, was in the setting of the tape delays ...'[120]

The grandly named Durrett Electronic Music Synthesizer was monophonic, so to create any multi-layered electronics Byrd had to multi-track in the studio, and when performing live, play along to tape recordings. In 1967 he struck out on his odd rock career with this little gadget under his arm, forming The United States of America. The 'population' (line up) comprised Byrd playing various keyboards and electronic music; his former partner Dorothy Moskowitz on vocals; the classically trained Gordon Mallon playing electric violin through a ring modulator; Rand Forbes on fretless electric bass; Craig Woodson on 'electric drums' – a conventional drum kit with contact mics on the drum skins that were used to modify the sounds; and occasional member Ed Bogas on additional keyboards. In contrast to Silver Apples, which came from of rock background, all the musicians in Byrd's band had associations with *avant-garde* music and ethnomusicology.

We were very conscious that we were plunging into rock without any real knowledge of, or experience in, the medium. We had played Cage and Stockhausen, African and Indian music, and I thought we could simply bring that all to rock. But we knew almost nothing about the roots of rock and roll.[121]

There was no place for rock's lead instrument, the electric guitar, although Mallon's ring-modulated violin managed a fair impression of one. In the context of the band, Byrd's electronics include tape music. But it is the Durrett Electronic Music Synthesizer that dominates, generating the sonic exclamation marks that punctuate The United States of America's songs. These, despite the band's apparent innocence of rock tradition, sound more or less in step with then-current West Coast psychedelic rock, Jefferson Airplane being an obvious reference point. The recording of the band's album was a fraught business. Byrd and Moskowitz's broken romance caused tensions amplified by the presence of another of Moskowitz's former partners, producer David Rubinson. Byrd's insistence on pushing the band to experiment caused more tension, and yet the finished product is cohesive – a balance of confrontational rock-outs and dreamy ballads in keeping with the spirit of the times. The Durrett was a limited instrument, offering some textural possibilities, but not really capable of much in the way of melody. This, along with relatively conventional songwriting, resulted in what is really a standard rock album with vivid electronic daubs, as opposed to Silver Apples' almost pure electronic music. With hindsight, The United States of America album provided a very early example of the problem rock musicians had with integrating electronic sound. Too often the electronics sound like attention-seeking gestures rather than a necessary component of the whole – impressive in moderation, but quickly over-bearing.

The United States of America got swept up in a Columbia Records rush for rock acts following the Monterey Pop Festival, but their album was only a very lowly chart entry. The band was widely heard, appearing on Columbia's big selling budget sampler album *The Rock Machine Turns You On* (1969), though the chosen song, 'I Won't Leave My Wooden Wife for You', was rather lame. They toured too, Byrd recalling an encounter with a hostile Velvet Underground, who toppled The United States of America's amp stack. But it all came to nothing. Civil war split the band in two, Moskowitz keeping the name and recording some demos before giving up. Byrd, for his part, released a second album of electronic rock for Columbia in 1969 under the name Joseph Byrd and the Field Hippies, but it passed almost unnoticed.

Before The United States of America's album was released Byrd's electronics were heard on a recording by the one-time protest folkie Phil Ochs. Ochs had already recorded three albums for Elektra when, in 1966, on account of his biting topical songs, factions of the folk community sought to adopt him as saviour elect after Bob Dylan's electric apostasy. But Ochs bridled at such expectations and in 1967 he moved to the A&M label, seeking a new direction ... at which point Joseph Byrd stepped into the picture.

Ochs' debut for A&M was *Pleasures of the Harbor* (August 1967). With its harpsichords and string quartets, this was a baroque chamber pop, Ochs revelling in a new direction. The album closed with the epic and extraordinary 'Crucifixion', an allegory about the death of John Kennedy arranged by Byrd. Nearly nine minutes in length, Byrd's dense amalgam of strings, flute, brass, backward tapes, organ, electric harpsichord, percussion and electronic oscillations from the Durrett was created in response to Och's request for an arrangement that referenced Schoenberg, Stravinsky, Cage and electronic sound. It was a daring musical statement that, staggering under the weight of its ambition, dragged Ochs a thousand miles from his earlier eager folk strumming. The recording process was tense and drawn out. Ochs, used to singing and playing his guitar simultaneously, was finding it hard to sing in time, so Byrd recorded a click track by hitting two drumsticks together. By the time it came to mix the track Byrd had fallen out with producer Larry Marks and wasn't invited to the session. To Byrd's chagrin, Marks left the click track in the mix, an ominous ticking constant as the swarming melee spreads ever further into dissonant territory.

Pleasures of the Harbor was not a great commercial success. Ochs never found a decent audience for his post-protest music and writer's block and alcoholism precipitated a steep decline that ended in suicide in 1976. Byrd, meanwhile, didn't get too many offers of arrangement work after 'Crucifixion', but his spectacular orchestration is one of the great audacious gestures of 1960's rock.

San Francisco's Fifty Foot Hose, with its detached, incorporeal female voice and its partly electronic instrumentation, bears some comparison with The United States of America. Led by Louis 'Cork' Marcheschi (born 1945) and David Blossom, the band entered the fray armed with a similarly serious aesthetic and considerable knowledge of *avant-garde* electronic music, courtesy of Marcheschi, who was then and still is an active visual artist.

Fifty Foot Hose formed in late 1966 after the split of Marcheschi's previous band, The Ethix. Though a working R'n'B outfit, The Ethix had released what now seems like one of the decade's most challenging singles, 'Bad Trip', which gave some indication of the more experimental direction Marcheschi's music would take. His deep roots in electronic music can be traced back to a youthful epiphany hearing Edgard Varèse's *Poème électronique*, played to him by the older brother of a girlfriend. 'I really didn't know what I was listening to,' he says 'but I was dumbstruck by the tonality, the sounds, the quality, the sense of movement, all of the visceral and visual imagery I got from it.' Advised by his friend's older brother to look out for anything with a theremin on it, Marcheschi picked up a copy of a Clara Rockmore album of pieces written specifically for the theremin, and 'got very interested in the magical concept of the instrument you played and never touched'. Like many early electronic musicians, Marcheschi uses esoteric language to describe his fascination with electronic sound. 'I clearly understood it as something scientific, electronic, mathematical, but my experience of it emotionally was rather magical.' [122] He became familiar, too, with work by other experimental composers, including John Cage, Terry Riley, and George Antheil, and was aware of the use of electronics in 1950s science fiction films. Ken Nordine's narratives, held together with music and sound, were another early influence.

A bassist by trade, Marcheschi met Blossom, a guitarist, and played him his collection of electronic and *musique concrète* albums. Blossom had no background whatsoever in electronic music, but was completely open to new influences. The pair set out to incorporate the concepts of serious electronic music into rock 'n' roll, with Marcheschi constructing a homemade rig of primitive noise-making devices from oscillators, radios, hobbyist kits and an old speaker from a Second World War Navy warship:

> I had the speaker mounted facing up. I would fill it with marbles – ball bearings, anything that could bounce and rattle. I would pump very low frequency sine waves through it and get the balls to dance and then add a second tone and they would show the waveforms in space. I also had an old microphone that I would put on a pendulum and swing it over the speaker for a doppler feedback. [123]

Blossom's wife, Nancy, was brought in to sing, and various other musicians augmented the three-piece core for recording and live work.

Although Fifty Foot Hose played the rock circuit, they were as much a part of San Francisco's art and *avant-garde* music scenes. The Mills College Tape Music Center started life as the San Francisco Tape Music Center. Morton Subotnick and Ramon Sender founded

Poster for the Fifty Foot Hose album.
Credit: © Cork Marcheschi

The beginning of Cork Marcheschi's electronic instrument set up. L–R
Hohner Echolette, Electrovoice microphone, two vacuum tube audio
generators, home-made theremin. Credit: © Cork Marcheschi

it in 1961, offering studio facilities and promoting concerts. In 1966 it relocated to Mills College, a liberal arts establishment in Oakland, California, changing its name to mark the move. By this time the emerging counterculture was finding its spiritual home in San Francisco, and the Center became a hub for experimental musicians and artists. It operated a non-profit, open-access policy, and anyone who wanted to could use its facilities, which included recording equipment and Don Buchla's synthesizer. Marcheschi and Blossom were involved and it was here, rubbing shoulders with the likes of Terry Riley, that they formulated their approach:

> I think because of our connection with the fine art world, and the Mills College Tape Music Center, being aware of Terry Riley and LaMonte Young, and thinking of things in art terms, in sculptural and painting terms, in performance terms, that put us slightly askew from other people who were concentrating on rock and roll venues and being in that scene.[124]

Yet despite this, there was much that was traditional in Fifty Foot Hose. The music was carefully considered, with a solid grasp of traditional song-craft and the dynamics of rock 'n' roll.

The band landed a deal with Limelight Records, a subsidiary of Mercury, leading to one album, *Cauldron* (1967). Mercury offered to hire a Moog and the Buchla for the album sessions, but the band made a conscious choice in favour of its own homemade devices. 'The attitude was always to create something, not to purchase something, not to buy a piece of equipment that another person could have, but personalize an instrument.'[125] Marcheschi's personalised instrument was by now a wobbling tower including two vacuum tube audio generators, a Hohner Echolette tape echo machine, various home-build organ kits and a saw blade with a contact microphone. The album was recorded on the first eight-track machine in San Francisco, but in an atmosphere of homespun improvisation. Effects were created by such primitive means as slowing the tape by putting a hand on the spool, and drilling a hole in a tape hub to make it wobble.

The album was a blend of R'n'B, jazz and psychedelic influences, the electronics generally mixed lower than on The United States of

America album, and to good effect. *Cauldron* sold few copies, but it is one of the best early attempts to incorporate electronics into rock. 'Red the Sign Post' is dense psychedelia, Nancy Blossom intoning over fuzz-guitar riffing and dive-bombing electronics. The ten-minute 'Fantasy', on the other hand, can be considered as the equivalent of Joseph Byrd's arrangement of 'Crucifixion' in its attempt to compress the ambition and daring of serious electronic composition into a rock template. In fact, in both cases, the template had to be re-shaped and enlarged. In 'Fantasy' trance-like intricate, interlocking bass and guitar parts and electronics open up into more standard electric guitar rock. Marcheschi notes that in this song, and in many others on the album, there was an improvisational element within a structure. Though solos were planned for particular points, and the atmosphere that those solos was designed to create was agreed and understood beforehand, the actual playing and performance of them was not pre-determined.

Fifty Foot Hose were aware of, and saw, most of the other under-ground acts then experimenting with electronics – Silver Apples, The United States of America, Lothar and The Hand People – but there was no sense of being part of a scene. Neither did they fully connect with the rock world, despite touring on apparently incongruous bills with artists as diverse as Blue Cheer, Chuck Berry and Fairport Convention. The obvious seriousness of intent, the integrity of the effort and the quality of the performances insured Fifty Foot Hose against hostile reactions from traditional rock audiences, though many were puzzled. Marcheschi recalls some fellow musicians showing interest in the approach, including members of Blue Cheer, and Dr John, when he encountered the bands in a rehearsal studio. But in common with all the acts in this chapter, the timing wasn't quite right for Fifty Foot Hose. 'It was a pretty conservative time,' says Marcheschi:

People looked different, people had their freakiness, but it's like anything else – you get any large group of people that think in one direction and they create a type of conservatism of their own. And this type of music was challenging. Jimi Hendrix feedback was very contextual. You could feel people not being as comfortable with something they might not understand.[126]

The band broke up in late 1969 when most of its members (though not Marcheschi) joined the cast of the musical *Hair*, Nancy Blossom becoming the lead in the San Francisco production, and later singing in *Godspell*.

Jazz had its own pioneer of home-brewed electronic venturing in the person of artist and musician Gil Mellé (1931–2004). He recorded for Blue Note and Prestige through the 1950s, at the same time creating cover art for albums by Miles Davis, Thelonious Monk and Sonny Rollins, while also becoming interested in electronic music and studying with Edgard Varèse. From 1959 Mellé began building his own electronic music devices, which he used on the 1968 Verve album, *Tome V1*. This he declared the first-ever album of electronic jazz, though actually the electronics are integrated with more conventional jazz playing, including Mellé himself on saxophone. After this Mellé moved into film and television composing. A 1968 made-for-TV film called *Perilous Voyage*, which wasn't screened until 1976, featured a ten-minute thunderstorm sequence with an entirely electronic accompaniment. His best-known film work is the electronic score for *The Andromeda Strain* (1971), which Mellé – never shy of making a controversial statement that put himself at the centre of the action – liked to declare the 'very first electronic score'. The Barron's soundtrack for *Forbidden Planet* was made on 'ordinary test sign wave generators – and that's not electronic music', he said, and so didn't count.[127]

The long arms of Frank Zappa's musical ambition gathered up pop, doo-wop, R'n'B, jazz, surf and twentieth-century classical and *avant-garde* composition. Varèse was a declared and pronounced influence, and much of the electronic content in Zappa's work shares Varèse's fascination with percussive sound. A musical director more than a front man, a composer more than a songwriter, Frank Zappa was never really a rock musician. His discography, even covering the few years after his band The Mothers of Invention debuted with *Freak Out!* in 1966, is too dense for a detailed examination here, but a few examples demonstrate the extent to which serious electronic music and *musique concrète* in particular permeated his imagination.

Zappa sometimes stated that his solo debut, *Lumpy Gravy*, was one of his favourite works. Originally released in 1967 on Capitol

Records and subsequently reedited and reissued by Verve Records, Zappa used it to take his montage approach to music making to the extreme. Combining orchestrations, spoken word passages, smooth jazz-rock, rocking instrumental surf guitar and *musique concrète*, it compares to little before or since. The lurches from style to style, sounding at times like abrupt cuts between The Ventures and the *Williams Mix*, are disorientating or exhilarating, depending on your disposition. This sort of thing was always going to be an acquired taste, and *Rolling Stone* was not convinced, calling it 'an idiosyncratic musical faux pas'.[128] 'The Chrome Plated Megaphone of Destiny' is even more of a stretch for the conservatively minded listener. The closing track on the Mothers of Invention's *We're Only In It For the Money* (1960), it creeps up on an electronic drone for more than six minutes of plucking, whistling and scraping sounds. Unravelling how all of this was done might not be feasible, but it demonstrates clearly an improvisational, experimental, home-built approach to electronic sound shared with everyone else in this chapter, even if the outcomes were different.

After his association with Del Shannon came to an end, Max Crook worked under the name Maximillion, or The Maximillion Band, for a few years in Michigan without much success. In 1964 he met Scott Ludwig (born 1942), a drummer and music graduate fascinated by new electronic music. Like Crook, he was an inveterate tinkerer, and had botched together reverb units and the like. As for Marcheschi, Mellé and Zappa, Varèse was an inspiration, and hearing *Poème électronique* for the first time had opened Ludwig's mind to the possibilities of electronic music, and he even completed some serious electronic compositions during his studies.

Ludwig was impressed with Crook's Musitron and found his own Clavioline to modify, calling it the Sonocon. The pair also had a collection of electric organs, electric pianos and home-made effects, which they put to use when they went out as The Sounds of Tomorrow on an estimated 200 gigs over 5 years. 'Music of today … played on the instruments of the future', claimed an advert for one residency. The multi-instrument and vocals act demanded considerable dexterity from both men, but particularly Ludwig, who used his left hand and knee for the Sonocon and other keyboards, while simultaneously playing the drums and singing. The duo took the

Scott Ludwig playing live with The Sounds of Tomorrow in early 1969, his Moog synthesizer on his left. Credit: © Scott Ludwig

Musitron and the Sonocon to some sessions at Stax, and contributed a wah wah-like effect to Carla Thomas's 'I Like What You're Doing to Me'. They also augmented the brass section on Johnnie Taylor's 'Take Care of Your Homework' and appear on The Goodees 'Jilted'.

During the life of The Sounds of Tomorrow Ludwig became intrigued by a succession of jingles, adverts and sound signatures he'd been hearing on television. On investigation, he discovered that Eric Siday made most of these using a Moog. This prompted Ludwig to investigate, and in early 1968 he ordered a catalogue from Moog, began saving, and eventually visited the company's base in Trumansburg, New York, meeting Bob Moog himself. Toward the end of the year Ludwig finally had enough money to place an order, purchasing a custom model the design of which he had sketched out himself. The keyboard and ribbon controller were standard, but the modules were contained in three cases lower than usual, as Ludwig wanted to be able to see over the top of the synthesizer when playing live. He paid $3,968 for the instrument – a lot of money, though cheap for a Moog – which arrived very early in 1969:

> I remember when I got it, I opened up the boxes and took it out, there was the keyboard, the ribbon controller, the three boxes [containing the modules] and the patch cords, and nothing else. There was absolutely no documentation or manual of any kind … it took me quite a while to get any sound out of the thing.[129]

Once he did get a sound out of it, Ludwig introduced the Moog into the The Sounds of Tomorrow's rig, and for the next six or seven months until the band split in late summer 1969, he gigged regularly with it. Years later Ludwig asked Moog if he was the first musician to use the instrument live. Moog, after a brief pause, replied that yes, he probably was.[130]

Clad in matching black and white check jackets, the futuristic yet simultaneously square duo entertained at weddings, dances, frat parties and school assemblies, but, hampered by a lack of original material, could not secure a record deal. As the decade drew to a close Crook's move to Los Angeles spelt the end of the band. There he bought his own Moog and took a course with Paul Beaver, learning how to use it. Though there were later collaborations with Del Shannon and Brian Hyland, Crook and Ludwig were by that time amateur musicians, Crook a firefighter, Ludwig a teacher.

The Sounds of Tomorrow was actually the sound of two men catching the most fleeting glimpse of the future and not really knowing quite how to respond. Both oddly visionary and kitsch to the point of bizarre, were they ahead of their time or out of time altogether? The tiniest of footnotes in music history they may be, but there is something bigger in their story that sums up the efforts of so many musicians who tried to breed electronic music with pop, only to end up with mutant hybrids: fascinating, flawed, with the occasional flash of insight.

Most of the acts profiled in this chapter used variations on an approach that was becoming obsolete even when they were active. Their moment had already passed, even as they were living through it. Roger McGuinn of The Byrds and Micky Dolenz of The Monkees had completed recordings using their new Moogs by the end of 1967, before The United States of America, Lothar and The Hand People and Silver Apples had made their debuts.

7

Moog men

The rise of the synthesizer

During 1966 Roger McGuinn of The Byrds introduced some homespun electronic experimentation into his band's music. In a manner worthy of Silver Apples or Fifty Foot Hose, he featured manipulated voice recordings and an oscillator controlled with a telegraph key on 'CTA-102' from *Younger Than Yesterday* (1966). There was also a physical assault on a piano sustain pedal that McGuinn called 'a sort of Stockhausen idea'.[131] He fits the profile of electronic innovator of the period – fascinated by technological advances, and with a wide-ranging interest in many styles of music, including recent *avant-garde* developments. It is therefore not a surprise to find that McGuinn was one of the first rock musicians to get interested in the Moog synthesizer and that The Byrds were one of the first bands to record with one.

McGuinn placed his order at The Monterey International Pop Festival, held from 16–18 June 1967, not because Moogs were used by any artists performing, but because enterprising Moog owners Paul Beaver and Bernie Krause had talked their way into becoming Moog's West Coast sales representative and had set up a stall at Monterey to promote Moog products. By the time of Monterey Moog had been marketing its instruments for a while, but sales were poor, partly because the synthesizers were so expensive. Most of the few that were sold went to universities. The instruments, with their many patch leads and potentiometers, were formidably complex too, yet Moog's journey from the simplest of electronic instruments, the theremin, to this had been swift.

Since launching RA Moog Co to build theremins in the 1950s, Robert Moog had continued his education, ending up with a BS in Physics from Queens College, a BS in Electrical Engineering from Columbia Engineering School and a PhD in Engineering Physics from Cornell University, and had got married to his first wife, Shirleigh. Throughout, he continued to sell theremin kits, culminating with the introduction in 1961 of the Melodia, a compact fully transistorized model sold assembled or as a $50 kit. The emergence of the transistor into the market in the early 1950s changed electronics as much as the emergence of the vacuum tube that it largely superseded had nearly fifty years earlier. Arguments about the superior sound of tubes were in the future. For now attention was fixed on the new technology, which was cheaper, lighter, smaller and more robust, characteristics that allowed a new phase in electronic musical instrument design. The tube generation of electronic instruments that appeared in the 1930s and 1940s were only viable because of that technology, but it also imposed limits on them. Hammond's Novachord was polyphonic and offered impressive sonic variety, but lots of tubes were needed to achieve that complexity. This meant a heavy, complicated, fragile and expensive instrument, impractical for most musicians. On the other hand, the Solovox and Clavioline and other piano attachments were relatively cheap and portable, and therefore much more practical, but complexity had to be sacrificed. They were monophonic and with limited sounds. With tubes you couldn't have it both ways, but with transistors you could.

The company shipped more than 1,000 Melodia kits alone, and Moog began to think that there was the basis of a viable full-time business in what had, up to that point, been a cottage industry that supported him through college. In the summer of 1963 he set up shop with two employees in Trumansburg, a small, isolated village in upstate New York, and added budget guitar and bass amps to the Moog catalogue, alongside theremins. But business was a struggle at first as the theremin market tailed off and the amps made little money.

In November of that year at a conference in Rochester Moog met Herbert A. Deutsch (born 1932), a musician, composer and educator

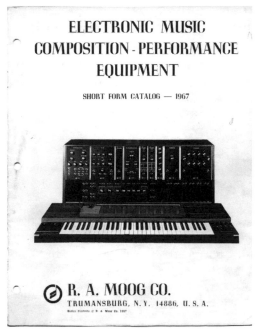

The front cover of Moog's 1967 catalogue.
Credit: from Scott Ludwig

with an interest in electronic music. Moog was selling theremins at the event, and Deutsch, who had built his own Melodia from a kit, struck up a conversation that lasted for three hours. He invited Moog to an electronic music concert planned for early 1964, which Moog attended, after which the pair (and their wives) had dinner and hatched plans to work together on electronic music equipment. In a letter written by Moog shortly after that concert he tells Deutsch that he is 'thoroughly excited about our plan to work together this summer', going on to say that he will have assembled some 'studio equipment' within a few months.[132] By the end of that summer Moog had constructed an operational prototype of what would become known as the Moog synthesizer, and in the fall of that year Deutsch composed the first ever Moog music on it, a piece called 'Jazz Images, a Worksong and Blues'. That first prototype bore scant resemblance to the familiar production Moog modular systems of a few years later, but it did include voltage-control, a process where controlled changes in voltage alter various parameters in the synthesizer, thereby changing its sound output.

Initially the pair was thinking in terms of equipment that would generate new sound colours for compositional use and less about performance. Electronic music was rarely performed live in those days anyway, so anyone setting out to make a new electronic instrument wouldn't necessarily have thought that much about how you would play it, more about the raw sound it would make. But as the partnership evolved the idea of creating a performance instrument – that is, one that could be played in real time – soon emerged, and with it the question of what to use as a controller, an interface between the performer and the technology. Vladimir Ussachevsky counselled against using a piano-style keyboard on the grounds that it would tempt people to treat the Moog as a novelty organ. As the director of the Columbia–Princeton Electronic Music Center, which housed the world's first programmable synthesizer, the room-sized RCA Mark II Sound Synthesizer, his opinion had weight. But Deutsch disagreed, arguing that a familiar interface would make the instrument more marketable and wouldn't necessarily be a barrier to original musical expression. It was Deutsch's view that prevailed, though hindsight shows that Ussachevsky had a point, as before the decade was out there would indeed be a glut of novelty Moog music. Deutsch was right too, though, as using a keyboard didn't automatically prevent other Moog performers from using the instrument creatively. And the keyboard did certainly make the Moog more marketable, the decision to use it opening up the possibility that the revolutionary instrument would find a place in popular commercial music. This wasn't just about practicality and playability, either. The addition of a familiar feature to something otherwise radically new took the edge off the fear of the unknown, a spectre that hovered persistently over electronic music's creeping advance.

Gradually, composers and musicians became aware of what Moog and Deutsch were up to. The pair visited the University of Toronto Electronic Music Studio where Hugh Le Caine, a pioneering physicist/inventor responsible for the electronic sackbut, designed much of the equipment. Here they demonstrated their system to the

resident composers, generating enthusiastic responses and suggestions for its refinement. Myron Schaeffer, who headed the studio,
was particularly encouraging. This endorsement from the academic
music establishment buoyed up Moog and Deutsch. Next, Moog
was invited to demonstrate prototypes at the Audio Engineering
Society (AES) convention in October 1964, where he also presented
a paper outlining his ideas that was published the following year.[133]
Moog was at this stage a very minor supporting player in the world
of music electronics, displaying his homespun wares on a card table,
but a few people were intrigued. At this convention he took the first
order for the new product, from *avant-garde* choreographer and
composer Alwin Nikolais.[134]

For the rest of 1964 and into the following year Moog's little
company began assembling modules in the Trumansburg factory.
Until the summer of 1965 this was still a part-time activity for Moog,
as he was finishing his doctoral thesis. Eric Siday visited Trumansburg
sometime after the AES convention in search of equipment he
wanted to expand his already burgeoning and profitable home studio
in New York, becoming Moog's second synthesizer customer (though
the term synthesizer wasn't yet being routinely used). Siday was by
this time one of the country's best-paid composer/musicians, on
account of a string of television and radio jingles. He was also versed
in the art of pre-synthesizer electronic music making. With money
to spend and a shopping list borne out of practical experience of
commercial music making, Siday ordered a set of Moog's modules,
with the added request that everything be housed in one cabinet and
controlled by a keyboard. This interaction between Moog himself and
his customers was an important feature of the Moog synthesizer's
development. Moog was always careful to point out that he valued
and needed the feedback of active musicians to make his instruments practical and useful. In a 1967 catalogue there is reference
to discussions with over 100 composers. It took Moog about six
months to build for Siday what was in effect the first commercial
Moog modular synthesizer, comprising an organ-style keyboard in a
dark wooden cabinet, with another cabinet containing the modules
resting on top of the keyboard. Moog himself packed the whole thing
into boxes and took them down to New York on an overnight bus,
arriving at Siday's apartment at 8am.[135]

As a commercial musician Siday was an exception amongst Moog's very small list of customers. It was serious, academic music that Moog saw as his market. In August 1965 Moog and Deutsch organised a three-week summer school at the Trumansburg factory. The twelve participants spent the time learning about electronic music history and composing and recording on equipment provided by Moog. Most were musicians and composers (or mathematicians) associated with universities. A concert of the compositions created during the three weeks was held at 4pm on the last day of the school, 28 August. It was a small event, attended by the participants themselves, Moog employees and a few friends. Much of the music played was made using Moog equipment, although some of it employed tape-editing techniques.[136]

Moog continued to develop and sell modular systems and individual modules in small numbers, to order, through the rest of 1965 and 1966. In 1967 the company commenced production of the first standardised range, the Moog 900 Series Electronic Music Systems. The primitive device Moog had built for Deutsch in 1964 had evolved into a complex set of oscillators producing different waveforms (saw-tooth, triangle, sine and so on – each with its own distinct sound), amplifiers, mixers, filters, noise generators and envelope shapers, with voltage control, housed in a cabinet mapped with a labyrinthine grid of knobs and patch cords. The performer was given, usually, both a ribbon controller (similar to the one Moog made for The Beach Boys) and a keyboard. The range was promoted by a 33-rpm demonstration record, with the same content on both sides, 'produced, composed and realized' by Walter (later Wendy) Carlos, another collaborator who Moog credited with making many suggestions which helped make the instruments user-friendly for musicians. The record combines snatches of music with demonstrations of various sounds and a didactic narration explaining what, it was assumed, would still be a mysterious process to most. The traditional electronic music studio is described, with emphasis laid heavily on its time-consuming nature, before the narrator Ed Stokes finally arrives at the sales pitch: 'The Moog 900 Series eliminates many of the problems through the systematic use of [electronic punctuation] voltage control ... virtually any sound can be produced [electronic explosion].'[137] The nine-minute advert ends with several minutes of a musical assortment ranging from free-form bleeping to rather lame Moog boogie that accidentally foretells the exploitation Moog cash-in albums that proliferated a few years later.

The 900 Series demonstration record probably had little impact, but hidden in the extended narrative that ran through the record was an acknowledgement that the Moog was intended for sound generation, composition *and* performance. This was reiterated in a catalogue Moog published the same year. The introduction contends that the 'classical' approach to electronic music making – oscillators, filters, tape splicing and so on – while 'certainly a valid means of musical expression' is restrictive. It goes on to single out the principle of voltage control in particular as the key that opens the door not only to increased control, but also real time performance.[138] The problem was that there weren't that many performers aware of the Moog. The breakthrough came when Beaver and Krause went to Monterey, though for them that was the last gamble in a game that threatened to bankrupt them.

By the time he got to Monterey, Paul Beaver (1925–75) had been making electronic music for years. He was already in his 40s and had been amassing a formidable arsenal of early electronic instruments since the early 1950s, many of which he modified, which included several Hammond organs, an RCA Theremin, an Ondes Martenot, a Hammond Solovox and as many as five Hammond Novachords. In 1960 he bought a crumbling one-storey warehouse in Los Angeles that became his base. Here he lived amidst his expanding collection of instruments, renting them out for film and television work, often finding that he would also get hired himself to operate the equipment.

A suit-wearing Republican, Scientologist and UFO enthusiast, with dark hair and chubby, boyish features, Beaver was an unusual man. Jac Holzman (founder of the Elektra and Nonesuch record labels), who contracted Beaver and visited the warehouse storeroom, comments that he 'absorbed some of the soul and characteristics of his collection' and that 'he definitely orbited a sun of his own'.[139] Beaver was born in Ohio. His father, also Paul, was a doctor. A trained organist, Beaver had a college career lasting until 1950, interrupted by war service in the Far East. A younger sister, Georgeanna, was a violinist and music teacher. He was a versatile musician and spent most of the 1950s playing jazz. His first known movie work was in an independent film called *Magnetic Monster* (1953).[140]

Although the titular monster is a human creation, not alien, *Magnetic Monster* fits into the 1950s American science fiction genre that provided a platform for so much electronic music. Beaver's involvement, contributing electronic textures to another composer's (Blaine Sanford) score, set a pattern for much of his subsequent work. The electronics are primitive and basic, but a distinct and precise change of note is audible at times, indicating that Beaver used some kind of keyboard drawn from his collection. As well as the keyboards, Beaver also amassed oscillators, tape echo devices, ring-modulators, filters and several small keyboard instruments he had built himself, including one he called the Canary.[141] At recording sessions he would line up the collection on long tables, in front of which he would run up and down, pressing buttons, flicking switches and turning dials as he went.

Beaver expanded his collection of instruments through the 1960s, renting them and himself out for a wide range of film and television work. He established a reputation as an eccentric oracle of electronic sound in the area. Maurice Jarre hired Beaver and a truckload of electronic gear to provide an undercurrent to his score for David Lean's *Dr Zhivago* (1965). This work pre-dated Beaver's Moog ownership, but even after he acquired the new instrument much of his work was accomplished using selections from his older instruments. Film composer Jerry Goldsmith regularly knocked at Beaver's door, using his services on *The Satan Bug* (1965*)*, *In Harm's Way* (1965), *Our Man Flint* (1966) and *In Like Flint* (1967). The Flint films, spy spoofs starring James Coburn, made particularly liberal use of Hammond's pre-war Novachord and Solovox, played by Beaver from his own collection. The all-star war film *In Harm's Way* used a modified Novachord in some naval battle scenes.

The prolific and multi-award winning Goldsmith (1929–2004) had been inspired to become a film composer by Miklós Rózsa's score for *Spellbound*. He drew on that score's approach of combining orchestral music with electronic sound in many of his own works. His first score to feature substantial electronic elements was *Freud* (1962), the title role taken by a bearded Montgomery Clift. The score harked back to *Spellbound*, with three disturbing dream sequences scored all electronically: 'The means were rather primitive, using tone generators, simple filters and a bank of tape machines.'[142] The score was nominated for an Oscar. After that Goldsmith frequently integrated electronic instruments into orchestral scores, often working with Beaver, and then in the early 1970s acquiring his own Minimoog and ARP 2500 synthesizers. He did at times feel it necessary to separate the electronic from the acoustic, revealing the influence of an earlier generation of Hollywood composers who tended toward the view that electronic music was suitable only in certain settings. One example was *Logan's Run* (1976), in which there was a distinction between what Goldsmith thought of as the more 'human' scenes that required pure orchestral music, and the futuristic settings suitable for electronic sound.

By 1967 Beaver was also picking up some pop sessions, including Hal Blaine's quick-off-the-mark psychedelic exploitation album, *Psychedelic Percussion*, on Dunhill Records. This instrumental collection, with twelve tracks representing the months of the year, sounds exactly as its title suggests: all deft percussion grooves decorated with period trappings. As well as Beaver and Blaine, the album featured percussionist Emil Richards, with whom Beaver had performed live in a project named Aesthetic Harmony Assemblage. All three also played on *The Zodiac: Cosmic Sounds* project for Elektra Records, as did Bernie Krause. It is this album which is generally hailed as the first rock recording to feature Moog, though Richards, speaking to Richie Unterberger for liner notes of a reissue of the album, posited that another recording in a similar vein, *Stones*, just preceded it.[143]

Born 1938 in Detroit. Krause was thirteen years Beaver's junior. His musical gift became apparent early in his life. He was studying violin at three and a half, classical composition at four, and by his teens was also playing cello, bass, viola and harp. By then he had fallen in love with the guitar, though, and as a young man he was playing jazz and even Motown sessions. Krause then joined a late line-up of the long-running folk institution The Weavers in 1963, the last of several replacements for Pete Seeger. He stayed with them until they disbanded a year later. Shortly afterwards he career took an abrupt left-turn, from acoustic folk into electronic music. He enrolled at Mills College Tape Music Center and began a serious study, hearing Stockhausen lecture and experimenting with the Buchla equipment to hand. While there Krause heard of Moog synthesizers through reading an article about how Siday used his instrument to get lucrative work making music for television commercials. Krause wasn't the only one. Although not a particularly high-profile figure Siday became a point of convergence for interest in Moog, being then the only person using one to make music that was widely heard. Scott Ludwig and Jean-Jacques Perrey were two other early Moog users who were inspired by Siday. Krause visited Siday at his studio in New York where the older composer gave a demonstration of the temperamental equipment. Krause was intrigued.

At this point, Jac Holzman stepped into the story. He contacted Krause having heard of his interest in electronic music, asking if Krause knew Beaver. At that point Krause had heard of Beaver, and had once seen him at work on a film sound stage, but the two had never met. Holzman (born 1931) was only in his mid-30s, but was already a music industry veteran. He had launched Elektra in 1950 when he was 19 and had released scores of mainly folk and blues albums. Like so many others in the story of emerging electronic music, Holzman had something of the technical nerd about him. As a younger man he had taken solace in oscillators, amplifiers and vacuum tubes, and as a label boss and a producer he had amassed considerable first-hand experience of recording equipment. An interest in electronic music was perhaps inevitable.

By the early 1960s Elektra had become an established folk label, and now Holzman was branching out in several directions. In 1964 he formed a budget imprint, Nonesuch, which concentrated on classical repertoire, and a little later began scouting around for rock and folk-rock acts for an expanded Elektra roster. Both labels would contribute to the popularization of electronic music.

By 1966 it was becoming apparent that a burgeoning counterculture was developing, drawing on rock music and psychedelics, against a backdrop of cultural exploration and upheaval. Holzman was still young enough to retain an insider's grasp of this, and perceived that electronics might contribute an appropriate accompaniment. This notion would find its first expression in *The Zodiac: Cosmic Sounds* (1967), one of Elektra's more eccentric releases.

Krause and Beaver were introduced by Holzman, probably sometime in late 1966, with a view to them working together on the album, which was then in the planning stages. They were an unlikely team, yet despite their differences the pair forged a strong partnership based on a love of electronic music and a hunch that somewhere in it lay hidden commercial prospects. 'We immediately hit it off, found creative synergy, and formed a team. We had a great time working together', says Krause '... as long as he didn't evangelize Scientology.'[144]

One of the first things the pair did together was visit Moog at his factory to discuss purchasing a modular system. One of their concerns was about the stability of the system and its ability to stay in tune, a concern borne out of Krause's earlier visit to Siday. Moog's answer to this was to push a system from a table on to the floor, pick it up, place it back on the table, turn it on and demonstrate that it still worked.[145] Beaver and Krause were persuaded, and each paid about $7,500 for their jointly owned Moog. This was a huge risk for freelance musicians to take. At the time, $15,000 would have bought you five top-of-the-range Ford Mustang convertibles. In time, Beaver and Krause bought another Moog, which they located in San Francisco. The first went to Beaver's studio in Los Angeles. There the pair spent many fraught hours trying to master the technology and failing to generate much interest in their investment in either the music or film businesses.

On the surface The Zodiac: Cosmic Sounds was another psychedelic cash-in concept album, a-rather-too rich a mix of light orchestral weirdness, ornate percussion, po-faced spoken-word interjections and electronics. Each of the 12 tracks represented an astrological sign, at a time when an interest in astrology was coming into counter-cultural vogue. It must, listeners were instructed in a note on the sleeve, be played in the dark. The music was composed and conducted by Mort Garson and the album produced by Alex Hassilev, both unlikely candidates for an attempt to conjure up an evocation of the emerging counter-culture. Garson had been around for years and had worked with Doris Day and Mel Torme among many others, while Hassilev was a novice producer who had previously been in commercial folk trio The Limeliters. The truth is that they were hired hands, the real driving force behind the album and the originator of the concept being none other than Holzman himself.

Whether or not this was the very first album to feature Moog, it was certainly a very early entry in the Moog discography. A master tape with half the album's tracks is dated April 1967, though the album wasn't released until November that year. *The Zodiac: Cosmic Sounds* was not a big hit, though it sold respectably and became quite well known. Very much of its time, the middle-of-the-road, mildly groovy psychedelic mood music underpinning portentous poetry could only have been recorded, with a straight face at least, in 1967. Its use of Moog as a counter-culture signifier was a first, though. The association of electronic sound with other worlds (space, ghosts), with fear and psychological distress, with humour, were by this time deeply ingrained through years of repetition in film and television music. Now there were the beginnings of an association between electronic music and the exotic, mystical, hallucinogenic aspects of hippy culture. Mort Garson went on to use Moog and other electronics on a succession of odd and obscure albums like *Electronic Hair Pieces* and *Wozard of Id*. Of more note was the work of Beaver and Krause.

By Monterey Beaver and Krause had spent a great deal of time learning how the Moog worked, but so far they had failed to persuade anyone at all to hire it and them. They went to the festival in some desperation, ready and able to demonstrate the instrument to anyone who was interested, but hard pressed financially. They bravely set up their Moog on a table in an open-air booth on Monterey Fairground in June 1967, sitting next to the weird apparatus like fortune-tellers offering a glimpse of the future. Displaying $15,000 worth of equipment on which your livelihood depends in an open-air pop festival and inviting all-comers seems reckless, but Krause points out that at the time there were so few Moogs in existence that if it were stolen it wouldn't have been too hard to trace, that security was good, and that, anyway, it would have been useless to any thieves, as they wouldn't have known how to operate it.[146]

The thinking behind this apparently incongruous enterprise made sound sales sense. Moog systems were expensive, so only wealthy musicians could afford them, and at Monterey in 1967 there were a lot of wealthy musicians. Rock grandees were present in strength, both on the festival's bill and mingling backstage. Performers included Simon and Garfunkel, Big Brother and the Holding Company, The

Byrds, Jefferson Airplane, Otis Redding, Buffalo Springfield, The Who, The Grateful Dead, The Jimi Hendrix Experience and The Mamas & the Papas. Meanwhile, in the audience members of The Beatles and the Stones walked like gods descended.

At first, business was slow on the Monterey Moog stall, but it gradually picked up. Soon there was a queue waiting to put on the headphones and hear the patches Beaver and Krause had set up, demonstrating electronic thunderclaps and simulated Hammond organs, among other things. By the end of the festival, Beaver and Krause had sold between six and a dozen systems (accounts differ) at prices between $12,000 and $15,000. By the fall of 1967, Moogs were being delivered to McGuinn, and also Micky Dolenz of The Monkees. By the end of the year, Moogs were in the charts.

At the same time that he recognized that electronic music might find a place in the youth counter-culture, Holzman was well aware of its more serious, highbrow manifestations. He commissioned Morton Subotnick to write and record *Silver Apples of the Moon* (1967) for Nonesuch, using Buchla's voltage controlled synthesizer. This was the first extended work of electronic music commissioned by a record company. He followed this with another curious entry in the canon of early electronic recordings. Holzman had sat with Krause on a flight to Monterey for the 1967 pop festival, talking about electronic music. By the end of the journey Holzman had conceived of what would become *The Nonesuch Guide to Electronic Music* and Beaver and Krause had their first recording contract as a duo.

Released in spring 1968, the double album was intended as an instructional demonstration record to explain the possibilities of electronic music rather than a complete musical work, and most of the 68 tracks are short sound examples. As such, it wasn't completely without precedent in Holzman's history, bearing some faint resemblance to a successful series of sound effects albums and a guitar tutor that Elektra had released earlier. Even so, the double album resisted easy classification. It came packaged with a 16-page booklet of explanation and instruction written by Krause. The text was derived from transcribed cassette recordings of agonizingly long sessions with Beaver, a nocturnal creature given to staying up into the early hours playing music, tinkering and reading. During these sessions the pair attempted to unlock the secrets of the Moog.

Krause did this for his own benefit as much as anyone else's, figuring that if he could codify the Moog's mysteries into a nomenclature that he could understand, then others could too.

With track titles like 'Periodic: Sine-Higher Frequency' and 'Low-Frequency Sawtooth-Tuning Through Harmonics', both album and booklet came across somewhere between an arcane gnostic text and an electronics manual. It was odd, then, that it sold so well, staying for 26 weeks on the Billboard classical chart, an indication of the growing interest in electronic music that the Moog was fomenting.

On 20 October 1967 The Byrds released the first pop single to use Moog, 'Goin' Back" b/w "Change Is Now'. Paul Beaver performed the barely audible part during a session on 9 October.[147] The song appears on *The Notorious Byrd Brothers* album released in January 1968, the sessions for which continued through the final months of 1967. Many other songs on the album featured the Moog, sometimes played by Beaver, sometimes by McGuinn himself. The most prominent of these is the album's closing track, 'Space Odyssey'. An ominous, funereal dirge of creeping Moog sweeps, over which McGuinn's folksy melody was given the traditional Byrds harmony treatment, it is the first example of an established rock band successfully integrating the Moog into its sound, not just as a texture in the arrangement or as ornamentation, but the very basis of it. The sessions also spawned 'Moog Raga', the very title encapsulating the marriage of counter-culture esoterica and electronics that Holzman had imagined with *The Zodiac: Cosmic Sounds.* Written, programmed and played by McGuinn, the experimental instrumental was not included on the album because of tuning problems, and only surfaced on an expanded edition in the 1990s. It can be understood as an audio account of a man grappling with the Moog's enormous potential and temperamental complexity. McGuinn later recalled having particular difficulty operating the ribbon-controller, which he used to create vaguely sitar-like lines.[148] Flawed it may be, but it is something of a lost landmark, a whole piece of music realized entirely on multi-tracked Moog.

Just before recording with The Byrds, Beaver had also played with The Monkees. Micky Dolenz's interest in the Moog is a surprise. The Monkees were manufactured pop, after all, and

Dolenz isn't generally regarded as a musically adventurous member of the band. Even so, he was one of the very first pop musicians to use a Moog. Session records show that at some point between 15 September and 4 October he played his new toy on 'Daily Nightly', from *Pisces, Aquarius, Capricorn & Jones Ltd*. Producer Chip Douglas says:

> Micky bought a new Moog and he had no idea how to run it or anything. We just kind of turned on the track and turned on Micky's input, plugged him in, and he just kind of fiddled around there on several different tracks. We just put the best little bits in there that we could. After Micky experimented with his synthesizer I thought, 'Well, let's find a real synthesizer player.' I'd heard about Paul Beaver; Micky had told me about him. So I met him through Micky and he was a player, a good player, and he knew what to do.[149]

A film of the band performing the song actually uses the Moog as a performance prop, Dolenz miming at the keyboard and even reaching over to twiddle a module control at one point.

Moog records show that Motown bought a modular system in December of 1967, marking an interest in electronic sound that would draw in Raymond Scott before too long. The classic 'Reflections' single by Diana Ross and the Supremes arrived with a bleeping introduction and featured various swoops and textures, all obviously electronic and sometimes attributed to a Moog. In fact, the single predated the arrival of the Moog, and the sounds come from a treated test oscillator operated by one of the Funk Brothers.

Beaver, along with Krause, notched up a third significant rock credit in the fall of 1967, working on The Doors' second album, *Strange Days*. The vogue for established rock bands of the time was towards ornamenting and extending their sound, and the Moog was an expression of that. But a tightly drilled young rock band raised on live work and fronted by a poet was not an easy fit with the hit-and-miss aesthetic of an eccentric middle-aged synthesist. Doors keyboardist Ray Manzarek gives an engaging account of minds failing to meet in his autobiography.[150] He paints Beaver in the studio, furiously tugging at patch leads and pressing buttons, sweat dripping from his brow, asking the band what they thought of this sound or that. From time to time Jim Morrison responded along the lines of 'I liked the sound of broken glass falling from the void into creation,' to which Beaver replied 'Which sound was that?' This wasn't just a clash of personality or working methods. The Moog was not only complex, offering innumerable combinations each of which had its own sound but not a name, but its oscillators were also unstable. This meant that getting the same sound that you'd got yesterday, or even a minute ago, wasn't always possible, even if you could remember the exact configuration of patch leads and dial settings. Furthermore, there was no instruction manual. That didn't come until 1970. The Moog was like virtually all other means of making electronic music then available, requiring of much time, consideration, thought and experimentation, though perhaps a little less than the traditional tape and oscillator approach – not a good match for rock bands that, even in those experimental times, were given to making whole albums in a week or so.

The Byrds, The Monkees and The Doors were the first, tentative flowerings of mainstream rock's cross-pollination with Moog synthesis, and because Beaver and Krause were almost alone in having a working grasp of the instrument, for a short while at least they had a virtual monopoly on the West Coast rock scene. But at the same time they were even more in demand for film and television work, through which means they reached a far larger audience. From the latter part of 1967 through to about 1970, when the work started to tail off, they contributed to dozens of big- and small-screen productions. Many of these used not only the Moog, but also other instruments from Beaver's collection. They include *The Graduate* (1967), *In Cold Blood* (1967), *Rosemary's Baby* (1968) and *Beneath the Planet of the Apes* (1970). In each of these, Beaver and Krause played a supporting role, adding electronic textures and detail at the instigation of whoever was composing the soundtrack music.

It was the fate of most early electronic musicians to remain in the background, and Beaver and Krause were not that well known in the starry sense, despite their music being heard by millions on account of their film work and their contributions to rock records. They boosted their profile somewhat when they began recording albums under the name Beaver and Krause. If the first of these, *The Nonesuch Guide to Electronic Music*, was something of an anomaly, the duo moved into more recognisable territory with *Ragnarok Electronic Funk* (1969) and *In a Wild Sanctuary* (1970). These instrumental albums combined bluesy and jazzy motifs with dreamy, gliding soundscapes of the sort that would attract a new age tag in the 1980s. Moogs were featured heavily on these albums, and subsequent similar releases, but so were drums, guitars and other conventional instruments. *In a Wild Sanctuary*, with its ecological themes and field recordings made by the pair as they wandered around San Francisco with a tape recorder, was Beaver and Krause's most intriguing album. The end section of one track, 'Spaced', starts with a single G note that fans out into multiple notes of a chord, each of which sweeps in unison through a long portamento before resolving on a D chord. It was a device much copied in television and film, to Beaver and Krause's chagrin.

As recording artists, Beaver and Krause were transitional figures, advance scouts serving a short tour of duty. By integrating synthesizers into blues, jazz and rock structures and creating entirely synthetic sound pieces they were blazing a trail. They acclimatized listeners to accept, even expect, electronic music in new settings. Commendably, they always tried to keep moving forward. Each album has its own identity, even if many of the ingredients are shared between them all, and each tends toward texture and atmosphere, not memorable melody. After all, Beaver in particular had carved a niche as soundscapist, adept at creating atmosphere, rather than a composer or performer in the conventional sense. This goes a long way to explaining why so little of their music is remembered. They are recognized for their influence, but it is hard to recall much of their music.

Beaver and Krause started making albums shortly before the film and session work that had been so lucrative began to tail off a little. It isn't a coincidence that this happened as synthesizers were becoming more numerous. Simply, by 1970 Beaver and Krause were no longer the only people in Los Angeles and San Francisco who owned and knew how to operate Moog synthesizers, and before long there were other synthesizers apart from Moogs readily available. Through the early years of the new decade Beaver and Krause would instruct people in the dark art of Moog operation. This passing on of trade secrets was generous, but it was inevitable that other people would learn the trade secrets whether they shared them or not. It was a process that would be repeated in the early 1980s with the arrival of the Fairlight. Rare, expensive and complicated, musicians needed the help of trained operatives to make use of it. These people, gatekeepers to a new phase of musical evolution, were destined to stand guard only briefly. As the technology became more readily available, cheaper and better understood, they became redundant. Krause, and particularly Beaver, were those gatekeepers for the Moog.

Several of that clutch of musicians and bands that were striving to make electronic rock and pop music before the Moog's arrival at the party did end up attracted it when it turned up. In some cases this was a brief flirtation, in others a warm embrace. Lothar and The Hand People, known for caressing the air around their Moog theremin, did feature Moog synthesizer in their recordings as well, courtesy of Robert Margouleff, a synthesist and Moog owner who produced the band's first album. In 1968 he was a novice producer, but he did have a very large modular Moog, which was enough to get him the job. He went on to programme and perform synthesizers for Stevie Wonder in the 1970s.

Jean-Jacques Perrey and Gershon Kingsley had recorded their first instrumental electronic pop album in 1966 without a Moog. In 1967 Perrey heard one of the new wonder instruments for the first time, on a tape of what was probably the Moog demonstration record made by Carlos. He was captivated. Still resident in Carroll Bratman's studio in New York, he asked his patron if he would buy a Moog. Bratman, always supportive of his protégé, obliged, and in due course Robert Moog brought the instrument down to Perrey's studio himself, as he had done two years earlier for Eric Siday. Records show that the Moog was purchased in February, and as Perrey and Kingsley got to work with it immediately, they might well be the first pop artists to work with a Moog, even if they weren't the first to release a Moog record.[151] The title of their second album, *Kaleidoscopic Vibrations: Spotlight on the Moog*, is self-explanatory. Although the Ondioline and tape editing were still a part of the mix, the Moog was now the feature instrument. As much of the album was comprised of covers of standards like 'Moon River' and 'Strangers in the Night', it has the dubious distinction of inaugurating a particular brand of Moog muzak that briefly flourished soon after. It also marked another aspect of early Moog releases, with the instrument itself becoming a focus of the record, with equal billing at least with the artists. Perrey continued to record with both Moog and Ondioline on future releases. Kingsley, too, went on the make many commercial Moog releases, including *Music to Moog By* (1969), which included his composition 'Popcorn'. This, when covered by Hot Butter in 1972, was a massive international hit.

Bruce Haack had heard about the Moog and in 1968 visited Perrey in his New York studio for a demonstration. Then, when signed to Columbia, Haack was given access to one owned by the company, which he made use of on *Electric Lucifer* (1970). However, although the album has retrospectively been described as a Moog album, according to Haack's manager and collaborator Chris Kachulis, most of the sounds in the dense electronic collages that make up the album come from Haack's room full of homemade instruments.[152]

By the end of 1968 the words Moog and synthesizer were becoming synonyms in the public mind, in America at least. The Moog, though, was not the only synthesizer then available. It wasn't even the only American voltage control synthesizer available. There was also the Buchla Series 100 Modular Electronic Music System, developed and produced in Berkeley. Its designer Don Buchla (born 1937) was just three years younger than Bob Moog, and like Moog was a musician, an electronics tinkerer and an inventor. Buchla had studied physics at the University of California, Berkeley, and in the early 1960s was attending concerts of electronic music at the San Francisco Tape Music Center. This led to a commission for Buchla from the Center's instigators, Morton Subotnick and Ramon Sender. They asked him to create an electronic music device that could be used for composition and performance, and which would help eliminate the laborious process of tape editing on which most electronic music up to that point depended. His response became known as Buchla's Music Box, or simply Buchla's Box, a modular electronic music system using voltage control that became the basis for the Buchla Series 100 Modular Electronic Music System.[153] Both Buchla and Moog commenced work on their systems in 1963 without any knowledge of what the other was doing. Both, though, were responding to requests from musicians and composers to make something that would enable a new approach to electronic music making.

Within a few years the Moog and the Buchla, which began their respective lives in similar circumstances, were diverging. Buchla locates himself on the fringes. He is by nature an explorer at the edge of things, not overly concerned with mainstream commercial success, and this inclination found expression in a series of decisions that kept his devices in their natural home, the *avant-garde* world. The musicians and composers who gathered around him and helped shape his music systems included John Cage and David Tudor, people who, like Buchla, saw electronic music as a means of going beyond traditional tonal music into unexplored regions.

Bob Moog liked to say that he wasn't much of a businessman, and indeed he did eventually lose control of his own company. Even so, by luck or judgement, he made some decisions that turned out well commercially, such as the theremin kits. Another was the decision to use a keyboard as a controller. Buchla thought that a keyboard would push composers down the well-trodden paths of more conventional tonal music and preferred a system of touch-sensitive pads. This meant that the Moog was more attractive to anyone interested in making commercial, tonally conventional music. And when those people came along – people like Eric Siday, and later the first rock musicians to embrace the Moog – Bob Moog was ready and willing to engage with them. In 1969 Buchla did enter into a brief commercial relationship with CBS, and although CBS Buchlas were made for a while, the venture soon petered out.

Buchla's predilection for the experimental meant that his instruments did not find many commercial users in the late 1960s. They were not widely heard at a time when Moogs were coming into vogue and hogging the limelight. An unlikely exception came courtesy of Subotnick, who made several albums using Buchla equipment in this period. The first of these was *Silver Apples of the Moon* (1967), commissioned by Jac Holzman and Tracey Sterne for Nonesuch Records.

This was the first-large scale electronic piece made specifically for record, and Subotnick arranged the thirty-one-minute composition into two halves, to fit the vinyl medium. Part A is a puckish, playful, abstract splatter of percussive bleeps and squelches, combined with softer whistling tones and cloudy textures. Part B evolves into a gradually building rhythmic set of repeated pattering phrases.

Critical response was varied. A review in *Gramophone* published more than a year after the album was released, which was broadly positive, made two telling comments. The first, that 'Jimi Hendrix's guitar would not be all that out of place on this LP', reveals an association between experimental electronic music and the freer end of rock, which surely was not unique to that writer. The review then reverts to another association, this one long established, saying '... a good deal of electronic music ... does put one in mind of science-fiction films'. A few years later the same magazine was grumbling that the album was a 'random technical exercise rather than a proper musical composition'.[154]

The repetitive patterns on the second side of *Silver Apples of the Moon* were made possible by a feature that Buchla had in his box from the start. This was a sequencer, a device that continuously produces a predetermined set of voltages that can then be applied to different parts of the synthesizer. Moogs didn't have sequencers initially, but when Buchla was creating his he was one of three people approaching a similar point, completely independently of each other. Raymond Scott was another. He claimed to have invented his sequencer in 1960. The third was Peter Zinovieff in London, who, like Sender and Subotnick who had commissioned Buchla's Box in the first place, thought tape editing a maze from which electronic music had to find an escape.

8

White noise

British electronic music in the swinging sixties

The Moog progressively infiltrated American popular culture from 1967 onwards but it didn't cross the Atlantic that year. Electronic music was continuing its gradual spread in Britain, though, using different means. The Radiophonic Workshop was in what has come to be seen as its golden period, making music for BBC television and radio, while Barry Gray and Daphne Oram remained active. Tristram Cary was still busy as a composer, educator and instigator too, and went on to form one third of EMS (Electronic Music Studios [London] Ltd) in 1969, along with Peter Zinovieff and engineer David Cockerell. By this time Zinovieff had become a leading player in British electronic music.

Zinovieff was born in 1933 to Russian aristocrat parents who had fled to London to escape the Revolution. His education included a spell at Gordonstoun School in Scotland, favoured by the Royal Family. This was followed by a lengthy stay at Oxford University, from which he eventually emerged with a doctorate in geology, having tried several other subjects. His career trajectory includes some of the familiar elements common to many electronic music pioneers, including an early fascination with radio technology and experimenting with sound:

> When I was a boy I used to make radio sets, and I used to love the howls and screams of the heterodyne whistles. When I was

at university I got together a band that would use odd instruments like biscuit tins and smashing glass to make curious sounds.[155]

In many other respects, though, the path Zinovieff took was atypical. His formal scientific training nurtured an analytical and experimental bent, and although he did compose and record music, much of his subsequent career was spent trying to find solutions to problems and devise new ways of doing things. After university he married his first wife and went to work as a mathematician with the Air Ministry. He gave this job up after a year as all his income was swallowed up in tax, his wife being independently wealthy. Freed from the need to earn a living, Zinovieff was able to devote his significant energy and resources to what had become his passion – electronic music. This phase of his life began in 1960, when he was living in central London. His first move was to do what most people did at the time if they wanted to make electronic music, which was to buy tape recorders and military surplus sound wave generators. He visited Daphne Oram's studio in Kent on a few occasions to learn the craft of tape editing, but very quickly decided that not only was the painstaking process not for him, but that it was a dead end: 'I couldn't stand the fiddliness of it. I decided very soon that sequencers were the answer … that's ultimately what led me to computers.'[156]

By 1966 Zinovieff had moved to Putney, London, living in a house with a garden that ran right down to the River Thames. In this garden he built a studio that overlooked the river for his expanding collection of electronic equipment, the hub of which was a Digital Equipment Corporation (DEC) PDP-8 computer. The American-made PDP-8, introduced in 1965, was the first mass-produced microcomputer and the ancestor of the home desktop machines that began to proliferate in the 1980s. About 50,000 had been made when production ceased in 1980. Zinovieff had paid about £4,000 for this machine, more than the average price of a house, and was probably the first person in the country to privately own a computer. It had 8k of memory and no hard drive. A later addition, a 32k hard drive, cost the same again. Zinovieff knew that computers were already being used in factories to automate production lines, and he planned to use his to issue commands to his sound generators to make music.

It was to this riverside studio that Paul McCartney came to meet Zinovieff, Delia Derbyshire and Brian Hodgson, collectively known as Unit Delta Plus. Formed sometime in 1966 and lasting for no more than a year, this was always an uneasy alliance. The idea was to use Zinovieff's studio and the expertise that Hodgson and Derbyshire had acquired at the Radiophonic Workshop to make commercial electronic music and put on events. One of its first efforts was a concert of electronic music held on 10 September 1966 at the Watermill Theatre, near Newbury. This featured a number of pieces composed and realized by several combinations of the three members of Unit Delta Plus and light projects by the Hornsey College of Art. Derbyshire was later to recall the poet John Betjeman falling asleep on the front row. Programme notes state that 'modern electronic computer technology' played a role in not only 'performing' the music, but composing it as well: 'The studio of Unit Delta Plus has specialised in electronic switching arrangements to reduce the manipulation, editing and copying of tape, and also in the development of controlled randomness in certain aspects of sound.' The programme goes on to explain that the computer is set up to select, either randomly or sequentially, one or more of up to 32 tones, each infinitely variable.

This was where Zinovieff's heart lay – in exploring electronic music technology. There seems to have been ambivalence about the actual music made from the start. When interviewed for this book, he described the music Unit Delta Plus made as terrible, and a profile published in 1973 notes that he frequently asserts that he doesn't like electronic music.[157] Any electronic music that he might have liked would have been serious, not popular. Zinovieff wasn't interested in pop music or commercial music: 'I was much more interested in Stockhausen coming than Paul McCartney coming … I myself steered clear of pop groups.'[158] Here is one reason why Unit Delta Plus didn't last. Derbyshire and Hodgson too made serious and experimental music, but their interests were broader than Zinovieff's. Their day jobs involved making short, snappy pieces for BBC television and radio, and they were aware of the counter-culture for which rock music provided the soundtrack. The programme of the Windmill concert hints at this tension. In the midst of more serious work was a selection of BBC introductions composed by

Derbyshire and a pop song, the result of a collaboration between her and Anthony Newley. Derbyshire later recalled Newley visiting her at her one-bedroom flat, dropped off by his wife, Joan Collins. This eccentric piece, titled 'Moogies Bloogies', was never properly completed and remained unheard after the concert until liberated online some 40 years later. The apparent reference to Moog in the title is probably coincidental. Newley pronounces the word 'mooj' and the moogies bloogies describe a state of depressed sexual frustration prompted by mini-skirted girls. Unit Delta Plus did manage one commercial assignment, an advert for Phillips, but Hodgson and Derbyshire split from Zinovieff after a lecture at the Royal College of Art in 1967.

If Unit Delta Plus represented the two opposing tendencies of British electronic music, the experimental and the popular, then McCartney's approach to them is entirely appropriate. He too was coming to electronic music through both routes. In February 1966 he went to hear the Italian composer Luciano Berio give a lecture in which he talked about electronic music, and Stockhausen's appearance on the cover of *Sgt. Pepper's Lonely Hearts Club Band* was a little more than icon grabbing. By that time McCartney and Lennon had put some effort into exploring areas of serious music far removed from Merseybeat. Simultaneously, McCartney was exposed to the considerable influence of The Beatles' producer George Martin, who himself had dabbled in tape manipulation. As a producer, he had already devised tape loops for comedy records by The Goons and Peter Sellers when, in 1962, he teamed up with Maddalena Fagandini from the Radiophonic Workshop under the name Ray Cathode. The pair released a middle-of-the-road pop instrumental, 'Time Beat' b/w 'Waltz in Orbit', that combined tape loops with conventional instrumentation. It just pre-dated Martin's involvement with The Beatles and wasn't a hit, but McCartney was aware of it and the Radiophonic Workshop, and it was to the Radiophonic Workshop that he was drawn when investigating electronic music. He was later to say that he arranged his meeting with Derbyshire by getting the number of the Workshop from the phone book. Maybe he did, but it seems he never went there.

Hodgson, who worked closely with Derbyshire both at the BBC and on freelance projects, has no recollection of McCartney visiting the workshop or of a sometimes-reported radiophonic version of 'Yesterday':

> I would have thought Delia would have mentioned it [working on 'Yesterday']. I would have thought Delia would have done it, quite frankly. So many rumours go around, so many legends. Chance meetings turn into long associations which didn't happen.[159]

Hodgson does, though, confirm that he, Derbyshire and Zinovieff met McCartney together at Zinovieff's Putney studio. Mills, who too worked with Derbyshire during this time, also knows nothing about the 'Yesterday' rumour, and suspects there is nothing in it. Finally, confirmation came from Derbyshire herself, shortly before she died. She said that although she and McCartney met and he heard her work, the association was fleeting. She also contradicted McCartney's memory of where the meeting took place. 'He [McCartney] never did come to the workshop ... He came to [Peter] Zinovieff's studio and I played him some of my stuff, that's all.'[160]

Evidence that The Beatles were beginning to absorb some of these influences emerged on the tape manipulation in *Revolver*, released in August 1966. 'I'm Only Sleeping' features controlled backwards guitar by George Harrison, but the closing track, 'Tomorrow Never Knows', goes far further. Here, Lennon sings over layered tape loops, sped-up tapes and backwards tapes running alongside a metronomic drum and bass pattern.

The tape experiments on *Revolver* almost certainly pre-date McCartney's visit to Unit Delta Plus. Although The Beatles returned to tape manipulation on Lennon's 'Revolution 9' (from The Beatles' *The White Album*), little of substance appears to have come from the meeting. The talk of a radiophonic version of 'Yesterday' seems confused, as, assuming McCartney's visit was in 1966, the song was already a year old. At most, he must have been considering an electronic reinterpretation, but if he was it didn't get far and Hodgson, Derbyshire's close friend at the time, thinks she had little further contact with McCartney. There was one collaboration of sorts, though, between The Beatles and Unit Delta Plus.

The Million Volt Light and Sound Rave was held in early 1967 at the Roundhouse Theatre in Chalk Farm, London. It was organized by designers Binder, Edwards and Vaughan and ran over two nights (28 January and 4 February 1967). The designers were known for decorating a piano for McCartney and their brightly collared Buick appeared on the cover of the Kinks' *Sunny Afternoon* album. The event included tape music by Unit Delta Plus and the solitary public airing to date of The Beatles' 'Carnival of Light'. This was a 14-minute sound collage assembled under McCartney's direction, which George Martin and George Harrison later vetoed for inclusion on the *Anthology* series of albums. According to Beatles researcher Mark Lewisohn it was made on 5 January 1967, and has four tracks: track one with organ and drums; track two, distorted electric guitar and sound effects; track three, more sound effects, a church organ, and John Lennon and Paul McCartney shouting; track four, tape echo, tambourine and more sound effects. Leaving to one side any speculation about musical merit, the inclusion of 'Carnival of Light' and the Unit Delta Plus contributions to what was quite deliberately a counter-culture celebration was another example of the emerging rapprochement between this counter-culture, of which rock was an integral part, and electronic music.

For Hodgson and Derbyshire, friends as well as colleagues, Unit Delta Plus was just a small part of a charge of activity. Remembering that both were employed full time at the BBC and that any other activities were extra-curricular – evenings and weekends only – their output was prodigious. But the Radiophonic Workshop remained at the centre of their professional lives. Hodgson (born 1938) first joined in 1962 and his career there spread over four decades. With a theatre background and experience as a studio manager at the BBC, his early work with electronic sound tended toward sound effects rather than music, but as his career developed he moved gradually toward a more conventional musicality. Although he has acquired a measure of retrospective fame as the man behind the Tardis sound and the Daleks' voice in *Doctor Who*, he is often cast as a background figure in this period of British electronic music. Actually, he was a constant throughout the decade and well beyond it, at different times a catalyst, an enabler and a creative presence.

Another of Derbyshire's associates was Dick Mills, who had assisted her with the *Doctor Who* theme. He took over from Hodgson as primary producer of the programme's sound effects in the early 1970s. Mills spent most of his working life at the Radiophonic Workshop, from 1958, six months after it opened, until 1993. He had previously worked as a recording engineer with the BBC. Like Hodgson, Mills had no formal musical training.

John Baker (1937–97) was another prolific operator in the golden age. He joined the BBC as a studio manager in 1960, having studied piano and composition at Royal Academy of Music. He joined the Workshop in 1963 and quickly demonstrated a flair for tape editing. Baker had a knack for turning out catchy tunes and was much employed to provide local radio indents and brief themes. Typical is an eight-second tune to cue the listeners' letters section of BBC radio *Woman's Hour*, a perfectly formed *musique concrète* pop miniature constructed from a recording of water being poured from a cider bottle. A jazz pianist in his spare time, Baker was renowned for his deft handling of the razor blade and the splicing block, with the capacity to edit into being a jazz feel. Baker sometimes combined tape edit rhythm tracks with live jazz musicians, an example being a piece for the suspense series *Vendetta* ('Vendetta – Ice Cream Man'). Saxophones honk over a skittering radiophonic rhythm track and the occasional abstract atmospheres.

Many other gifted and original artists also served. Space does not permit examination of all of them. But it was Derbyshire's appeal that endured. Her temperament, her thoroughness and attention to detail, her enthusiasm and her unwillingness to compromise creatively gave her the mental resources to produce great work, but also exhausted her. Working in a service department at the BBC had its advantages – access to equipment, a regular wage – but there were pressures for someone like Derbyshire too. Mills recalls, 'Delia was a law unto herself. Getting through to her was difficult. She was wildly enthusiastic at the start of any commission, and then it tailed off in direct proportion to the nearness of the deadline.'[161] Derbyshire herself recognized this trait: 'I think I must have reverse adrenalin. As the deadline gets closer most people speed up – I just get slower.'[162]

The BBC Radiophonic Workshop's location in a national institution ensured that it remained a focal point for British electronic music. The Workshop composers weren't the only people making electronic music for the masses in Britain by any means, but they were the most visible. It was named in the credits of hundreds of television and radio programmes. Virtually everyone in the country would have listed to some BBC radio or watched some BBC TV in the 1960s, and all of them were hearing radiophonic music. There had been a marked shift in the department's output since its inception, but there were still tensions within it, between sound and music, between the experimental and the commercial. As late as 1962 *The Guardian* was reporting Desmond Briscoe as still displaying a rather ambivalent attitude: 'It is easy to be unpleasant in manipulated sound, but much more difficult to be beautiful, because it is basically inhuman.'[163] But as the decade progressed there was a gradual but marked shift in emphasis. Although more abstract sound for radio and television was still produced, there was a greater emphasis now on more conventional music, to be used for indents, theme tunes and incidental purposes. Most of the various employees of the workshop became adept at knocking out pop tunes using tape techniques, whether that was where their inclinations lay or not. A sampler album titled *BBC Radiophonic Music* released in 1968 by the BBC Radio Enterprises label, and then reissued on BBC Records in 1971, drew attention to this shift. Many short, cute pieces built up from recordings of cash registers, doorbells and items of cutlery surround a few longer, more mysterious and abstract compositions. Among the latter category is a piece by Derbyshire that came to be amongst her most acclaimed. 'Blue Veils and Golden Sands' was first heard in a 1968 *World About Us* documentary about nomads in the Sahara and then again in a 1970 episode of *Doctor Who*. A gong-like sound is a recording of a Derbyshire hitting a green aluminium lampshade that has since acquired the status of something like a holy relic of the Workshop. In the track listing of the album it is preceded by Baker's eight-second *Woman's Hour* piece.

Being such an established part of the nation's audio life, it is understandable that the Workshop became a first port of call for anyone wanting to investigate electronic music. Luminaries from the rock world actively took an interest in what was happening. Brian Jones of The Rolling Stones visited and invited Hodgson and Derbyshire to come and take a look at a Moog recently acquired by the band. He died before the visit could be arranged. Members of Pink Floyd visited too, but not McCartney.

While all of this was going on Tristram Cary was keeping himself busy as a composer, though not exclusively an electronic one. In

1963 he moved his studio, which Zinovieff considered the best-equipped tape-based electronic music facility in the country, to the family home in Fressingfield, Suffolk. Here it was reassembled in a corrugated iron-clad outbuilding in the garden. The electronic music community in Britain was still very small, and Cary was probably the best-connected member of it, with contacts spreading into both the popular and serious fields. Although never a part of the Radiophonic Workshop, he knew everyone there, and also kept in touch with Daphne Oram. It was inevitable that he would encounter Zinovieff, and the two became friends, sharing a taste for convivial pub conversations during which much EMS business would be conducted.

Cary's electronic and partly electronic compositions appeared in both popular and serious ends of the musical spectrum simultaneously. His name featured often in early British concert hall presentations of electronic music, while at the same time he was contributing to industrial and corporate films and television programmes. As well as working on that Radiophonic mainstay, *Doctor Who*, Cary had another indirect connection with the Workshop on account of his soundtrack for the film version of *Quatermass and the Pit* (1967, entitled *Five Million Years to Earth* in the US). Made by Hammer, this was a cinema adaptation of the third instalment of the 1950s BBC TV series, one of the earliest BBC productions to use Workshop-generated electronic effects. The plot, which closely follows the original television production, revolves around the discovery of an object buried in the ground at a London Underground station, which turns out to be an alien spacecraft that has lain buried for five million years. Also dug up are the fossilized remains of pre-human bipeds, which, Quatermass deducts, have been influenced by power from the alien craft, thus implying that all human evolution since has been similarly infected. Once it has been dug out of the London clay, the spacecraft begins to exert a destructive influence over anyone in its vicinity, growing in strength as it feeds on their energy. Its power is broken in a climactic scene when the archaeologist Dr Roney (played by James Donald) swings a crane, which acts as a conductor, into the centre of the force, dissipating its energy and sacrificing himself.

Cary's compelling score mixed brass-heavy orchestrations with electronics. It is a powerful soundtrack, full of violent emotions of fear and suspense expected in any Hammer film. What is most notable is that it conforms exactly to the now-established cinematic convention of electronic sound as a signifier of alien activity, while conventional orchestration represents human events and emotions. Churning overlapping tape-loops pulsate as the film builds towards its climax, and the boiling alien force begins to suck the life out of London. Then, as Dr Roney climbs the crane in a desperate bid to stem the tide, Cary sets a tape loop running for a full two minutes, building the tension with a repetitive phrase dominated by one high note. When this stops, to be replaced briefly by a lower, rumbling loop, it is clear that the end is near. The crane tumbles into the projection of alien power, and both are destroyed to an explosion of electronic noise.

After leaving the Radiophonic Workshop in 1959 and setting up her own private studio, Daphne Oram began taking varied freelance assignments. One of these was for her old paymasters at the BBC – a collection of six short electronic pieces for a children's dance and movement series called *Listen, Move and Dance*. These exercises in spartan melodicism were released on an album alongside spoken word pieces by Vera Gray and on their own in 1962 on a seven-inch EP. The nature of this release allowed for the inclusion of some didactic sleeve notes that also served as an advert for Oram's studio:

> People who are interested in sound production may like to know that these sound patterns were created by Daphne Oram at her Electronic Studio in Kent. By using audio generators, many tape recorders, filters, ring modulators and other electronic devices she built up the tone colours, pitched each of the notes separately, gave them duration and dynamics and finally spliced the notes together to obtain the required rhythms and sequences.[164]

This was just one aspect of Oram's campaign to induct the country into the mysteries of electronic music. From 1960 onwards she gave many lectures and demonstrations in universities and arts institutions, led workshops in schools and also held tape-editing tutorials at her studio. Fred Judd accompanied her in some of this work.

It was hard for electronic musicians of the time to avoid science fiction. Oram's encounter with the genre came in 1962 with the sound for *Rockets in Ursa Major*. This was a play for children written by the astronomer, mathematician and science fiction author Fred Hoyle, with 'music and electronic sound' by Daphne Oram. It ran to mixed reviews for about six weeks from April 1962, most of which failed to notice Oram's contribution. *The Daily Sketch* did comment that there were 'enough blips and bleeps to burst a galaxy' while the *Financial Times* spoke of 'whirrings, roarings, blips, bleeps'. These glib summations don't do justice to a sophisticated set of atmospherics including a syncopated rhythmic tape loop and some slurring, overlapping tones. Another commission was for a piece of electronic music to accompany a kinetic light sculpture initially installed in the headquarters of Mullard Electronics, off Tottenham Court Road in central London, and later relocated to Harrods. Then there were the uncredited electronics in the film *The Innocents* (1961). A British adaptation of the Henry James novella *The Turn of the Screw,* the film didn't attract a big audience on release, but has come to be seen as a classic of the psychological horror genre. Directed and produced by Jack Clayton, it stars Deborah Kerr and Michael Redgrave, with the script written by Truman Capote. Miss Giddens (Deborah Kerr) is governess to two children, Flora and Miles, who are in the care of a bachelor uncle (Michael Redgrave). Although the children are polite and the country house setting idyllic, a creeping sense of unease gradually encroaches on the atmosphere. We learn that the previous governess died suddenly, the children start to behave oddly, and Miss Giddens is troubled by unexplained voices and appearances. The genius of the book, and this adaptation of it, is the way in which the question about Miss Giddens is held in balance: is she really seeing ghosts or is she mad? Oram's spectral massed sine tones cast a diaphanous shroud over this question and are powerfully evocative, particularly when set against the innocence of a tinkling music box.

There were, too, several adverts for commercial television. One, for Nestea (1962), combined a cheery fluting melody underpinned by a bubbly four-note pattern, while a later one for Lego (1966) is little more than a collage of echoed voices. While all of this work was going on, Oram's heart was elsewhere. There's an unmistakable sense that these adverts in particular were knocked out in a hurry. Her true passion was her dream of drawn sound, and two grants from the Gulbenkian Foundation, in 1962 and 1965, enabled her to pursue it. The first of these, for £3,500, was considerable, at a time when an average British salary was about £800 and a house £2,670. The second grant (£1,000), though smaller, was still significant. This money enabled Oram to take fewer commercial commissions and concentrate on building her longed-for machine, which she called the Oramics system. With this, the composer interacts with the tone generators not by pressing keys or turning dials or plugging in patch cords, but by painting ink on to strips of 35-mm film that scroll over light beams. The Oramics machine was never finished to Oram's satisfaction and much about how it worked and what music she was able to make with it remain shrouded in mystery. The idea, had it been fully realized, would have provided a new method of composing. Even so, on the evidence of an archival compilation of her work that includes some Oramics recordings, the machine didn't lead her to compose music radically different from the music she made using conventional electronic music techniques. A piece dated 1969/70 called 'Brociliande', based on a poem by the Christian mystic Charles Williams, is not radically different in form or content from a lot of her earlier tape and tone generator work. Perhaps this is because she was putting so much effort into making the system work that there was little left for composing. Although the Oramics system holds a certain retrospective fascination, it is a story of what might have been, and it marks Oram's exit from this story. Her preoccupation with it led her away from the mainstream of electronic music. Concentrating her resources on developing Oramics, there was little left to develop her tape studio, which became obsolete. Although she continued to lecture and teach for many years, she wrote little music that anyone heard.

The success of Gerry Anderson's succession of 'supermarionation' television programmes kept Barry Gray busy through his sixth decade. *Stingray*, *Joe 90* and most famously, *Thunderbirds*, all featured music composed and arranged by Gray. He was the master of the rousing theme and rarely made exclusively electronic compositions. Even so, he often turned to his Ondes Martenot and Miller Spinetta for electronic interjections, or musifex, as he would have it. He had a vast audience. Much of the music was released on a run of 7-inch, 33-rpm mini-albums from 1965 to 1967, on the Anderson-owned Century 21 label. Many of these might well have sold enough to warrant a chart placing. Sales of the first batch of six mini-albums, released for the Christmas market in 1965, sold out of their total pressing of 240,000. But the unconventional format of the records, plus the fact that they were often sold through non-standard (for the record industry) retail outlets like toy shops, meant that most sales didn't count in chart terms. Record sales aside, the TV series themselves reached millions in the 1960s. Many are still regularly repeated around the world.

In 1969 Gray composed a complete score for a Gerry Anderson live-action movie, *Doppelgänger* (also known as *Journey to the Far Side of the Sun*). Given his own views on the suitability of electronic music for science fiction, this might have been an opportunity for more overt electronics. Instead, he opts for a sparing and conservative use of Ondes Martenot. In a theme titled 'Sleeping Astronauts', used for space scenes, Gray integrates a Martenot played by the French Ondist Sylvette Allart with dreamy slow-motion strings. Gray also augmented the scores of other film composers. He contributed electronic music and effects to *Dr. Who and the Daleks* and *Daleks' Invasion Earth 2150 AD* (both 1966), spinoffs from the BBC television series. On the second of these Martenot ribbon controller swoops were grafted into Bill McGuffie's main theme, and what sounds like a tape loop to a jazzy 'Daleks' Suite'. Other films Gray contributed to in this way were *Island of Terror* (1966) and François Truffaut's *Fahrenheit 451* (1966), where he provided effects alongside a score by Bernard Herrmann. This type of work sums up Gray's attitude to electronic sound – that it was suitable as a means to add a dimension to music, but didn't really stand on its own. He rarely realized completely electronic compositions, apart from a few adverts.

In 1967 Anderson launched *Captain Scarlet and the Mysterons*. It was darker than previous Anderson programmes, the sense of threat more palpable, the action more violent. Scarlet himself faces all manner of threats with the sort of courage that derives from the knowledge of one's indestructability. Gray used the storylines as cues for some of his most eerie music, and because it was sci-fi, in his mind it qualified for electronic experimentation. Electronic instruments, treatments and sound effects abound, like the 'electronic voice' in the series end title theme, a treatment of Gray's own soft northern burr. Hidden in the middle of this series is one of his most fully realized predominantly electronic compositions, 'Lunarville 7 – Suite', which appears in an episode of that name. As well as Martenot, with Gray making the most of the ribbon controller, the piece uses an electric accordion played by Jack Emblow, tremolo electric guitar and vibes.[165] The evocation of the cold, desolate expanses of the moon is impressive.

Britain didn't really have a comparable set of electronically inspired underground rock bands like The United States of America, Silver Apples or Fifty Foot Hose. But in the years 1966 to 1968 several bands including The Pretty Things and Pink Floyd joined The Beatles and embarked on their own journeys of electronic experimentation. The Rolling Stones, too, were expanding their sound in several directions by 1966. For this, Brian Jones tends to get a lot of credit, the received wisdom being that as Jagger and Richards ousted him as bandleader he, for a while, found another role exploring new sounds. It is true that he introduced Appalachian dulcimers, sitars and more to the band in this period, but the Jagger/Richards songwriting team was branching out as well, moving some distance on from its R'n'B starting point. Released in early 1967 but largely recorded the previous year, *Between the Buttons* contains much evidence of this shift, and, on one song, includes a first tentative step into electronic experimentation. The song in question, 'Please Go Home', appeared only on the UK version of the album. It is a microcosm of The Rolling Stones in transition. From the past there's a pounding Bo Diddley beat, from the future generous use of echo as an effect, heavily distorted guitars and what is sometimes described as a theremin, played by Brian Jones. The nature of the tone and the smoothness and accuracy of the portamento point to this sound actually coming from a dial-controlled audio test oscillator. Brian Jones probably played it, though. His interest in electronic music is confirmed by his later visit to the Radiophonic Workshop, and he spoke in interviews of experimenting with electronic sound and tape at home.

At the end of 1967 the band released *Their Satanic Majesties Request*, routinely and lazily dismissed as a poor psychedelic album. It is an anomaly in the band's discography, but warrants closer attention. Recording had been strung out over much of the year, with the sessions self-produced after Andrew Loog Oldham walked out. That tiniest hint of a nod to electronic sound on 'Please Go Home' becomes a much more considered gesture on several songs on the album. Double-tracked oscillators and hissing tape effects combine on an extended prelude to 'She's a Rainbow', and a backwards chords spend 40 seconds introducing '2000 Light Years from Home', in which oscillator squiggles and swirling tape effects can be hard as the song progresses. Given the protracted and flexible nature of the sessions, it is not possible to trace the origin of this experimentation, but based on bootlegs of the sessions it is reasonable to assume that Jones had a big hand in it all. After *Their Satanic Majesties Request* was released to poor reviews the Stones inaugurated their mature blues-based style with 'Jumpin' Jack Flash' in May 1968 and 'Street Fighting Man' in August 1968 and never again strayed down those experimental avenues. It could have been different. In September 1968 the band took possession of a Moog synthesizer.

According to Frank Trocco and Trevor Pinch, writing in their book *Analog Days*, Moog employee Jon Weiss was dispatched to London with the instrument to give Mick Jagger a week's tuition. The idea was, apparently, that Jagger would become the band's synthesist. This might just have been understandable if it had happened a year earlier, in the midst of the explorations of *Their Satanic Majesties Request*. But the Moog arrived just after the release of 'Street Fighting Man' and just before the release of *Beggars Banquet*, with all thoughts of psychedelic exploration apparently abandoned. Weiss's stay extended well beyond that first planned week, and Jagger proved to be a quick and willing learner. At the time he was in the closing stages of work on the film *Performance*, and the idea came up of using the instrument in the film.

Directed by Donald Cammell and Nicolas Roeg, and starring James Fox and Anita Pallenberg alongside Jagger, the film had a troubled gestation and was not released until 1970. The cloudy plot drifts around the stories of an East End gangster Chas (Fox) and a washed-up recluse of a rock star Turner (Jagger). As the action progresses, Chas takes refuge in Turner's retreat, and the characters of the two men melt into each other. A recording studio is set up in the basement of Turner's refuge, a mirrored room where four huge speakers stand on guard, two on each side, a tape recorder set up between one pair. They form a corridor that leads to the Moog, the three module cabinets arrayed like a triptych altarpiece, the keyboard on the floor in front of them. Before it, Turner sits cross-legged on an Eastern rug, patching leads as the Moog breathes heavily over first some tinkling dulcimer music, and then Merry Clayton singing 'Poor White Hound Dog'. In this room occurs the hallucinogenic scene without which no 1960s counter-culture movie was complete. It ends with Turner feinting with a fluorescent tube against a rising surge of distorted Moog noise. By the time the film was released in 1970 the Moog was well known and came with a whole new set of associations, some of which linked it with light entertainment and middle-of-the-road easy listening. In 1968, when the film was shot, it appears as an object of veneration, a symbol of psychedelic peculiarity, unsettling, haunting and inscrutable.

While The Rolling Stones were stretching out the recording of *Their Satanic Majesties Request*, a core of musicians, engineers, producers and technicians at EMI's Abbey Road studio were raiding electronic music's box of tricks for the epochal British recordings of the summer of love.

Work on The Beatles' *Sgt. Pepper's Lonely Hearts Club Band* had begun in late 1966, with the album ready for release in June 1967. Although there was no equivalent of the out-and-out experimentation of *Revolver*'s 'Tomorrow Never Knows', George Martin and engineer Geoff Emerick spun tape loops made of spliced cut-ups of old calliope recordings into 'Being for the Benefit of Mr Kite!'. The Beatles' next and last foray into tape music came the following year with 'Revolution 9' from *The Beatles* (*White Album*). A *musique concrète* collage assembled by John Lennon while Paul McCartney was absent from the studio, it was an equivalent on record of what McCartney had created 18 months earlier with the unreleased 'Carnival of Light'.

An avuncular presence at Abbey Road who had worked on earlier, more conventional Beatles recordings was Norman Smith. He went on to have several hits in the 1970s under the name Hurricane Smith. In 1967 he was 44 years old, a down-to-earth sort with, he said himself, no understanding whatsoever of psychedelia. An RAF glider pilot during the war, a sometime jazz musician and a songwriter, he had become an apprentice engineer at EMI in 1959 at the ripe age of 35 (he said he was 28 on the application). He went on to engineer all The Beatles' EMI recordings up to and including *Rubber Soul*. By

1967 he had been promoted to producer, and was working with new EMI signings Pink Floyd and The Pretty Things.

The arc of The Pretty Things' career up to 1967 is like a pale reflection of that of The Rolling Stones. They too progressed from long-haired rhythm and blues malcontents through a gradual stylistic broadening and more varied instrumentation to psychedelia, but with much less commercial success at every point. Their hit-making days seemed over when in 1967 the album *Emotions*, with its brass and string arrangements, attracted the interest of Smith. The band signed to EMI's Columbia label and in November they released the overtly psychedelic 'Defecting Grey' single, produced by Smith. It was an edited version of a wildly ambitious epic that originally extended over five minutes in length. When eventually retrieved from the vaults for issue on CD this extended version revealed a rich vein of electronic experimentation even more apparent than on the single itself. An ominous bass oscillator drone and extended backwards guitar collages vie with vogue-ish cod-music hall stylings and hard rock. The single failed, but Smith and the band pressed on undeterred. Another single, 'Talking About the Good Times'/'Walking Through My Dreams', reined in the experimentation a little, but by the time it was released the band had embarked on its masterpiece, the concept album *SF Sorrow*. Recording lasted through most of the following year, with the album finally released in November 1968. Electronic guile abounds, though it is hard to trace its sources. There is plenty of tape trickery, but guitarist Dick Taylor mentioned Smith dispatching the Abbey Road technician Ken Townsend to make many a 'special little box'.[166] Two ascending distorted tones in 'Old Man Going', the echoed collage of 'Well of Destiny', a static scratching effect at the end of 'Death' – all of this was the product of long hours experimenting in the studio, with Smith all but inaugurated as a member of the band.

If The Pretty Things were veterans embarking on the third stage of their career by the time Smith got to them, he was involved with Pink Floyd almost from the start of their recording life. The band's first single, released in March 1967, had been produced by Joe Boyd, but Smith was in place for the second, 'See Emily Play', and the band's first four albums. Their debut, *The Piper at the Gates of Dawn*, was recorded from January to July 1967 and first released in August. The US release, when it appeared in October, was a substantially different album with an altered track listing, titled simply *Pink Floyd*. It would be the one album over which doomed leader Syd Barrett reigned, and Smith recalled later finding it difficult to engage with a man already slipping away from reality. Any tension turned out to be creative, though, with the album, marinated in reverb and detailed with multiple esoteric sounds of uncertain provenance, a classic of psychedelia. It closes with 'Bike', a song equal parts Barrett's Lewis Carroll pop whimsy and *musique concrète*. Barrett invites the girl he is addressing in the song into a room of 'musical tunes', which turns out to be a collage of ringing bell-like tones and clock mechanisms, which in turn segues into a tape loop of duck-like quacking noises.

Barrett was leaving the building by the time Pink Floyd embarked on a follow-up album, *A Saucerful of Secrets*. Recorded between January to April 1968, it is the sound of a band in transition, with both Barrett and his replacement David Gilmour involved. Remnants of an earlier Floyd were everywhere, but so were palpable traces of the band's mature sound. From its first bass drones the album's cacophonous 12-minute title track has the most electronic content: backwards tapes, spiralling oscillators, distorted subterranean rumbles.

All of these records co-opted the language of electronic music for psychedelia and helped normalize the sounds for the rock audience. Tape manipulation and oscillators became orthodox. Backwards tapes in particular were everywhere. But although these techniques were derived from what was now considered as classical electronic music, the way they were used was subtly different from the way the same approaches were used by the American bands, Silver Apples, United States of America and Fifty Foot Hose. This difference was one of intent. For each of those American acts the electronics were the *point* of the band; they had formed to blend electronic music and rock. In the case of the British bands at EMI, and The Rolling Stones, the electronic sound was an aspect of the broader sonic exploration of the psychedelic era. It was just one part of a tendency that also embraced experiments with sitars, the use of harpsichords and French horns, and studio effects like phasing. None of the British bands were trying to become electronic bands, and only Pink Floyd would go on to explore electronic music more seriously to the point that it became integral to their sound.

One album that came out London in 1968 that did bear a superficial resemblance to the American underground electronic rock was White Noise – *An Electric Storm*. Another project bearing the fingerprints of Derbyshire and Hodgson, it was made by a band of sorts that saw the pair joined by an American-born classical bass player called David Vorhaus:

> I was on my way to an orchestral gig when the conductor told me that there was a lecture next door on the subject of electronic music. The lecture was fantastic and we got on like a house on fire, starting the Kaleidophon studio about a week later!

This lecture was at Goldsmiths College, south London, and Kaleidophon was a studio in Camden where the album was made. Vorhaus found he had many ideas in common with the slightly older workshop duo, and started working with them immediately, also starting a relationship with Derbyshire. The three completed a couple of tape compositions with added vocals that found their way to Island Records boss Chris Blackwell. To the embryonic band's surprise, Blackwell offered them a deal, and *An Electric Storm* was pieced together over the following year. Although sometimes compared to the American experimental electronic bands, White Noise's work is in a different category. Whereas the Americans created their sounds mainly using primitive homemade electronic instruments, White Noise relied entirely on the tape-manipulation skills of Derbyshire and Hodgson. Although Vorhaus did later acquire a very early EMS VCS 3 synthesizer, reports that it was used on the album seem mistaken. *An Electric Storm* was released at the end of 1968, a full year before the VCS 3 went on sale.

In contrast to Derbyshire's dalliance with Anthony Newley, White Noise was a much more serious business occupying a niche firmly in the hinterland between psychedelia and the emerging progressive rock. According to Hodgson, it was mainly the work of Vorhaus and Derbyshire, and his role was more peripheral. Six of the album's seven tracks are credited to Vorhaus, with or without Derbyshire, the last, 'Black Mass: An Electric Storm in Hell', being attributed to the whole band. With the exception of percussion by free jazz improviser Paul Lytton, the arrangements are generally considered to be entirely electronic, though string-like sounds can be heard.

The vocals of John Whitman, Annie Bird and Val Shaw give the album its surface resemblance to The United States of America and Fifty Foot Hose. It is in a deeply disorientating category of its own, though; spooky, comic and intriguing all at once. The declamatory disembodied voices intone melodies of contrasting folksiness against a shifting background of free-ranging drumming and electronic sound that lurches from fiercely angry to ethereal. Anyone familiar with Derbyshire's will recognize the trademark twangy guitar-like plucking. 'My Game of Loving', with its orgasmic moaning varisped into a climax, is harmony pop cut into *avant-garde* pornography. 'Here Come the Fleas' is a novelty that betrays a debt to Hodgson's and Derbyshire's theatre experiences. Though not short of melody and displaying a good grasp of traditional song craft, the album was too plain odd to make an impression. Island's initial enthusiasm waned, possibly because the record took so long to complete, and it crept out at the end of 1968 almost unnoticed. Over the years it sold quite well and was hailed as a bizarre one-off. Vorhaus continued to make White Noise records from the Kaleidophon studio, but without Derbyshire and Hodgson. Talking a few years before her death, Derbyshire said that the White Noise project gave her the opportunity to write extended melody, which she considered she had an aptitude for, and for which there was little call in her BBC work.

The unresolved tension in British electronic music, between the serious and the popular, continued until late in the 1960s. The predicament of the two key figures in early British electronic music – Daphne Oram and Tristram Cary – was typical. Both aspired to make serious, experimental electronic music for the concert hall, and both were compelled for many years to seek commercial outlets for their music to make ends meet. Cary seems to have been better equipped, temperamentally, to deal with this. Through the 1950s and for most of the following decade there were no funded academic electronic music facilities where they might have found a home. Delia Derbyshire too inclined toward the serious and experimental. And although the BBC Radiophonic Workshop where she did most of her work was publicly funded and did do some experimental work, mainly in the field of radio drama, at the same time it devoted much of its energies – and by extension hers – to radio indents and popular television shows. It seemed like the only way to wholeheartedly pursue experimental electronic music was to have a private income, like Zinovieff, although even he got embroiled in the same difficulty with Unit Delta Plus, itself a sort of embodiment of the problem. But by the middle of the 1960s there were small signs emerging that this tension might finally ease, and the serious music establishment in Britain began to embrace electronic music, though rather awkwardly and tentatively at first. Oram continued to lecture and demonstrate at universities around the country and the Arts Council began to take an interest, holding several electronic music events. On 21 November 1966 the Society for the Promotion of New Music held its Electronic Music Forum 1, chaired by Cary, to explore the subject.

This activity was not a formally orchestrated campaign by any means, but neither was it a succession of unconnected events. There was a very small group of people pushing this agenda, and the names of Cary and Oram in particular, and Derbyshire and Zinovieff as well, often appear in accounts of these events. Those accounts often reveal, too, not so much hostility and suspicion as head-scratching puzzlement. A review of an Arts Council concert in London in 1963 by the critic Edward Greenfield struck an even-handed tone, even praising some of the music, before declaring of another piece that 'music as most of us understand it was left behind'.[167] A concert organised by Zinovieff and Cary at Queen Elizabeth Hall, London, on 15 January 1968 got a similarly ambivalent critical reaction. This event is often mistakenly billed as the first concert of electronic music in Britain, ignoring that other 'first' concert put on by Unit Delta Plus in September 1966 and various Arts Council-funded events before. Even so there was something of the big occasion about it, which television cameras were there to capture. Located in London's Southbank Centre, the Queen Elizabeth Hall is right at the heart of London's cultural life, and the venue itself lent the concert a certain gravitas. A capacity audience of 1,800 heard performances of music by several leading British composers, including Cary, Oram and Zinovieff. It might not have been the first electronic music concert in Britain, but it was the first concert featuring computer music. Zinovieff's DEC PDP-8 was wheeled on for an exercise in controlled randomness.

The critic Hugo Cole said of the computer piece that 'the effect on the listener is often baffling', going on to say of the concert in general that 'we are all innocents when faced with this music, and the most we can hope for is to misunderstand in a fruitful manner'.[168] Even this studious, beard-stroking event was marked by the schism in British electronic music: the opening piece was 'Potpourri' by Delia Derbyshire, which had also been used at the earlier Windmill concert. This was actually several of her more commercial BBC pieces spliced together. Yet for all this, and despite obvious reservations, the heavy doors of the establishment did begin to creak open. Around the same time as this concert modest electronic studios were being established in universities across the country, including Manchester, York, King's College, Cambridge, Goldsmiths College and at the Royal College of Music, where Cary began teaching a class.

9

It rhymes with vogue

Switching on

The unwritten person specification for an electronic music pioneer included some combination of musical and technical aptitude, acquired either through formal education or self-motivated exploration. Wendy Carlos (formerly Walter, born 1939) fits this profile, starting piano lessons at the age of six, and going on to study music and physics at Brown University, Rhode Island. In Carlos's case, the combination of interests led to home experiments with *musique concrète* as a teenager in the 1950s, and after graduating with a masters in composition at Columbia University, studying with Vladimir Ussachevsky and Otto Luening between 1962 and 1965. This was the heyday of the Columbia-Princeton Electronic Music Center, a stronghold of formal electronic music. Carlos was completely out of step with the prevailing mood there, favouring melody, harmony and rhythmic structure and scornful of serialism and atonalism. After graduating from Columbia, Carlos spent three years working as an engineer at Gotham Recording studios, and while there bought a small Moog set-up in 1966 that was gradually expanded. Carlos and Bob Moog became friends and collaborators, a relationship that influenced the development of Moog's instruments. Carlos placed demands for all manner of improvements and extra features to her modular system. These included a portamento control, a touch-sensitive keyboard and a filter bank that all became standard Moog features in time. The growing Moog became the centrepiece of a home electronic studio that included a self-made eight-track recorder and mixer.

At about the same time that Carlos was setting up this home studio she befriended Rachel Elkind, who came from a musical theatre background and was working as a secretary for Goddard Lieberson, then president of Columbia Records. So, by 1967, a set of relationships and circumstances had fallen into place that precipitated subsequent events. Carlos had a Moog synthesizer, a home studio and the technical skill to operate them, the confidence and attention of Bob Moog, and a friend with keys to the corridors of power at Columbia Records. There was a period of casting around for a direction, making a couple of adverts and a demo Moog version of 'What's New Pussycat?' before Elkind heard a rendition of a Bach piece that Carlos had synthesized and suggested a whole album along the same lines. With Carlos as performer, Elkind as producer, and a friend, Benjamin Folkman, in a rather vague advisory role, the recording of what became *Switched-On Bach* began, concluding at the end of the summer 1968. Elkind's contacts at Columbia helped secure a deal with the company and the album was released later that year.

The impact of the 40 minutes of electronically interpreted Bach pieces that made up *Switched-On Bach* has been lost. Has there ever been a record so popular and so talked about in its time and now so rarely listened to? The very idea of playing selections from the classical canon electronically seems prosaic and ersatz now, a budget commercial device suitable for the elevator or the telephone call-centre. But in 1968 it was a subversively radical concept, a cavalry charge at cherished assumptions. For many, electronic music wasn't *real* in some essential but hard-to-define sense. It was artificial and sterile, lacking human emotion. In this mindset a composer like Bach, on the other hand, was a paradigm of authenticity. It was this juxtaposition, between the perceived real and unreal, inauthentic and authentic, which made *Switched-On Bach* an attention-grabbing story in its day.

Leaving aside aesthetic judgements about the appropriateness or otherwise of rendering classical music electronically, in a technical sense the closely interlocking precision of Bach's music made it ideally suited to a synthesizer performance in 1968. Carlos's Moog, like all Moogs of the time, was monophonic, so the only way to build up any sort of musical complexity was to painstakingly multi-track one line at a time. Carlos achieved dynamic nuances in the performance with the touch-sensitive keyboard, but also by carefully switching between timbres and sounds, sometimes using tape splicing. Carlos avoided the debate about whether synthesizers should be used to mimic existing instruments by opting for a sort of aural impressionism, hinting at harpsichords, French horns, violins and so on, without trying to replicate them precisely.

The cover art of *Switched-On Bach* used a similar idea to that of Jean-Jacques Perrey's *Mr Ondioline* EPs nearly a decade earlier, with a visual emphasis on the electronic technology. Although the names of first Walter then Wendy Carlos were added in time, initially the credit was 'Virtuoso electronic performances of [Bach pieces listed] performed on the Moog synthesizer'. A bewigged, costumed model poses as the composer in an approximation of a period drawing room. Behind him where we might expect to see an ornate harpsichord sits a Moog modular system – actually one owned by Columbia Records, and not the one Carlos made the music with. A power cable snakes across the floor, though there are no patch leads plugged into the module, so the instrument couldn't have made a sound. The intention is clear: to draw attention to the instrument itself, and mark the clash of cultures – the old and the new. The recording artist is rendered almost irrelevant and the Moog itself is the star, reinforcing, perhaps unintentionally, the prejudice that electronic music is inhuman, that the machines really were taking over.

Switched-On Bach started its commercial life slowly, though by March 1969 it had entered the Billboard charts. In Britain and elsewhere it had a lower profile. Reviews were mixed, and even with the positive ones there is a sense of critics who don't quite grasp what is going on trying to keep up. *Gramophone* magazine said: 'generally the registrations used are very pleasing, particularly when known sounds are synthesized. However some unusual new sounds … made one wonder if one's equipment had not developed a buzz' before concluding that the album 'will not be everyone's choice', though it 'opens up a new range of possibilities'.[169] *The Guardian*, meanwhile, considered that this 'outrageous record has an insidious quality that makes it compulsive listening', going on to refer to the Moog as an electronic computer.[170]

The *New York Times* critic Donal Henahan published an opaque review that sums up the confusion lurking in many responses to *Switched-On Bach*. He managed to strike a positive tone, using words like astonishing and significant, without actually praising the album. There are signs of bewilderment about what a synthesizer was and what it could do. The involvement of Folkman and Carlos seems to have persuaded him that two people were needed to operate the Moog, which he compares to a 'great organ'. He writes that there has been talk for some time of traditional instruments being replaced by synthesizers with little evidence to back it up. 'But here,' he continues 'almost at one leap, is the much-promised revolution: not only can traditional sounds be imitated, but new sounds found that can be musically valid.' Then, the recording is 'genuinely baroque in sound and style', and yet 'no musician would … be fooled'. The review ends with a worry that although a vaguely defined essence of Bach is retained, an equally ill-defined authenticity is sacrificed.[171]

In March 1970 *Switched-On Bach* was awarded three Grammys, for Best Classical Album, Best Classical Performance – Instrumental Soloist or Soloists, and Best Engineered Classical Recording. But this apparent acceptance of electronics in the traditional classical establishment is illusory and never really led to anything. Electronic realizations of works from the classical canon did not become the norm, or even an accepted alternative. In the world of classical music *Switched-On Bach* was a freak storm. The album's massive commercial success was less to do with a groundswell of interest in electronic music among the classical music audience than with a general emerging interest in the Moog in particular as a convenient peg on which to hang electronic music. It was an archetypal crossover album that sold way beyond the usual audience for classical music, catching a wave of interest that had been building up since 1966.

By the time the album was released, most of the American population were hearing the Moog every day on television courtesy of Eric Siday and others, and the instrument itself was acquiring a sort of personality. *Switched-On Bach* appeared at the right moment to satisfy a curiosity about the Moog. The album hasn't endured as a classic but the time was right for it, and by virtue of the attention it attracted it was another milestone in the emergence of electronic music. A series of articles about synthesizers and the Moog were published through 1969 that reiterate the aspirations and fears associated with electronic music voiced at various points since Thaddeus Cahill's Telharmonium. A *Time* feature published in March caught the mood, talking of music of the future, a 'bizarre collection of buzzes, bleeps and squawks', made by a hybrid of a composer and a technician, not a performer.[172] It had a familiar ring to it.

Carlos followed up *Switched-On Bach* with the similar but less-successful *The Well-Tempered Synthesizer* (1969), by which time an industry of copycat Moog albums had sprung up. Many of these were electronic realizations of classical composers, while others meted out the same treatment to pop artists or popular music genres. In 1969 alone there was *The Moog Strikes Bach* by Hans Wurman, *Switched On Bacharach* and *More Switched On Bacharach* by Christopher Scott, *Switched-On Rock* by The Moog Machine, *Music to Moog By* by Gershon Kingsley, *Moog Power* by Hugh Montenegro, and *The Age of Electronicus* and *Moog: The Electric Eclectics of Dick Hyman* by Dick Hyman. Similar releases poured out through the early part of the 1970s, most of little consequence musically or commercially and destined for the remainder bins. This might not have been a legacy Carlos or Moog would have wished for, yet *Switched-On Bach* and the subsequent torrent of cash-in releases gave electronic music an identity in popular culture. Now it had if not a face, then at least a new set of associations. In reduced and simplified form, if the popular understanding of electronic music in the 1940s and early 1950s was focused on the theremin, and then for a while on *musique concrète* and tape techniques, after *Switched-On Bach* it switched to the Moog in particular, and synthesizers in general.

In 1969 this association was much stronger in America than it was in Britain for the simple reason that there were very few Moogs in the country at that time. An error-strewn article in a special feature in *Melody Maker* about organs and electronic keyboards reveals how little was known about the instrument. In it the writer describes the Moog as a 'computer-like device which tapes basic tones and pitches' before declaring 'what is believed to be the only Moog in the country resides in the home of Beatle George Harrison'.[173] Actually, The Rolling Stones' Moog that arrived in Britain in September 1968 was the second of the instruments to cross the Atlantic. The first had gone to Manchester University shortly before. Harrison got his early in 1969, one of a tiny band of British rock and pop musicians and producers who acquired them that year. Gradually, the instrument established itself in public consciousness.

On Christmas Eve 1969 ITV screened *With a Little Help from My Friends*, a Yorkshire TV production described as 'George Martin ... presenting an hour of pop and comedy' and featuring Lulu, Spike Milligan and Ringo Starr, among others. Martin himself did a spot playing the Moog synthesizer. Yorkshire TV claimed this was the first time the instrument had been performed on British television, which wasn't quite true. *With a Little Help from My Friends* was the third of three programmes taking very different approaches to electronic music that aired on British television in the closing months of the decade. The first, *The Same Trade as Mozart*, was broadcast on BBC2 in August 1969. Featuring the elders of British electronic music Tristram Cary and Daphne Oram alongside Peter Zinovieff and the august presence of Stockhausen himself, the programme was a serious attempt to explain what electronic music was and where it might go. In September 1969 the BBC 1 technology programme *Tomorrow's World* ran a short feature introducing the Moog. This probably *was* the first time a Moog has been seen on British television. In the programme, Mike Vickers demonstrates the instrument to an explanatory narrative by Derek Cooper.

Vickers had been guitarist, flautist and saxophonist in Manfred Mann, leaving the band in late 1965 for a session and scoring career that took in films, television, The Beatles and much library music. He acquired a Moog in 1969, producing a library album called *A Moog for More Reasons* in 1975. The feature is notable not just for introducing on prime-time early evening television an instrument that it assumed would be unfamiliar to viewers. As Vickers plays the Moog, Cooper comments that the performer can set up in a few minutes what 'would normally take radiophonic experts with their complicated equipment days of work'.[174] In saying this, he takes for granted that viewers would know what term 'radiophonic' means, acknowledging the strong association between electronic music and the BBC Radiophonic Workshop in Britain at the time, while also identifying a transition in electronic music. The age of the test oscillator and tape manipulation, radiophonic music, was passing. Like mechanical musical instruments – player pianos and barrel organs – tape music was superseded by technology's relentless advance and it became redolent of a brief period in which it seemed like the sound of the future. Now the synthesizer was the future. Both Vickers and George Martin were on hand for The Beatles album *Abbey Road*, which shadowed this transition from the tape to the synthesizer era.

After *Switched-On Bach* became the first charting synthesizer album, Dick Hyman followed the same year with the first charting Moog single 'The Minatour'. Hyman (born 1927), a jazz keyboardist and composer, had already recorded dozens of albums when he added two Moog collections in 1969, *The Age of Electronicus* and *Moog: The Electric Eclectics of Dick Hyman*. 'The Minatour' was taken from the second of these. Nearly nine minutes of Moog grooves over a repetitive drum machine, it has something of the style that would become familiar on television cop shows of the 1970s.

Hyman recorded 'The Minatour' and indeed all of his two Moog albums with the assistance of Walter Sear, the Moog salesman and later proprietor of the famed analogue refuge, Sear Studio. It comprises three tracks of improvised Moog over a drum machine pattern made up of combined waltz and bossa nova presets. The lead Moog line makes liberal use of the Moog's portamento feature, originally specified by Carlos. In an interview in 2002 Hyman said he considered that Keith Emerson's famous Moog solo on the Emerson Lake & Palmer hit 'Lucky Man' (1970) was a 'little too close' to 'The Minatour' and briefly considered pursuing legal action.[175] The scarcity of Moog solos at the time meant that perhaps comparisons were inevitable, and any perceived similarity between the two is attributable to portamento use.

Emerson was another British early Moog adopter. Born in 1944, he had been playing blues and jazz organ since he was a teenager, and with his band The Nice had cultivated a flamboyant act that involved hurling daggers into his Hammond organ. He was also interested in exploring the limits of the organ's potential and coaxed unusual effects out of it by hitting the reverb spring and turning the power supply on and off while playing. He first heard the Moog when a London record store manager played him *Switched-On Bach* in 1969. He was fascinated, but not convinced:

I thought, 'What the hell is this?' There was a picture of the thing it was played on, on the cover, and I wasn't too impressed to be honest, it sounded a bit boggy, too heavy sounding, too laboured.[176]

Emerson asked his manager Tony Stratton-Smith to enquire if anyone in London had a Moog, which led him to Mike Vickers. By this time Vickers was London's Beaver and Krause rolled into one, the person you went to for all things Moog, having had a modular system long enough to have a firmer grasp than most of how to operate it. Emerson visited Vickers for a demonstration and asked if he could borrow the instrument for a forthcoming Nice concert. Vickers voiced reservations, explaining that the Moog was complex and unstable, and not really intended for live performance, but he gamely agreed to let Emerson have a go. The condition was that Vickers would nurse the temperamental synthesizer through its public debut.

In February 1970 The Nice appeared at the Royal Festival Hall in London with the Royal Philharmonic Orchestra. Alongside Emerson's familiar Hammond was Vickers' Moog, behind which was Vickers himself, wearing headphones and occasionally darting out to switch a patch lead. Describing the event, Richard Green of the *New Musical Express* wrote:

> The Moog was introduced for the first time on a British stage during 'She Belongs to Me'. It's a weird thing, resembling a switchboard and takes some playing. Mike Vickers, its owner, was on hand to programme it and Keith got laughs when he almost made the thing talk.[177]

Stratton-Smith sent a begging letter to Moog asking for a free modular synthesizer for The Nice to use in exchange for publicity for the company. Moog salesman Walter Sear replied saying that the company never gave out promotional instruments on account of their cost, and anyway, it would be unfair on The Beatles and The Rolling Stones, as both bands had already paid for their Moogs.[178] Later in 1970 Emerson broke up The Nice and formed Emerson Lake & Palmer. Flush with a big record company advance, he was able to buy his own Moog, and took delivery of an instrument that had been used in a 1969 concert at the Museum of Modern Art (MOMA). There is symmetry in this, as that concert was devised to demonstrate that the Moog could be used as a live performance instrument, which is exactly what Emerson was interested in doing with it.

Jazz in the Garden was a series of outdoor concerts held at MOMA in late summer 1969. The last of these featured two Moog quartets performing on specially constructed modular systems that had only been finished two days before the concert. The two bands, one led by Herb Deutsch and the other by Chris Swanson, used these instruments to perform sets of semi-improvised electronic jazz entirely live, with no backing tapes. They played to a capacity crowd and the concert was considered a success for Moog, although it got mixed critical notices. In the audience was Jean-Jacques Perrey's former partner, Gershon Kingsley. He was inspired to form the First Moog Quartet, which debuted at Carnegie Hall in January 1970 and afterwards toured and released a live album. A staple of the Quartet's set was a throwaway Kingsley tune called 'Popcorn', which when covered two years later by Hot Butter became one of the biggest ever synth pop hits.

Audio magazine declared of Jazz in the Garden: 'One thing was clear; from now on the Moog will have an established place in live performance.'[179] This was fair enough, if you happened to have Bob Moog and virtually his entire staff on hand to set up and monitor the equipment, which is what happened at Jazz in the Garden. Or if, like Kingsley, you'd secured a $30,000 record company advance to buy the synthesizers you needed.

Before forming The Nice in 1967 Emerson had played with 'Rn'B' band the VIPs, in which he had honed some of his organ stunts. After Emerson left, the VIPs morphed into Spooky Tooth, who recorded for Island. The band released two moderately successful albums of melodic blues-rock before, in 1969, embarking on an odd collaboration with the French composer Pierre Henry, one of the period's more uncomfortable marriages of electronic music and rock. Henry (born 1927) was a pioneer of *musique concrète* and had worked extensively with Pierre Schaeffer. In 1969 he approached Island Records with a proposal for a Christian concept album, not unlike the two Electric Prunes collections *Mass in F Minor* and *Release of an Oath*. The idea was that a band would write and record a set of songs based on the Catholic mass, which Henry would then subject to an electronic make-over. Spooky Tooth were selected and duly obliged, knocking out six bluesy pieces and handing over a master tape to Henry, who they met just once. Henry then surrounded these recordings with his tape-music textures and the end result was released as *Ceremony* in late 1969, without Spooky Tooth hearing it until it was in the shops. It was an anomaly for both members of the team, sounding for the most part like two different recordings playing simultaneously, which in a way it was. It also struck an anomalous note in the emerging relationship between rock and electronic music. By 1969 most rock musicians that had flirted with tape and *musique concrète* techniques were looking to synthesizers. George Harrison was one of these, and in May he released an entire album of Moog music, *Electronic Sound*, the second and final release on the Zapple Records label.

The album is made up of two long, meandering Moog pieces, the origins of which were later disputed by Bernie Krause in his autobiography. He claimed that much of the music on the album was recorded at a demonstration of the Moog he had given to Harrison in 1968. The inaccurate *Melody Maker* feature that spread misinformation about the Moog did make an interesting point about Harrison's album, suggesting that it was more successful artistically than *Switched-On Bach* because it was not imitative. It 'never tries to reproduce sounds produced originally by humans. That is the way it must go.'[180] The cover art of Harrison's album was a twist on the convention of making the instrument itself a focus, featuring a naïve self-portrait of the artist sitting at the keyboard, the Moog's modules lined up behind like a backing band.

Around the time that Harrison's album was released The Beatles and George Martin convened one last time at Abbey Road to record the album that bore the studio's name. Harrison's Moog was present, and so was Mike Vickers. His job was to set up the patches and coax sounds out of the instrument, which all The Beatles except Ringo Starr played. It was used on 'Because', 'Here Comes the Sun', 'I Want You (She's So heavy)' and 'Maxwell's Silver Hammer'. The Beatles' myth-reinforcing machine has tended to make rather too extravagant a claim for the revolutionary nature of the band's synthesizer use on *Abbey Road*, forgetting that The Byrds and The Monkees had pre-empted them by two years and many other rock bands had used the instrument since then. But even so, the Moog was more than a decorative device on *Abbey Road*, and the biggest band in the world making much of its presence was indicative of a sea change. 'Maxwell's Silver Hammer' features multi-layered ribbon-controlled Moog, 'Because' a brass approximation in the middle eight. 'I Want You (She's So heavy)' succumbed to a rush of Moog white noise before its abrupt closure, while Harrison himself used the instrument to more melodic effect on his 'Here Comes the Sun'.

Back in the last years of the nineteenth century Cahill's patent for the Telharmonium had spoken of the art and the apparatus of electronic music. They needed each other. The art could only develop as far as the limits of the apparatus, and the apparatus itself often developed at the prompting of the artist, as Carlos and Moog's relationship shows. The synthesizer was a giant leap forward for the apparatus, but if it were to take the art along with it needed to become a more practical tool. Moog modular systems were big and expensive. Most musicians couldn't afford them, and they were not suited to live performance. The art needed smaller, cheaper, performance synthesizers, and it soon got them. Scott Ludwig playing light Moog music in lounge bars with The Sounds of Tomorrow was an exception that proved the rule. As Jazz in the Garden, the First Moog Quartet and Keith Emerson demonstrated, using Moog synthesizers as live performance instruments was not a replicable experience for most musicians. You needed access to rare equipment that only a lot of money could buy and considerable technical expertise and/ or support to take a Moog out on the road. Electronic music was approaching the same high hurdle it fallen at before. It needed an apparatus suitable for live performance. It needed portable, affordable and reliable instruments.

Peter Zinovieff had been convinced since 1960 that tape manipulation as a means of making electronic music was a dead end. He saw computer sequencing as the way forward and he would be proved right, in part. Electronic music would in time embrace computers, but before it did it embraced the synthesizer. Zinovieff had a part in that phase of history too, almost in spite of himself. By 1969 his studio in Putney had developed a consuming appetite for cash. Zinovieff was pressing on with his experiments with computers, acquiring new equipment and expanding, while at the same time allowing composers including Harrison Birtwistle and Stockhausen to use the facilities. He entertained groups sent by the Arts Council too, but all at no charge. There was a compelling need to earn money.

Another composer who visited the Putney studio was Tristram Cary. At some point he, Zinovieff and David Cockerell, Zinovieff's engineer, conceived of what became the first affordable synthesizer, the Voltage Controlled Studio 3, better known as the VCS 3 (sold as The Putney in America). This was a development of the VCS 1 (there doesn't seem to have been a VCS 2), a few of which were made, one going to the Australian composer Don Banks. The idea of the VCS 3 was that it would be a cheap modular synthesizer in miniature, suitable for schools in particular. With that goal in mind, the price of components and size were strong factors influencing the end product. The team came up with a voltage-controlled system comprising three oscillators, a filter, an envelope generator and a ring modulator in a neat case about the size of a small desk. In some respects it looked like a familiar modular system, but scaled down, with an angled upright panel of dials and controls attached to an almost flat desktop panel. But patch leads were dispensed with in favour of a 16x16 matrix panel with connections made with coloured pins, which looked like a children's game. And there was no keyboard, but a little joystick adapted from the radio control mechanism of a model aeroplane. It also featured an integral amplifier and stereo speakers, and stereo inputs. This last feature turned out to be particularly attractive to musicians, who were able to use the VCS 3 not only to make sound, but to process sound from other sources too.

The VCS 3 first went on sale in November 1969 at a price of about £330, well over the original £200 EMS was aiming at. By comparison, at the time you could buy a Fender Stratocaster guitar for about £240. So the VCS 3 wasn't a budget instrument, but it was cheaper than the equivalent small Moog and ARP synthesizers that appeared a little later, both of which were more expensive in Britain than they were in America. The VCS 3 was flawed and limited, yet successful too. It was known to be unstable, which meant that getting the same sound twice was always a challenge, and the absence of a keyboard meant that it wasn't really viable as a melodic instrument, though a

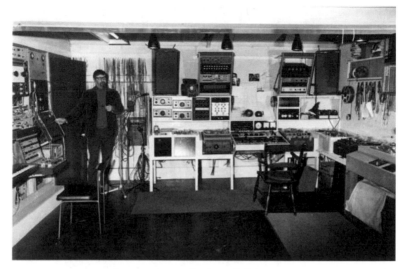

Tristram Cary's studio in Fressingfield, Suffolk, circa 1969. Note an early EMS VCS 3 to the left; a collection of tape loops hanging on the wall behind Cary; a bank of oscillators beneath the left-hand speaker. Out of shot was a Bechstein upright piano, and behind the camera, Cary's work table looking out on to the vegetable garden. Credit: © Tristram Cary Estate 2012

monophonic keyboard could be added as an extra. A later, cheaper version of the instrument packed into a briefcase. An emphasis on cheapness and portability makes the VCS 3's relationship to large modular synthesizers similar to the Hammond Solovox's relationship to the Novachord: an entry-point electronic musical instrument, with very obvious limitations. It did sell well in the educational market and was adopted by a number of British rock bands including The Who, Pink Floyd, Hawkwind and Roxy Music. The later Minimoog and ARP Odyssey were pitched at the same gap in the market.

The VCS 3 occupies a curious place in the history of EMS. It very quickly became, and remains, the recognizable face of the company, yet for Zinovieff in particular it was little more than a sideline to earn cash, a commercial afterthought. As far as he was concerned the heart of the work was developing the massive computer studio in Putney. As a product the VCS 3 was little more than an infant sibling of that studio, its capabilities correspondingly dwarfed, yet it was this bijou device that found its way into the music departments of schools and colleges, and into the hands of Pete Townsend and Brian Eno.

In 1969 there were three companies marketing synthesizers: Moog and Buchla in America and EMS in Britain. After a brief brush with commercial manufacturing, Buchla would remain a specialist concern. That year another American synthesizer company was formed. Alan Robert Pearlman (born 1925), an engineer who had worked for NASA, had long harboured an interest in electronic music. As far back as 1948, when a student at Worcester Polytechnic Institute, Massachusetts, he had written a paper on the subject, saying:

The electronic instrument's value is chiefly as a novelty. With greater attention on the part of the engineer to the needs of the musician, the day may not be too remote when the electronic instrument may take its place …[181]

In 1969 Pearlman, like lots of people in America, heard *Switched-On Bach*. He began to investigate the instrument used to make it. Discovering that the Moog had a reputation for going out of tune and that the Buchla, the only other American synthesizer, didn't have a keyboard, he set himself the goal of making performer-friendly, playable synthesizers. With $100,000 of his own money matched by a small group of investors he started ARP Instruments, Inc. The company launched its first product, the ARP 2500, in 1970. This did succeed in improving on the Moog by virtue of keeping in tune, and unlike the Buchla it did have a keyboard, but it was as large and as expensive as its competitors. ARP developed rapidly in the early 1970s and was bigger than Moog by 1975. But that was all to come: 1969 was the year of the synthesizer, and for almost everyone who cared synthesizers were Moogs.

The 1970s began with electronic music heard as a matter of routine, day in day out, on television, on the radio and in film. The record companies, after decades of suspicion, finally decided that electronic music was the coming thing and opened the gates to release herds of weird mutants into the market. There were the first hit electronic albums and singles. Affordable and usable equipment was beginning to emerge – practical electronics at last. But still there was lingering suspicion and a sense of otherness surrounding the music. Critics continued to routinely air all the time-honoured worries about machines taking over, musicians being out of work, of music losing its soul. This persisted for a while longer, yet by the end of the 1970s electronic music was normal. There was no eureka moment in between, just a speeding up of the advance of the art and the apparatus.

In 1969 Moog started work on a small performance synthesizer and leant a prototype to Sun Ra, never to see it again. In 1970 a Moog brochure proclaimed the launch of the production version with the words: 'Here it is! A compact, moderately priced electronic music synthesizer designed and built for live performance ...'[182] This was the Minimoog, a monophonic 44-key instrument that packaged up the most popular features of the modular systems in a case small enough to take on the road. ARP launched its Odyssey in 1972 with the same idea in mind. In the same period the main Japanese instrument companies Korg, Yamaha and Ace Electronics (the forerunner of Roland) were creeping up unnoticed. Korg's first product appeared in 1963, an electro-mechanical rhythm box called the DA-20 Disk Rotary Electric Auto Rhythm Machine, also known as the Donca Matic, inspired by the Wurlitzer Sideman. It was superseded by a solid-state all electronic version, the DE-20, in 1966. The following year Korg branched out into the electric organ market, and its first synthesizer, the miniKORG 700, appeared in 1973. Ace Electronics was another drum machine pioneer, the Ace Tone FR1 Rhythm Ace (1967) being the first in a series of successes. Ace Electronics founder Ikutaro Kakehashi left to launch Roland in 1972, marketing the company's first synthesizer, the Roland SH-1000, in 1973. That same year, Yamaha, which had been making organs and pianos since the nineteenth century, also entered the fray with the GX-1 (first released as Electone GX-707). In a few more years these companies would sweep aside EMS, Moog and ARP and dominate the synthesizer market. The apparatus of electronic music in the 1970s was synthesizers, drum machines and sequencers, and as the decade progressed there were more and more of each.

While the apparatus kept on getting refined, reduced, edited, made understandable and usable and portable, the art grew in all directions. No self-respecting progressive rock keyboard player's rig was complete without an Minimoog or an ARP Odyssey; Pink Floyd lined up the EMS synthesizers; Wendy Carlos retooled Beethoven for the soundtrack to *A Clockwork Orange*; Hot Butter's 'Popcorn' was an international hit, as was 'Pepper Box' for The Peppers and 'Son Of My Father' for Chicory Tip; Stevie Wonder began a long association with Tonto's Expanding Head Band (featuring Robert Margouleff, former producer of Lothar and The Hand People); Suicide updated the home-made electronic aesthetic for the 1970s; Tangerine Dream moved from tape collage to synthesizers, won the support of John Peel, signed to Virgin and started to have hit albums; Kraftwerk coalesced into an electronic quartet and made an international breakthrough with *Autobahn*. Giorgio Morodor's insistent sequenced arpeggios on Donna Summer's 'I Feel Love' launched a thousand house records. David Bowie and Brian Eno were listening. So was Gary Numan, and future members of Soft Cell, The Human League, Heaven 17, Depeche Mode, Sparks, New Order, OMD, Ultravox, Visage and every other musician to forsake an electric guitar for a synthesizer.

Most of the pioneers of electronic music missed out on the gold rush. In temperament many were more like scientists or inventors or writers. Few were natural performers. They tended to prefer a back room warned by vacuum tubes and solder to a stage hot with lights. Once electronic music started to become performance music they didn't fit in. This was one reason why many of them slipped from view, if indeed they were ever particularly visible in the first place.

Another reason was the acceleration in technology. The 1960s ended with electronic music in transition from the tape age to the synthesizer age. That change was swift and some were unable or unwilling to adapt. As most synthesizers were keyboard instruments, some cut-and-splice pioneers thought them restrictive. For them the excitement of the tape approach lay in the absence of limits, of creating sound that nobody had ever heard before and might never hear again, of liberation from the tyranny of the tone and the semitone. Now, they thought, anyone with the money to buy a synthesizer had access to the same sounds as whoever else had bought that same model. Actually, there was a misunderstanding here, as many of those early synthesizers were infinitely variable and did not rely on pre-sets. Perhaps people had just become attached to their own belief systems and their own way of doing things, just as their critics had before them. Or maybe many of the musicians and composers who had their heydays sometime between the late 1940s and the late 1960s would have been happier to vault over the synthesizer and sequencer era and go straight to computers and samplers, with the boundless scope for sound manipulation they offer. But for most of them, by the time that technology became available it was too late.

Epilogue

Daphne Oram continued to lecture about electronic music until the 1980s. She wrote a curious book, *An Individual Note of Music, Sound and Electronics* (1972), which appeared on the Galliard imprint, a music publisher that released a pair of Tristram Cary EPs at about the same time. It is part cheerfully didactic introduction to electronic music, part arcane rumination on the nature of sound. In her very first sentence, Oram declares her intention not to write another sober academic textbook, and in this aim she succeeds. Instead, she gives us a discursive mix, including hand-drawn diagrams, technical explanation, quotes from Montaigne, ancient Chinese symbols, and wistful musings on life and art. If the text in any sense represents Oram's inner life, it reveals an eccentric, original woman of eclectic interests, a freelance scholar. Reading it, you can see how Oram went from being an important motivating force in British electronic music to a marginalized figure. Not surprisingly, it didn't sell well, and soon disappeared into obscurity.

By the time the book was published it appears that Oram had all but given up composing, or if she was still composing nobody heard what she was coming up with. Most of her energy was expended on trying to perfect the Oramics system. Electronic music was now becoming mainstream and synthesizer technology condemning to obsolescence the test oscillators and tape that Oram's generation worked with. Working alone and afraid of others stealing her ideas, Oram drifted away from the expanding community of electronic musicians, and without further financial backing and the involvement of anyone else, the Oramics system never achieved its full potential. When computers became sufficiently powerful, Oram began working on a digital version, but two strokes in the 1990s ended her working life. Dolia Derbyshire visited Oram for a while after the older woman had moved into a nursing home, but the friendship fell apart in acrimony. Daphne Oram died in the nursing home in 2003.

The sequestered artist/scientist working on alone in her tower may be a romantic image, but a background hum of missed opportunity sounds through Oram's later life. She never fully realized her vision of drawn sound and her experiments occupied her to the extent that she stopped creating music. The dismantled and non-functioning Oramics machine was retrieved by Goldsmiths College, which curates Oram's archive. When displayed in London's Science Museum from 2011 it was apparent, even in its unrestored form, that it never progressed beyond the working prototype stage. Oram kept trying to raise further funds, but didn't succeed. A handwritten note on her file at the Gulbenkian Foundation, dated 16 November 1973, records that Oram had made a recent approach asking for further funds. The writer of the note records that she or he told Oram she had 'no chance' of securing another grant and commented that Oram, although nice, was 'not terribly businesslike'.[183]

A similar background hum runs through Derbyshire's last decades. She continued to work at the BBC into the 1970s and was briefly enamoured of synthesizers, buying an EMS VCS 3 and developing an affinity for the Workshop's massive EMS modular system, only to see that particular utopia fade into frustration. She found the technology in some ways more restrictive and less controllable than the laborious tape splicing she was used to. By the late 1990s digital synthesizers and software could do what she always wanted technology to do, but by then it was too late for her. Working constantly on commissions coming in at short notice, which were then often changed at the last moment, she was gradually worn down and left the Radiophonic Workshop in 1973:

I didn't want to compromise my integrity any further. I was fed up with having my stuff turned down because it was too sophisti-cated, and yet it was lapped up when I played it to anyone outside the BBC.[184]

According to Hodgson, her friend and colleague for many years:

Delia always said she liked the preparation, the concept, the planning. She just found it very difficult to get those concepts through in a manner she liked. She just thought, 'What's the point in doing all this planning when you can't actually do what's in your mind.' The tragedy was that by the time the sort of equipment came along that Delia would have absolutely reveled in she was no longer capable of picking up the technology.[185]

When she left the BBC Derbyshire worked briefly with Hodgson at his Electrophon Studio before drifting away from music. Stories of her later years reveal a sad decline. Chaotic, volatile and alcoholic, she moved from job to job and house to house, hoarding newspapers and obsessively writing notes. There was a brief, unsuccessful marriage. For two decades few beyond the world of *Doctor Who* fan conventions recognized her contribution to music. However, in the 1990s a new generation of electronic musicians embraced her and a cult began to develop. Derbyshire conformed exactly to the requirements for a troubled lost genius: pioneering work, alcoholism, a mercurial personality, decades of creative silence, a seemingly wilful slide into obscurity. A 1997 interview broadcast on BBC Radio Scotland gives some insight into her state of mind as this reassessment of her work was underway.[186] With much nervous and probably drunken giggling she told stories of her life in music, revealing occasional flashes of an opinionated, forceful, uncompromising temperament. She seemed to be relishing the attention, enjoying the role of elder stateswoman, and beginning to believe the myth growing up around her.

That myth posits a capricious, beautiful, forgotten pioneer of electronic pop, hemmed in and ultimately crushed by establishment forces. Like most myths it contains much truth, but is reductionist. Her achievements were considerable, but by most accounts she was her own worst enemy, her temperament eating away at her talent just as much as the circumstances in which she found herself restrained it. Those circumstances – the vast, slow moving machine of the BBC – did provide her with opportunities, facilities and an audience that she would never have found anywhere else. And although she bridled at what she considered unreasonable BBC deadlines, once that structure was removed, her musical career soon ended. In later life her interest in music never waned, but there was little to show for it. The British musician Pete Kember (Sonic Boom, of Spacemen 3) befriended her toward the end and the pair did dabble with software and synthesizers together. How much music they made and the extent of Derbyshire's contribution to it remains unclear. She died of renal failure in 2001.

Hodgson himself left the BBC in late 1972 to start Electrophon, an electronic music studio, and recorded several synthesizer albums. He returned in 1978 as organizer, then, on Briscoe's retirement in 1984, as head, remaining there until 1995. Like Hodgson and Derbyshire, John Baker remained at the BBC into the 1970s, and combined his work at the Radiophonic Workshop with much extra-curricular activity. Over-work may have contributed to a growing tendency to drink heavily. He had a breakdown in 1970 and was edged out on account of his unreliability in 1974. He never worked again, and died on the Isle of Wight in 1997.

Under Hodgson's stewardship during his second tenure the BBC Radiophonic Workshop itself was re-equipped as a midi studio and thrived once again. At the time much midi, sampling and computer equipment was extremely expensive and only available to well-funded professional studios, which by this time the workshop was. It was just like the early days of the synthesizer, with most of the means of production in the hands of a small elite. But history repeated itself and as the decade wore on the equipment got cheaper, smaller and more readily available. It became possible to build a home studio with modest resources, and this became the natural habitat of the television soundtrack composer. There was no longer a need for a specialist establishment like the Radiophonic Workshop, and its doors were finally closed for good in 1998. In its 40 years it completed nearly 6,000 separate projects, from single-line radio indents to multi-episode television series. From the beginning it kept copies of its work and often the radiophonic soundtracks to television programmes survive even though the visual element was lost decades ago. Composer Mark Ayres took on the considerable task of organizing this archive, contained on thousands of reels of flaking, fragile tape. Many of these he snatched from the jaws of oblivion, retrieving them from a BBC anteroom where they were awaiting disposal.

EMS synthesizers started the 1970s brightly, with the VCS 3 becoming popular in Britain at least, though much less so in America, where it was sold as the Putney. EMS did things the other way round from Moog, starting with a small synthesizer and building up to much larger and more complex instruments. Many more EMS products appeared through the 1970s, including the Synthi 100, the equivalent of a Moog modular system. One of these found its way to the BBC Radiophonic Workshop, where it was known as the Delaware. Although Peter Zinovieff remained in charge of the company, for him it was always a sideline. He reserved his passion for the studio, which moved from the garden in Putney into the house when he bought the building next door and knocked through. Then it went to a manor house in Great Milton, Oxfordshire. By the end of the 1970s Zinovieff's marriage had broken up and he was out of money. EMS went bankrupt in 1979 and the company passed through several hands before Robin Wood acquired it in 1995, having worked for all incarnations of the company since 1970. The studio was moved back to London and put into storage in a basement at the National Theatre, a few miles along the south bank of the Thames from where it had started its life. Water got into the room and the equipment was destroyed. Zinovieff retired from music for many years, though he has recently started work again. When interviewed for this book in September 2011 he was working on a radio piece called 'Horse', a collaboration with the poet Katrina Porteous, which was broadcast on BBC Radio 3 in November of that year. All of Zinovieff's music for the piece was assembled from the sounds of a chain ferry that crosses the River Fal in Cornwall. Not far away, in a barn near Truro, Wood still sells EMS VCS 3s built to original specifications.

Tristram Cary remained productive and active into old age. In 1974 he moved to Australia, teaching at Adelaide University until 1986. He then returned to freelance composition, taking commissions until his death in 2008. British electronic musician and archivist Mark Ayres, who knew Cary and worked with him on compiling an album of his *Doctor Who* music, identified ambivalence in Cary about his career:

He really wanted to be a serious music composer – he wanted to be taken seriously for his concert work – and he was deadly serious about electronic music. He resented his success as a media composer, he felt it was prostituting his art to put food on the table.[187]

Ayres suggests that one of the reasons Cary left Britain to take up an academic post in Australia was to get away from media composition.

As an academic he would, by definition, be taken seriously; he'd have a regular income; and he'd be able to compose his serious music in his spare time. The frustration of what you really want to do not being commercially viable is a common experience to many creative people, yet through all the compromises it entailed Cary was able to keep working without being consumed by bitterness or overwhelmed by disappointment. Brian Hodgson considers Cary the nicest person he encountered in electronic music.[188]

Barry Gray continued to collaborate with Gerry Anderson, composing and orchestrating music for a live-action series, *UFO*, and the first series of another, *Space: 1999*. This was his last substantial professional engagement. He had moved to Guernsey, in the Channel Islands, while working on *UFO* and here he saw out his days in semi-retirement. He found a new home for his ageing collection of electronic instruments in a studio he built in a former German bunker dating from the wartime occupation, 15 feet underground. He played piano in the restaurant at the Government House Hotel and from time to time took along his Ondes Martenot. He died in 1984, and sometime after his studio equipment, instruments, tape archive and papers were moved to a garage in Chelsea. There they remained until Gray's family contacted an Anderson enthusiast named Ralph Titterton in the early 1990s, having seen an article about Gray he had written in *Record Collector* magazine. Titterton and his partner Cathy Ford were tasked with putting Gray's archive in order. They retrieved Gray's Ondes Martenot and passed it to the film composer Francois Evans, who restored it and uses it in his own work.

Much of Fred Judd's electronic music was compiled on a Studio G library album *Electronic Age* (1970), from where it found its way into various television programmes, including *The Tomorrow People*. By now Judd was drifting away from electronic music, and by the time of his last book on the subject, *Electronics in Music*, a note of disillusionment can be detected in his writing. He died in 1992, his music forgotten. Desmond Leslie seems to have abandoned electronic music in the early 1960s. He went on to write several more eccentric books, and then restored the family home of Castle Leslie. He died in 2001.

A French composer, Jean Ledrut, claimed that Joe Meek plagiarized the tune of 'Telstar' from a piece he had written for a film called *Austerlitz* (1960). He sued, and Meek's royalties were frozen while the case dragged on for several years. This put Meek's fragile mind under increasing stress, as did an arrest for importuning and increased drug use. There were more hits, but Meek's career faltered as tastes changed. On 3 February 1967 Meek argued with his landlady and shot her dead before turning the gun on himself.

The part-time thereminist Samuel Hoffman did less work from the mid-1950s onwards, though he never stopped completely. His oeuvre extends way beyond his best-known film work and the trilogy of albums he recorded in the 1940s, encompassing some heart-rending religious music and even rock 'n' roll. One of Hoffman's last appearances was with Captain Beefheart on the 1967 album *Safe as Milk*, where he appears on two tracks, 'Electricity' and 'Autumn's Child'. Hoffman died later that year.

After 10 years in America, Jean-Jacques Perrey returned to France in 1970. He was disappointed to find that his success overseas meant little at home and he had to start all over again. He ended up with a portfolio career including writing music for ballet, recording a series of library music albums, playing piano in restaurants and working at Radio Luxembourg, while never really recovering the momentum he had built up while based in New York. The Ondioline was obsolete, and despite efforts by its inventor Georges Jenny to update it by using transistors and a restyled cabinet, no one was interested anymore and it was forgotten. Perrey himself was forgotten too, spending the 1980s in retirement, but then the samplers found him. In 1990 Gang Starr borrowed from Perrey's 1970 track 'E. V. A.' and the Frenchman was rediscovered and reappraised by a new generation, leading to a protracted Indian summer second career. There was a lengthy interview in the book *Incredibly Strange Music, Volume 11*, reissues of the Vanguard recordings, live appearances and a succession of new recordings. On some of these Perrey collaborated with Dana Countryman, his biographer, picking up where he left off with the 1960s Vanguard albums, making instrumental pop with the Moog and the Ondioline.

The various proponents of 1960s self-build electronica, including Silver Apples, Fifty Foot Hose and The United States of America, were prophets without honour in their homeland, or any other land for that matter. They all had short careers, most ending before the decade was out. The CD reissue boom of the 1990s saw their once-hopelessly obscure albums made available again for new audiences, which were often considerably bigger and more enthusiastic than their original ones.

Joseph Byrd of The United States of America did manage to continue a low-profile, intermittent career in music. He made albums of synthesizer music and co-produced Ry Cooder's *Jazz* album. He is currently a teacher. The British band Broadcast is one of several contemporary acts to hail his influence. After The United States of America split up Richard Durrett took back his synthesizer. Neither has been heard of since.

Simeon Coxe gave up music in 1970 after financial pressures forced Silver Apples to split. He stored the Simeon under a house in Mobile, Alabama, during the 1970s. Hurricane Frederic swept the house away in 1979, taking the Simeon with it. Coxe worked as an artist for many years. In the mid-1990s he discovered by chance that the Silver Apples albums had a cult following amongst a new generation of musicians. This prompted a re-engagement with music and a subsequent low-profile career performing and recording once again under the Silver Apples name, helped by the endorsement of Damon Albarn from Blur. Despite a serious road accident in 1998 after a reunion gig with drummer Danny Taylor, Coxe remains active. Taylor died in 2005.

Cork Marcheschi gave up playing music professionally when most of Fifty Foot Hose decamped in 1969. He has been an artist ever since. In the 1990s he formed a new incarnation of the band, complete with a revised version of his electronic rig. Marcheschi and Fifty Foot Hose remain active.

With hindsight, Beaver and Krause's albums sound like a forerunner of a particular type of synthesized new age music. They signpost a shift in electronic music, which for so long had been the music of the unknown, the occult, of anxiety and fear, of UFOs and outer space, of comedy. Now it could also be the music of serenity, of peace, meditative and calm. The duo remained active as the 1970s wore on, though with decreasing returns as the need for specialist synthesists declined as synthesizers became readily available. Beaver continued to share enthusiastically his knowledge of electronic music, holding informal classes at his studio and lecturing at schools and colleges.

1n 1975 he suffered a ruptured aneurysm while giving a lecture at a high school and died the following day. Krause moved away from music after Beaver's death and now travels the world recording natural sounds.

In 1970 Berry Gordy came to visit Raymond Scott, accompanied by a large entourage. He was interested in Scott's perpetual work in progress, the Electronium. There was an interest in electronic music at Motown at the time, with representatives of the company approaching Scott Ludwig, formerly of The Sounds of Tomorrow, to ask him if he would consider operating the company's Moog, an offer he declined. Scott moved to California in 1971 and took up the position of Director of Electronic Music Research and Development at Motown, a position he held until 1977. During those years he continued to work on the Electronium, seemingly to little avail. If Motown did make any recordings with it they remain unissued. In 1988 the systems began to shut down for Scott. After years of failing health, including two heart bypass operations, the family ailment caught up with him and a series of heart attacks and strokes left him disabled, unable to work or communicate. He died in 1994. After many years lying forgotten in a garage, the Electronium was rescued by Mark Mothersbaugh of Devo, and is being restored to working order by Darren Davison.

Scott's friend and contemporary Eric Siday predeceased him by many years. He had continued to work on diligently in the 1970s, making widely heard and lucrative commercial electronic music that, an obituary in the *New York Times* noted, was as well known as the products it promoted. Siday himself, ever the quiet man of electronic music, remained an obscure figure. He died of a heart attack in 1976. His music was used on television for many years after his death, but so far has escaped the attentions of reissue labels. Scott had once been famous, but in the last decades of his life he too had become obscure. In contrast to Siday, his legacy has been attentively curated. A lavish double CD and book package called *Manhattan Research Inc* collected many previously unissued recordings and was followed by reissues of the *Soothing Sounds for Baby* series. In 2010 Stan Warnow, Scott's son by his first marriage, released the aforementioned documentary about his father, *Deconstructing Dad*.

Louis and Bebe Barron broke up in 1969 and divorced in 1970. Although some accounts report that they continued to work together after the divorce, their son Adam Barron thinks that they composed little new work. Instead, they occasionally cultivated their legacy, doing interviews, attending science fiction conventions, and releasing the *Forbidden Planet* soundtrack music on album several times, starting in 1976.

Despite their connection with John Cage, the Barrons escaped serious critical attention until film studies scholars began to reassess *Forbidden Planet* in the 1980s. Even then they remained on the fringes of the academic electronic music community. From 1985 to 1987 Bebe served as the first Secretary of the Society for Electro-Acoustic Music in the United States. An article in *Keyboard* magazine from 1986 has a photo of the couple in their studio. Louis and Bebe, older and greyer, were still surrounded by the same equipment they'd been using for 30 years, now relocated from the Greenwich Village apartment to a garage in California. Like Bjorn Borg making his comeback with a wooden tennis racket, they hadn't been able to move on, and they could no longer compete. In the article they talk ambivalently about synthesizers and computers. Louis Barron died of cancer three years later. Bebe Barron didn't compose for a decade, but in 1999 she was invited to create a new work at the University of California, using the latest digital technology. *Mixed Emotions*, completed in 2000, sounded remarkably similar to the *Forbidden Planet* music. She died in 2008.

Two men whose names had become almost synonymous with phases of early electronic music, Leon Theremin and Bob Moog, met in 1991. Theremin had left America and gone home to Moscow in 1938 after a decade of celebrity. In the West he was assumed dead for years after, but by the mid-1960s rumours began to filter through that Theremin was still alive. The truth was that he spent fifty years subject to the vicissitudes of the Soviet regime, falling in and out of favour with the authorities while working on state-sponsored electronics projects including listening devices. After the Iron Curtain fell in 1989, Theremin, now in his nineties, was found living in penury in Moscow, 'with all of his life's work and belongings distilled down into this little heap of furniture and icons sitting around this sad little room'.[189] The man who had once demonstrated his invention to Lenin had lived through the entire Soviet era, in the process outlasting the other electronic instrument inventors from the early twentieth century who owed him a debt. Georges Jenny had died in 1975, while Maurice Martenot, who had continued to oversee the limited manufacture of Ondes Martenots, was killed in a road traffic accident in 1980 four days before his 82nd birthday.

Theremin returned to America after more than half a century away at the invitation of John Chowning, who amongst other things is the inventor of FM synthesis, and the filmmaker Steve Martin, who was making a documentary about Theremin. Martin dated his fascination with the theremin to when he watched *The Day the Earth Stood Still* as a boy.

On 27 September 1991 at Stanford University's Frost Amphitheater a concert was given in Theremin's honour. A crowd of 1,500 gave the old man a standing ovation of several minutes when he was presented with the Stanford Centennial Medal. Among them were many of America's pioneering synthesizer makers, including Don Buchla and Moog. Theremin died in November 1993 at the age of 97, the day after Martin's film *Theremin: An Electronic Odyssey*, was first broadcast on British television, on Channel 4.

Although Moog the man started the 1970s preeminent in the synthesizer world, the decade was not an altogether happy one for him professionally. Always more an ideas man than a businessman, he gradually lost control of his own company, which had been renamed Moog Music in 1972, finally leaving in 1977. The company itself struggled on in the face of increasing domestic and international pressure before going bankrupt in 1986.

After leaving the eponymous company Moog went back to where he started and began making theremins again under the Big Briar name. He consulted to Kurzweil Music Systems, lectured, and gave many interviews to the music technology press. The original Moog instruments fell out of favour in the 1980s as dozens of cheaper, smaller and more versatile Japanese synthesizers succeeded each other on the market with bewildering speed. For a few years in the middle of the 1980s you could pick up a Minimoog for a song. This didn't last, though, as a new generation of musicians, particularly dance musicians, came to appreciate the sounds of the analogue generation of synthesizers. The price of second-hand Moogs rose and the name itself recovered something of the allure it had in 1970. In 2002 Big Briar won the rights to manufacture under the Moog name and promptly launched the Minimoog Voyager, an update of the original Minimoog. Bob Moog had the satisfaction of seeing his name on his instruments once again, even if most customers mispronounced it. He died in 2005.

Moog was an engineer and an inventor who thought like an artist and a visionary. He had a technical background, but he also had a spark of intuition. Both facets surfaced in Moog's last years, as the man who had done so much to make electronic instruments accessible, practical and usable for musicians, the man who had humanized the circuits began talking of them in almost-mystical terms. In *Moog*, a 2004 documentary by Hans Fjellestad, there is some something faintly otherworldly about him, with his kindly face topped with a head of snowy hair. He drives around the countryside in a battered station wagon hand-painted with bright, child-like flowers and rocks on a chair on his porch, making gnomic pronouncements. Waving his arms above his head, he talks about the ideas coming from 'out there' and 'through' him: 'I can feel what's going on in a piece of electronic equipment,' he says.

Notes

1 *Moog*, by Hans Fjellestad, 2004.
2 Jay Williston, 'Thaddeus Cahill's Teleharmonium', http://www.synthmuseum.com/magazine/0102jw.html (Accessed May 2012).
3 'Magic Music from the Telharmonium', *New York Times*, 16 December 1906.
4 'Twain and the Telephone', *New York Times*, 23 December 1906 and 'Mark Twain and Twin Cheer New Year's Party', *New York Times*, 1 January 1907.
5 *The Guardian*, 2 January 1907.
6 'An Invisible Rival for the Hurdy Gurdy', *New York Times*, 12 January 1907.
7 *Review of Reviews*, April 1906.
8 British Pathé, 1934.
9 'Listeners to Hear the Martenot with the Inventor at the Keyboard', *New York Times*, 4 January 1931.
10 'Piano-Like Device Uses Radio Tubes', *New York Times*, 14 December 1930.
11 'Better Music from the Air', *The Guardian*, 9 June 1928.
12 'Martenot Plays his Ondium for the BBC', *The Guardian*, 20 April 1947.
13 Young and Vail, *The Hammond Organ*.
14 'The Solovox Owners (Model L Solovox)', Hammond Instrument Company.
15 Constant Martin published a book in 1950 titled *Musique électronique de l'instrument de musique le plus simple aux orgues électroniques, amélioration d'instruments classiques, cloches électroniques, constructions pratiques*.
16 In October 1956, when the Selmer Clavioline still had another 8 years of its production life to run, the company was placing adverts claiming sales of more than 7,000 units.
17 'Music from the Air', *The Guardian*, 20 June 1934.
18 *Downbeat*, 1951.

19 Novachord is featured in the soundtracks to *Our Man Flint*, *In Like Flint* and *The Satan Bug*.

20 Audio tapes of Rózsa speaking about his career, made by Alan Hamer circa 1975, later used as source material for his autobiography, *Double Life*.

21 Rózsa/Hamer audio tapes.

22 *Radio Life*, 14 April 1946.

23 Tiomkin was a Novachord user, employing the instrument to bolster strings in many scores.

24 Shure also played theremin on the 1996 film *Batman Returns*.

25 Smith, *A Heart at Fire's Centre*.

26 Steve Rubin, *Cinefantastique*, vol. 4 no. 4, 1976.

27 *Radio and Television News*, January 1954.

28 Countryman, *Passport to the Future*.

29 *Masterworks from France*, programme no. 428. New French Instruments presented at the Brussels World's Fair. GRC 5394.

30 *New York Times*, 16 November 1968.

31 Toward the end of her life Bebe Barron was interviewed by Susan Stone for NPR (7 February 2005). In this interview she gave this account of the gift, though in other earlier interviews she sometimes referred to a friend, not a cousin.

32 3M started life as a mining company at the beginning of the 20th century, but began manufacturing magnetic tape as the direct result of being diverted into researching and producing materials for defence during World War II.

33 Burman, *Projections 7*.

34 Adam Barron, son of Louis and Bebe, has located copies of all of the records listed, but has not found or ever heard of anyone else finding a copy of a Tennessee Williams record, although Bebe did mention recording Williams in interviews she gave late in her life.

35 E-mail to author, 23 May 2011.

36 Juno and Vale, *Incredibly Strange Music Volume 2*.

37 Burman, *Projections 7*.

38 *Los Angeles Times*, 26 February 1956.

39 Undated resumé supplied by Adam Barron.

40 Ted Greenwald, *Keyboard 12* 1986.

41 Schary, *Heyday*.

42 Frederick S Clarke and Steve Rubin, *Cinefantastique*, vol. 8 nos 2 and 3, 1979.

43 *Current Population Reports* (Consumer Income US Department of Commerce/Bureau of the Census, April 1957).

44 Juno and Vale, *Incredibly Strange Music Volume 2*.

45 Clarke and Rubin, *Cinefantastique*.

46 *Films in Review*, April 1956.

47 Greenwald, *Keyboard 12*.

48 Ibid.

49 Burman, *Projections 7*.

50 *Variety*, 27 March 1957.

51 'Space Monsters', *The Guardian*, 10 June 1956.

52 *New York Times*, 4 May 1956.

53 Undated resumé provided by Adam Barron.

54 Author's interview, 12 January 2012.

55 Greenwald, *Keyboard 12*.

56 Burman, *Projections 7*.

57 Bernstein, *The San Francisco Tape Music Center*.

58 Information about Tristram Cary's early life is drawn from an unpublished autobiography, excerpts of which were provided by John Cary.

59 Information provided by Elizabeth Wells, Archives and Records Manager, Westminster School, April 2011.

60 Information provided by Sherborne Old Girls Office, April 2011.

61 Author's interview, 28 July 2004.

62 Andrew Pixley, liner notes to *The Quatermass Collection* (BBC DVD, 2005).

63 *The Composer: Journal of the Composers' Guild of Great Britain*, Spring 1962.

64 Briscoe and Curtis-Bramwell, *The BBC Radiophonic Workshop – The First 25 Years* (BBC, 1983).

65 Jo Hutton, 'Radiophonic Ladies', http://web.archive.org/web/20060517133312/http://www.sonicartsnetwork.org/ARTICLES/ARTICLE2000JoHutton.html (Last accessed January 2012).

66 Author's interview, 6 March 2011.

67 For a detailed account of the genesis and realization of the *Doctor Who* theme, see http://ourworld.compuserve.com/homepages/Mark_Ayres/DWTheme.htm (Last accessed November 2011).

68 *Boazine 7*, Scottish fanzine, circa late 1990s.

69 Information provided by Hannah Westall, archivist at Girton College, Cambridge, May 2011.

70 Author's interview, 6 March 2011. The book in question was *Electronic Music and Musique Concrète* by F. C. Judd (Neville Spearman, 1961).

71 Jo Hutton, 'Radiophonic Ladies', http://web.archive.org/web/ 20060517133312/http://www.sonicartsnetwork.org/ARTICLES/ ARTICLE2000JoHutton.html (Last accessed January 2012).

72 *SoundTrack*, September 1993. Interview conducted by Randall D. Larson in 1982.

73 Fragment of recorded autobiography on www.barrygray.co.uk (Last accessed May 2012). Much information about Gray's early life comes from this source and a written biography on the same website.

74 Author interview with Jocelyn Goodey, employee of The Miller Organ Company, who visited Barry Gray's home studio several times in the 1960s to service his Spinetta. 1 June 2011.

75 *SoundTrack*, September 1993.

76 Ibid.

77 Some of Eric Siday's electronic music was used for the first episode of this story.

78 Interview with Irwin Chusid, 1993, *Manhattan Research Inc* CD book (Basta Records, 2000).

79 http://RaymondScott.com/jjperrey.html.

80 Track 23, CD 1 of *Manhattan Research Inc* features Scott talking about this event

81 Track 17 CD 1 and track 7 CD 1, *Manhattan Research Inc.*

82 *Manhattan Research Inc.* Jeff Winner confirmed in an e-mail dated 1 February 2012: 'I transcribed those quotes from an audio recording of an electronic music lecture Raymond Scott presented in Chicago on July 31, 1962.'

83 Information about Eric Siday's early life was provided by Kathryn Adamson, librarian at The Royal Academy of Music, from Academy archives. 22 November 2011.

84 *Variety*, 5 July 1947.

85 'Composers: Swurpledeewurpledeezeech!' *Time*, 4 November 1966.

86 *Billboard*, 9 March 1957.

87 'Composers: Swurpledeewurpledeezeech!' *Time*, 4 November 1966.

88 Rhea was researching his PhD dissertation, *The Evolution of Electronic Musical Instruments in the United States* (1972). He visited Siday, Raymond Scott and Wendy Carlos at the suggestion of Bob Moog.

89 When writing this book I mentioned in passing the advert to an American friend, born in the 1950s and resident in England since the 1980s. He immediately knew the music, and was able to hum it from memory.

90 *Musique Electronique*, 78-rpm disc of library music released on Inter-Art Music Publishers, London.

91 E-mail to author from Tom Rhea, 9 December 2011.

92 Correspondence dated 29 June 1965 and 22 July 1965, held in the Eric Siday Archives, New York Public Library.

93 US Patent 2,871,745.

94 *Manhattan Research Inc* CD book.

95 The Electronium is owned by Mark Motherbaugh of Devo. It is being restored by Darren Davison, who has supplied much of the technical detail in this book about how the machine works.

96 E-mail to author, 23 February 2012.

97 Raymond Scott, *The Raymond Scott Electronium*. Short paper dated May 1970, provided by Darren Davison.

98 *Deconstructing Dad* by Stan Warnow, 2010.

99 E-mail to author, 9 December 2011.

100 Scott, *The Raymond Scott Electronium*.

101 Ibid.

102 Bruce Haack, interview on Canadian Radio CKUA (1970). Included as a bonus track on a reissue of *The Electric Lucifer* (Omni Recording Corporation, 2007).

103 E-mail to author, 23 February 2012.

104 E-mail to author, 9 December 2011.

105 *Manhattan Research Inc* CD book.

106 Author's interview, 14 February 2012.

107 *Manhattan Research Inc* CD book.

108 Author's interview, 14 February 2012.

109 *Manhattan Research Inc* CD book.

110 *New York Times*, 15 March 1959.

111 Copland, *The New Music 1900/60*.

112 Author's interview, 30 January 2004.

113 Author's interview, 9 February 2004.

114 Undated letter to author from Chris Kachulis, received November 2011.

115 Badman, *The Beach Boys*.

116 Pinch and Trocco *Analog Days*.

117 Author's interview, 23 January 2004.

118 Author's interview, 6 July 2004.

119 From essay supplied by Joseph Byrd to Sundazed Records, 2002.

120 Author's interview, 6 July 2004.

121 From essay supplied by Joseph Byrd to Sundazed Records, 2002.

122 Author's interview, 1 December 2011.

123 E-mail to author, 16 December 2011.

124 Author's interview, 1 December 2011.

125 *Ptolemaic Terrascope* fanzine, 1997.

126 Author's interview, 1 December 2011.

127 Randall D Larson, interview conducted March 1983, published in *The Cue Sheet*, January 2005.

128 Jim Miller, *Rolling Stone*, 22 June 1968.

129 Author's interview, 5 March 2012.

130 In 2005 I researched and co-produced a The Sounds of Tomorrow compilation on RPM records (RPM 300), which assembled previously unavailable archive recordings of the band. Ludwig passed on this story to me in a conversation I had with him when researching the liner notes.

131 *Zigzag* no. 30, March 1973.

132 Letter from R. A. Moog to H. Deutsch, 11 February 1964. http://moogarchives.com (Accessed May 2012).

133 R. A. Moog, *Journal of the Audio Engineering Society*, vol. 13 no. 3, July 1965, pp. 200–206.

134 Vail, *Vintage Synthesizers*.

135 Pinch and Trocco, *Analog Days*.

136 http://www.moogfoundation.org/2010/mooghistory-unveiled-brian-kehew-explores-1965-r-a-moog-co-electronic-music-workshop/ (Last accessed February 2012).

137 *Moog 900 Series Electronic Music Systems*, demonstration record, 1967.

138 *Electronic Music Composition – Performance Equipment*. Catalogue published by RA Moog Co. 1967.

139 E-mail to author, 3 November 2011.

140 Sherk, *Paul Beaver*.

141 E-mail to author, 30 November 2011.

142 Jerry Goldsmith, *Variety*, 14 October 1997.

143 Richie Unterberger. Liner notes for *The Zodiac: Cosmic Sounds*, Elektra/Runt 2002.

144 E-mail to author, 30 November 2011.

145 In time musicians discovered that one way to make the Moog's tuning more stable was to leave it turned on for a long time. Reportedly, Beaver got into the habit of leaving his instrument on 24 hours a day.

146 E-mail to author, 30 November 2011.

147 Hjort, *So You Want to be a Rock 'n' Roll Star*.

148 Ibid.

149 Sandoval, *The Monkees*.

150 Manzarek, *Light My Fire*.

151 Countryman, *Passport to the Future*.

152 Undated letter to author, received November 2011.

153 The original Buchla Box still resides at Mills College, the Center's home from 1966.

154 *Gramophone*, January 1969 and August 1972.

155 Author's interview, 12 September 2011.

156 Ibid.

157 *The Guardian*, 15 January 1973.

158 Author's interview, 12 September 2011.

159 Author's interview, 30 June 2004.

160 *Boazine* 7, circa late 1990s.

161 Author's interview, 28 July 2004.

162 Delia Derbyshire obituary, *The Guardian*, 7 July 2001.

163 'Engineering Music', *The Guardian*, 15 March 1962.

164 Daphne Oram. Sleeve note for *Electronic Sound Patterns* (His Master's Voice, 1962).

165 Session and broadcast information supplied by Ralph Titterton, 25 January 2005.

166 Liner notes to reissue of *SF Sorrow* (Snapper, 1998).

167 'Electronic Music', *The Guardian*, 14 May 1963.

168 'Electronic Music', *The Guardian*, 16 January 1968.

169 *Gramophone*, April 1969.

170 'The Mono Fade Out', *The Guardian*, 3 March 1969.

171 Donal Henahan, 'Switching on to Mock Bach', *New York Times*, 2 November 1968.

172 *Time*, 7 March 1969.

173 'Is George's the Only Moog in the Country?', *Melody Maker*, 15 November 1969.

174 *Tomorrow's World*, 30 September 1969.

175 http://erman.iobloggo.com/archive.php?eid=33 (Accessed May 2012).

176 Hanson, *The Nice*.

177 Ibid.

178 The letter from Walter Sear, dated 16 January 1970, is reproduced in Vail, *Vintage Synthesizers*.

179 'Moog Jazz in the Garden', *Audio*, November 1969.

180 'Is George's the Only Moog in the Country?', *Melody Maker*, 15 November 1969.

181 Vail, *Vintage Synthesizers*.

182 'Introducing... the Mini Moog Model D', advert by RA Moog Inc, 1970.

183 Gulbenkian Foundation archive file, e-mailed to author, 6 June 2011.

184 *Surface*, American art and culture fanzine, May 2000.

185 Author's interview, 30 June 2004.

186 BBC Radio Scotland interview with John Cavanagh, October 1997.

187 Author's interview, 6 May 2011.

188 Author's interview, 6 March 2011.

189 Albert Glinsky, speaking on BBC Radio 4, 21 October 2004.

Watch and listen

Chapter 1

Films

The Birds
Directed by Alfred Hitchcock
1963

Theremin: An Electronic Odyssey
Directed by Steven M. Martin
1994

Recordings

We'll Meet Again
Vera Lynn with Arthur Young on the Novachord
Circa 1939/40

Turangalîla Symphony
Olivier Messiaen
1948

The Art of the Theremin
Clara Rockmore
1992

Other

Newsreel clip of Leon Theremin demonstrating the theremin in
London, 1927

Newsreel clip of Georges Jenny demonstrating the Ondioline in Germany, 1948

Chapter 2

Films

Rebecca
Directed by Alfred Hitchcock
1940

The Maltese Falcon
Directed by John Huston
1941

The Lost Weekend
Directed by Billy Wilder
1945

Spellbound
Directed by Alfred Hitchcock
1945

The Red House
Directed by Demer Daves
1947

Rocketship X-M
Directed by Kurt Neumann
1950

The Day the Earth Stood Still
Directed by Robert Wise
1951

The Thing from Another World
Directed by Christian Nyby
1951

Spartacus
Directed by Stanley Kubrick
1960

Recordings

Music Out of the Moon/Perfume Set to Music/Music for Peace of Mind
Dr Samuel J. Hoffman
Released 1947–50; reissued 1999

L'âme des Poètes
Charles Trenet
1951

Song of the Second Moon
Electrosonics (Tom Dissevelt and Kid Baltan)
1957

Mr Ondioline
Jean-Jacques Perrey (as *Mr Ondioline*)
1960

Television

You Asked For It
Appearance by Samuel Hoffman
1953

Dutch television excerpt of Tom Dissevelt and Kid Baltan, 1959

Other

British Pathé newsreel footage of Musaire, 1937

Newsreel footage of Martin Taubman, 1938

Poème électronique
Edgard Varèse
1958

Chapter 3

Films

Bells of Atlantis
Directed by Ian Hugo
Circa 1953

Jazz of Lights
Directed by Ian Hugo
1954

Forbidden Planet
Directed by Fred M. Wilcox
1956

Bridges go Round
Directed by Shirley Clarke
1958

Space Boy
Directed by Florence Marly
1973

Recordings

Williams Mix
John Cage
1953

Seduction through Witchcraft
By Louise Huebner
1969

Chapter 4

Films

The Delian Mode
Directed by Kara Blake
2009

Practical Electronica
Directed By Ian Helliwell
2011

Recordings

Time Beat/Waltz in Orbit
Ray Cathode (BBC Radiophonic Orchestra)
1962

Telstar
The Tornados
1962

BBC Radiophonic Music
(various BBC Radiophonic Workshop composers)
1968

The Radiophonic Workshop
(various BBC Radiophonic Workshop composers)
1974

I Hear a New World
Joe Meek
1991 (recorded circa 1959/60)

Music of the Future
Desmond Leslie
2005

Oramics
Daphne Oram
2007

Soundings: Electroacoustic Works 1955–96
Tristram Cary
2008

BBC Radiophonic Workshop: A Retrospective
(various BBC Radiophonic Workshop composers)
2008

Stand By For Action! – The Music of Barry Gray
Barry Gray
2009

It's Time for Tristram Cary
Tristram Cary
2010

Stand By for Adverts: Rare Jingles, Jazz and Advertising Electronics
Barry Gray
2011

Electronics Without Tears
F. C. Judd
2012

Television

Quatermass and the Pit
1958/59

Space Patrol (also known as *Planet Patrol*)
1963

Doctor Who
From 1963

Chapter 5

Films

Deconstructing Dad
Directed by Stan Warnow
2010

Recordings

Manhattan Research Inc.
Raymond Scott
2000

Soothing Sound for Baby volumes 1, 2 and 3
Raymond Scott
1964

Sounds of Now Volumes 1 and 2
Eric Siday
1971

Television

Maxwell House 'perking coffee pot' advert, from 1960
Screen Gems identitone, from 1965

Chapter 6

Films

Strait-Jacket
Directed by William Castle
1964

Recordings

Music for Heavenly Bodies
Andre Montero and his Orchestra, featuring Paul Tanner
1958

Runaway
Del Shannon
1961

Music from Outer Space
Andre Montero and his Orchestra, featuring Paul Tanner
1962

Mondo Cane, No. 2
Kai Winding
1963

Soul Surfin'
Kai Winding
1963

Good Vibrations
The Beach Boys
1966

I Just Wasn't Made for These Times
The Beach Boys
1966

The In Sound from Way Out
Kingsley–Perrey (Gershon Kingsley and Jean-Jacques Perrey)
1966

No Time Like the Right Time
Blues Project
1967

Wild Honey
The Beach Boys
1967

Cauldron
Fifty Foot Hose
1967

Crucifixion
Phil Ochs
1967

Presenting ... Lothar & The Hand People
Lothar and The Hand People
1968

Silver Apples
Silver Apples
1968

Tome V1
Gil Mellé
1968

The United States of America
The United States of America
1968

The Way-Out Record for Children
Miss Nelson and Bruce (Haack)
1968

Contact
Silver Apples
1969

The Electronic Record for Children
Bruce Haack
1969

Space Hymn
Lothar and The Hand People
1969

The Electric Lucifer
Bruce Haack
1970

The Sounds of Tomorrow
The Sounds of Tomorrow
2005

Television

I've Got a Secret
Appearances by Jean-Jacques Perrey
1960 and 1966

I've Got a Secret
Appearance by Bruce Haack
1966

My Favourite Martian
1963–66

Chapter 7

Films

Magnetic Monster
Directed by Curt Siodmak
1953

Freud
Directed by John Huston
1962

In Harm's Way
Directed by Otto Preminger
1965

Moog
Directed by Hans Fjellestad
2004

Recordings

Kaleidoscopic Vibrations: Spotlight on the Moog
Kingsley-Perrey (Gershon Kingsley and Jean-Jacques Perry)
1967

Pisces, Aquarius, Capricorn & Jones Ltd.
The Monkees
1967

Silver Apples of The Moon for Electronic Music Synthesizer
Morton Subotnick
1967

The Zodiac: Cosmic Sounds
Composed, arranged and conducted by Mort Garson, words by
Jacques Wilson, spoken by Cyrus Faryar
1967

The Amazing New Electronic Pop Sound of Jean-Jacques Perrey
Jean-Jacques Perrey
1968

The Nonesuch Guide to Electronic Music
Paul Beaver and Bernard L. Krause
1968

Notorious Byrd Brothers
The Byrds
1968

Ragnarok Electronic Funk
Beaver and Krause
1969

In a Wild Sanctuary
Beaver and Krause
1970

Chapter 8

Films

The Innocents
Directed by Jack Clayton
1961

Daleks' Invasion Earth 2150 AD
Directed by Gordon Flemyng
1966

Dr. Who and the Daleks
Directed by Gordon Flemyng
1966

Fahrenheit 451
Directed by Francois Truffaut
1966

Island of Terror
Directed by Terence Fisher
1966

Quatermass and the Pit (also known as *Five Million Years to Earth*)
Directed by Roy Ward Baker
1967

Doppelgänger (also known as *Journey to the Far Side of the Sun*)
Directed by Robert Parrish
1969

Performance
Directed by Donald Cammell and Nicolas Roeg
1970

Recordings

Tomorrow Never Knows
The Beatles
1966

Between the Buttons
The Rolling Stones
1967

Carnival of Light
The Beatles
1967

Defecting Grey
The Pretty Things
1967

The Piper at the Gates of Dawn
Pink Floyd
1967

Sgt. Pepper's Lonely Hearts Club Band
The Beatles
1967

Their Satanic Majesties Request
The Rolling Stones
1967

Revolution 9
The Beatles
1968

A Saucerful of Secrets
Pink Floyd
1968

SF Sorrow
The Pretty Things
1968

An Electric Storm
White Noise
1969

The John Baker Tapes Vol 1 and 2
John Baker
2008

Television

Captain Scarlet
1967

Chapter 9

Recordings

Switched-On Bach
Wendy Carlos
1968

Abbey Road
The Beatles
1969

The Age of Electronicus and *Moog: The Electric Eclectics of Dick Hyman*
Dick Hyman
1969

Ceremony
Spooky Tooth/Pierre Henry
1969

Electronic Sound
George Harrison
1969

Moog Power
Hugh Montenegro
1969

The Moog Strikes Bach
Hans Wurman
1969

Music to Moog By
Gershon Kingsley
1969

Switched On Bacharach and *More Switched On Bacharach*
Christopher Scott
1969

Switched-On Rock
The Moog Machine
1969

The Well-Tempered Synthesizer
Wendy Carlos
1969

Lucky Man
Emerson Lake & Palmer
1970

Moog Indigo
Jean-Jacques Perrey
1970

Television

The Same Trade as Mozart
1969

Tomorrow's World
1969

Selected compilations of early electronic music

Ohm+: The Early Gurus of Electronic Music 1948–80
2005

Forbidden Planets – Music from the Pioneers of Electronic Sound
2010

Panorama de Musique Concrète
2010

Forbidden Planets Volume Two
2011

Sources

Interviews*

Mark Ayres, Adam Barron, John Cary, Dana Countryman, Simeon Coxe, Darren Davison, Alan Entenman, Joss Goodey, Alan Hamer, Ian Helliwell, Brian Hodgson, Jac Holzman, Mike Kellie, Bernie Krause, Scott Ludwig, Cork Marcheschi, Ted Pandel, Tom Rhea, Stan Warnow, Jeff Winner, Peter Zinovieff.

Interviews conducted for previous projects: Mark Ayres, Joseph Byrd, Simeon Coxe, Max Crook, Brian Hodgson, Dick Mills, Paul Tanner.

* Interviews include face-to-face conversations, telephone conversations or extended correspondence. More limited correspondence is referenced in the footnotes.

Books

Babiuk, Andy. *Beatles Gear* (revised edition). Backbeat, 2002.
Badman, Keith. *The Beach Boys*. Backbeat, 2004.
Baines, Anthony. *The Oxford Companion to Musical Instruments*. Oxford University Press, 2002.
Bernstein, David W. *The San Francisco Tape Music Center: 1960s Counterculture and the Avant-Garde*. University of California Press, 2008.
Brend, Mark. *Strange Sounds: Offbeat Instruments and Sonic Experiments in Pop*. Backbeat, 2005.
Briscoe, Desmond and Curtis Bramwell, Roy. *The BBC Radiophonic Workshop: The First 25 Years*. BBC Books, 1983.
Burman, Mark. *Projections 7*. Faber & Faber, 1997.
Cleveland, Barry. *Creative Music Production: Joe Meek's Bold Techniques*. Mix Books, 2001.
Copland, Aaron. *The New Music 1900/60*. Macdonald: London, 1968.

Countryman, Dana. *Passport to the Future:The Amazing Life and Music of Electronic Pop Music Pioneer Jean-Jacques Perrey.* Sterling Swan Press, 2010.

Glinsky, Albert. *Theremin: Ether Music and Espionage.* University of Illinois Press, 2005.

Griffiths, Paul. *A Guide to Electronic Music.* Thames and Hudson, 1979.

—*Modern Music: A Concise History* (revised edition). World of Art, 1994.

Hanson, Martyn, *The Nice: Hang On to a Dream* (Helter Skelter, 2002).

Hjort, Christopher. *So You Want To Be a Rock 'n' Roll Star: The Byrds Day-by-Day 1965–73.* Jawbone, 2008.

Holmes, Thom. *Electronic and Experimental Music* (2nd edition). Routledge, 2002.

Holzman, Jac and Daws, Gavan. *Follow the Music.* First Media, 1998.

Houghton, Mick. *Becoming Elektra: The True Story of Jac Holzman's Visionary Record Label.* Jawbone, 2010.

Judd, F. C. *Electronics in Music.* Neville Spearman, 1972

Juno, Andrea and Vale, V. *Incredibly Strange Music Volume 2.* Research, 1994.

Krause, Bernie. *Into a Wild Sanctuary: A Life in Music and Natural Sound.* Heyday Books, 1999.

Lanza, Joseph. *Elevator Music: A Surreal History of Muzak, Easy-Listening, and Other Moodsong.* Quartet Books, 1995.

Lewisohn, Mark. *The Complete Beatles Recording Sessions.* Hamlyn, 1988.

—*The Complete Beatles Chronicle.* Pyramid Books, 1992.

New Grove Dictionary of Musical Instruments, The. Macmillan, 1984.

Mackay, Andy. *Electronic Music.* Phaidon, 1981.

Manzarek, Ray. *Light My Fire: My Life with The Doors.* Berkley, 1997

Niebur, Louis. *Special Sound: The Creation and Legacy of the BBC Radiophonic Workshop.* Oxford University Press, 2010.

Oram, Daphne. *An Individual Note of Music, Sound and Electronics.* Galliard, 1972.

Peel, Ian. *The Unknown Paul McCartney.* Reynolds and Hearn, 2002.

Pinch, Trevor and Bijsterveld, Karin. *The Oxford Handbook of Sound Studies.* Oxford University Press, USA, 2012.

Pinch, Trevor and Trocco, Frank. *Analog Days: The Invention and Impact of the Moog Synthesizer.* Harvard University Press; New Ed edition, 2004.

Repsch, John. *The Legendary Joe Meek.* Cherry Red Books, 2000.

Rózsa, Miklós. *Double Life: The Autobiography of Miklós Rózsa.* The Baton Press, 1982.

Sandoval, Andrew. *The Monkees*. Backbeat, 2005.

Schary, Dore. *Heyday: An Autobiography*. Little, Brown, 1979.

Sherk, Warren M. 'Paul Beaver: Analogue Synthesist Extraordinaire' from *Film Music 2*. The Film Music Society, 2004.

Smith, Steven C. *A Heart at Fire's Centre: The Life and Music of Bernard Hermann*. University of California Press, 1991.

Smith Brindle, Reginald. *The New Music – The Avant-Garde Since 1945* (2nd edition). Oxford University Press, 1995.

Vail, Mark. *Vintage Synthesizers*. Backbeat, 2000.

Wierzbicki, James. *Louis and Bebe Barron's Forbidden Planet*. The Scarecrow Press, 2005.

Young, Alan and Vail, Mark. *The Hammond Organ: Beauty in the B*. Backbeat, 1997.

Magazines, Newspapers and Periodicals

Billboard
Boazine
Cinefantastique
Downbeat
Electronics and Music Maker
Gramophone
Jimpress
Keyboard
Los Angeles Times
Melody Maker
New Musical Express
New York Times
Ptolemaic Terrascope,
Radio and Television News
Record Collector
Rolling Stone
Sounds
Sound on Sound
SoundTrack
Surface
The Guardian
The Wire
The Cue Sheet
Time Magazine
Variety
Zig Zag

Websites

www.moogarchives.com
www.synthmuseum.com
www.barrygray.co.uk
www.moogfoundation.org
www.RaymondScott.com

Notes about chapter titles

The title of Chapter 1 is taken from a feature about the Telharmonium published in the *Review of Reviews* (1906). Edgard Varèse provided the title for Chapter 2, as quoted in a feature in the *New York Times* dated 16 November 1958. The title for Chapter 3 comes from Louis Barron, speaking to *Keyboard* magazine in 1986. The title of Chapter 6 is taken from *The Song of Wandering Aengus* by W. B. Yeats.

Acknowledgements

Thank you to David Barker at Continuum, who commissioned this book, and thank you also to that nameless (to me) member of the design team who made the cover that I like a lot.

The Sound of Tomorrow would not have been possible without the contributions of all of the people I've spoken to over the years about electronic music: Mark Ayres, Tony Bacon, Adam Barron, Joseph Byrd, John Cary, Dana Countryman, Simeon Coxe, Max Crook, Darren Davison, Jason Draper, Alan Entenman, Joss Goodey, Alan Hamer, Ian Helliwell, Brian Hodgson, Jac Holzman, Chris Kachulis, Mike Kellie, Bernie Krause, Scott Ludwig, Cork Marcheschi, Dick Mills, Ted Pandel, Tom Rhea, Tom Seabrook, David Sheppard, Paul Tanner, Richie Unterberger, Stan Warnow, Dan Wilson, Jeff Winner, Peter Zinovieff.

Ian Helliwell and Jeff Winner were particularly generous with their time and considerable knowledge.

I dedicate this book with love to Madeleine, Georgia and Gideon.

Index

Terms are given in abbreviated form. An 'n.' after a page number indicates an endnote; a page number in italics indicates a photograph.

Abbey Road 188
Abbey Road (Beatles) 204–5
Ace Electronics 117, 209
Ace Tone 117
Adams, Dave 101
Adventures of Twizzle, The 95
adverts 91, 108, 111, 130, 183,
     225n. 16
  humour 106–7
  Ondes Martenot 94
  scope 106, 107, 110, 229n. 89
  sequencers 111
  sound quality 107
  Spinetta 94
  uncertainty 110–11
AEG 22
AES 155
air raid sirens 80–7
alcoholism 35, 215
  theremins 36
All That Fall 78
Ampex 51
Amphitryon 38 79
Anderson, Gerry 95, 184, 185,
    218
Andromeda Strain, The (Wise)
    147
Apthorp, The 109
Arctic 39
Armstrong, Neil A. 42
Armstrong, Neville Spearman 90
Arnold, Kenneth 37
ARPs 208
Art of Noises, The (Russolo) 7

Artists Club 55
Arts Council 193
Atomium 48
  Ondioline 48–9
Ayres, Mark 216, 217

Bacon, Francis 80
'Bad Trip' (Ethix) 142
Baker, John 179, 216
  decline 216
  tape recorders 179
Barrett, Syd 190
Barron, Bebe and Louis 52–3, 57,
    58–9, 60, 65–6, 67–8,
    70–1, 103
  decline 66–7, 68–70, 221–2
  equipment
    limitations 69
    tape recorders 51–2, 53–7,
      61–2, 63–4, 226n. 31
  funding 59, 60
  lawsuit 66
Baxter, Les 42
BBC 74, 77–8, 79, 82, 96–7, 110,
    175–6, 178, 182, 200,
    215
  Clavioline 21
  Novachord 16
  Ondes Martenot 14
  oscillators 77
  punch-up 96
  see also Radiophonic
    Workshop
BBC1 200

BBC2 200
BBC Radiophonic Workshop 180
Beach Boys, The 133, 134
Beatles, The vii, 176
　Moogs 204–5
　scope 188
　tape recorders 177, 188
Beaver, Paul 69, 157–8, 159, 160,
　　　161, 163, 220–1
　decline 167–8
　instruments and 158
　Moogs 161, 162, 163, 164,
　　　165–7
　Novachord 16
Beckett, Samuel 78
Bells of Atlantis (Hugo) 56
　tape recorders 56–7
Bendix 107
Bernauer (Bernelle), Agnes 96
Between the Buttons (Stones)
　　　186
Big Briar 223–4
'Bike' (Pink Floyd) 190
Binder, Edwards and Vaughan
　　　177–8
Birds, The (Hitchcock) 15
Blackwell, Chris 191
Blaine, Hal 159
Blossom, David 143, 145
'Blue Veils and Golden Sands'
　　　(Derbyshire) 180
Borge, Victor 130
Brackett, Charles 35–6
Bratman, Carroll 126–7
Briscoe, Desmond 77–8, 79,
　　　81–2, 180
Britain 73–4, 173
　classical and popular appeal
　　　192–4
Britten, Benjamin 81
Broadway House 3, 4
'Brociliande' (Oram) 184
Brussels World's Fair 48, 82
　Ondioline 48–9

scope 82–3
Bryant, Barry 137
Buchla, Don 169–70
　sequencers 114
Buchla Series 100 169
Buchlas 208
　keyboard 170
　models 169
　scope 170–1
　sequencers 171
Buchla's Box 169
Busoni, Ferruccio 6
Byrd, Joseph 139, 140–2, 220
　Durrett 139–40, 142
Byrds, The 151
　Moogs 151, 164

Cage, John M. 55, 57
　tape recorders 55, 56
Cahill, Thaddeus 1
　Telharmonium xi, 1, 2–5, 6–7
Captain Scarlet 185–6
Carlos, Wendy (Walter) 156, 195,
　　　197
　Moogs 195–7
'Carnival of Light' (Beatles) 178
cartoons 104
Cary, Tristram O. 73, 74–5, 76–7,
　　　82, 83, 180–2, 192, 193,
　　　207, 217–18
　radar operator 76
　synthesizers 206
　tape loops 182
Cathode, Ray 176
Cauldron (Fifty Foot Hose) *144*, 145
　scope 145–6
Ceremony (Spooky Tooth–Henry)
　　　204
*Chants pour les Eternites
　　　Differentes* (Cittanova)
　　　48–9
Chowning, John 223
Christianity 40, 203–4
Cittanova, Darius 48–9

Clair, Leslie 95
Clara Rockmore 10–11
Clavioline 19
  adverts 225n. 16
  brochure *20*
  instruments and 20, 101
    piano and 152
  keyboard
    amplifier/speaker 19
    controls 19–20
  licensing 20–1
  scope 21–2
  Solovox and 19–20
  see also Musitron; Sonocon
Clavivox
  controls 112
  disparities 112–13
  keyboard 112
  limitations 119
  scope 112
Cockerell, David 206
Cocteau, Jean 126
cold war 40
Cole, Hugo 194
Collins, Dorothy 106
Cologne 76
Columbia-Princeton Electronic
    Music Center viii–ix, 195
Columbia Records 23, 141, 196
computers vii, viii
  funding 205–6
  microcomputers 174, 193–4
  scope 175
Concert de Bruits (Schaeffer) 23
concrete music viii–ix, 23, 76, 96,
    178, 188
  Elektronische Musik and 26,
    123
Contemporary Classics 52–3,
    226n. 34
Cooper, Derek 200
Cooper, Giles Stannus 78
Copland, Aaron 124
Corday 42

counter-culture 160, 165, 178
  disparities 161
  Moogs 162, 187–8
Coxe, Simeon 137, 138–9, 220
  oscillators 135–8
Crook, Max 126, 148, 150
  Musitron 125–6
Crosby, Bing 23
'Crucifixion' (Ochs)
  disparities 142
  Durrett 142
  scope 141–2
Cybernetics (Wiener) 54

'Daily Nightly' (Monkees) 165
Daleks' Invasion Earth 2150 AD
    (Flemyng) 185
Dalí, Salvador 35
Davis, Miles 81
Day the Earth Stood Still, The
    (Wise) 40
  scope 41–2
  theremins 40–1, 61, 65
de Forest, Lee 7
'Defecting Grey' (Pretty Things)
    189
Dorbyshire, Delia vii, viii, 84, 86–7,
    175–6, 177, 178, 179,
    180, 191, 192–3, 194
  decline 214–16
  synthesizers 214
Dermatron 130
Destination Moon (Pichel) 38
Deutsch, Herb 120, 152–3
  equipment
    Moogs 154–5, 156
    playing and 154
Dimension 5 129–30
Disagreeable Oyster, The 78
Dissevelt, Tom 49
Doctor Who 85, 96–7, 110, 178–9
  disparities 85–6
  films from 185
  scope 85, 87–8

Dolenz, Micky 164–5
Doors, The 165–6
Doppelgänger (Parrish) 185
Douglas, Chip 165
Dr Zhivago (Lean) 158
drama 58, 67, 77
    science fiction 182–3
    scope 78
drum machines 117
    scope 113, 209
Duncan, Trevor 82
Durrett Electronic Music
        Synthesizer 139–40
    classical and popular appeal
        142
Durrett, Richard 139–40

Edison, Thomas 2
Electric Lucifer, The (Haack) 131,
        169
'Electric to Me Turn' (Haack) 131
Electric Storm, An (White Noise)
        191
    disparities 191, 192
    scope 191–2
electricity generation 1–2
electro-theremin 131–2
    decline 134–5
    disparities 134
    keyboard 132
    mechanics 132
    scope 132–4
Electronde 31
electronic music ix
    classical and popular appeal
        viii–ix, 26, 91–2, 124,
        175–6, 181
    complexity 27
    constraint 209
    disparities 84, 90
    equipment
        creativity and 5–6, 7, 22,
            119, 205
        limitations 81

instruments and 5, 46–7
    limitations 63
    mechanics
        transistors 152
        tubes 7, 152
    people and x
    scope x–xi, 84, 123, 208–9,
        210
    union and 60–1
    see also individual terms
*Electronic Music and Musique
        Concrète* (Judd) 87, 90
*Electronic Record for Children,
        The* (Haack) 130
Electronic Sound (Harrison) 204
Electronics in Music (Judd) 90
Electronium 221, 229n. 95
    co-composition and 115–16
    intelligence and 116–17
    uncertainty 116
    limitations 118, 119
    mechanics 115
    scope 117
Electrosonics 49
Elektra 160
Elektronische Musik viii–ix, 76
    musique concrète and 26, 123
Elizabeth II coronation 74
Elkind, Rachel 196
Emerson, Keith
    Moogs 201–3
    organs 201
Emerson Lake & Palmer 201,
        202–3
EMI 188–9, 190
Emotions (Pretty Things) 189
EMS synthesizers 208
    destruction 217
    disparities 214, 216
    models 206, 207, 216–17
Entenman, Alan 117
Ethix, The 142
Expo 58 48
    Ondioline 48–9

extra-terrestrials 38, 40, 58, 99,
    181–2
    tape recorders 63–4, 65, 182
    theremins 39, 41

Fagandini, Maddalena 176
Fahrenheit 451 (Truffaut) 185
Fairlight 168
'Fantasy' (Fifty Foot Hose) 146
fantasy films 56–7
Festival of Britain 73–4
Fifty Foot Hose 142, 143, *144*,
    145, 146, 190
    break-up 147
    constraint 146
    disparities 219–20
    scope 145–6
film noir 32
films 26–7, 33, 34, 58–9, 158–9,
    187, 223, 224
    funding 57
    Moogs 166, 187–8
    Novachord 32–3
    scope 21
    theremins 36
    see also individual genres
First Moog Quartet 203
Five Million Years to Earth (Baker)
    181
    scope 181–2
    tape loops 182
'Flight of the Bumblebee'
    (Rimsky-Korsakov) 29
flying saucers 37–8, 40
    theremins 41
Forbidden Planet (Wilcox) 57–8,
    60, 62–3, 222
    disparities 65–7
    lawsuit 66
    scope 61
    tape recorders 59, 60–1, 63–4,
    65
Ford, Cathy 218
Ford Startime 133

Freeman, Rod 99
Freud (Huston) 158–9
Frost Amphitheater (Stanford)
    223
futurism xi, 6–7 *see also
    individual terms*

garden sheds vii, 97, 174, 175,
    177, 205–6
Garson, Mort 161
Giants of Steam 86
Gibson, Clavioline 20–1
'Glob Waterfall' 99
    scope 99–100
Goddard, Geoff 101
'Goin' Back' (Byrds) 164
Goldsmith, Jerry 158–9
Goldsmiths College 191, 214
'Good Vibrations' (Beach Boys)
    133, 134
Gordy, Berry 221
Grainer, Ron 86, 87
Grantham, Cyril 21
Gray, Barry 91–3, 94–5, 107–8,
    184, 185–6, 218
    archive 218
    Ondes Martenot 93, 94, 95,
    185, 218
    Spinetta 93, 94
    tape recorders 92, 93
Green, Johnny 59
Green, Richard 202
Green Hornet, The 29
Greenwood, Jonny 14
GRMC 25
Grofé, Ferde
    Novachord 15, 39
    theremins 39
Guernsey 218
Gulbenkian Foundation 183–4,
    213

Haack, Bruce 128–31
    Dermatron 130

Electronium 117
Moogs 169
Hal Hope's Electronic Trio 31–2
Haley, Bill 21
Hammer 181
Hammond
   Novachord 15, 17–18, 152
   organs 201
   Solovox 16–18
Hanert, John 16, 17
Happiest Girl in the World, The
   67
'Happy Whistler, The' (Scott) 114
Harrison, George 204
Hassilev, Alex 161
Hawks, Howard 39
Heavenly Menagerie (Barron) 55
Henahan, Donal 198
Hendrix, Jimi 138
Henry, Hathaway 34
Henry, Pierre 25, 203–4
Herrmann, Bernard 39–40
   theremins 40–1
Hindemith, Paul 14–15
Hitchcock, Alfred 33
   Novachord 32
   theremins 32, 33–5
Hodgson, Brian vii, viii, 85, 86,
      175, 176–7, 178, 191,
      214–15, 216
Hoffman, Dr Samuel J. 32, 42,
      131
   theremins 31–2, 34, 36, 39,
      43, 219
Holzman, Jac 53, 157, 160, 161,
      163
Hope, Hal 31–2
Hornsey College of Art 175
horror films
   Mixtur-Trautonium 15
   scope 183
'Horse' (Zinovieff–Porteous) 217
Hoyle, Fred 182–3
Huebner, Louise 67–8

Hugo, Ian 52, 56
Huston, John 32
Hyman, Dick 201

I Hear a New World (Meek) 99
   disparities 98, 100
   scope 99–100
'I Just Wasn't Made for These
      Times' (Beach Boys)
      133–4
IBC 98
In Sound from Way Out, The
      (Kingsley–Perrey) 128
In a Wild Sanctuary (Beaver–
      Krause) 167
*Individual Note of Music, Sound
      and Electronics, An*
      (Oram) 213
Innocents, The (Clayton) 183
Island Records 191, 203
ITV 74, 88, 200
   adverts 91
I've Got a Secret
   Dermatron 130
   Ondioline 127, 128

Jagger, Mick 186
   Moogs 187, 188
Japanese Fishermen, The 77
Jarre, Maurice 158
jazz 179
   Moogs 203
   scope 147
Jazz in the Garden 203
Jazz of Lights (Hugo) 57
Jennings Univox 21–2
Jenny, Georges 18, 19, 44–5, 48
Jingle Workshop, The 106
jingles 179
   108–9, 111
Johnny Carson show 43
Johnson, Austen (Ginger) Croom
      108
Jones, Brian 180, 186

Journey to the Far Side of the Sun (Parrish) 185
Journey into Space 77
Judd, Fred 88–90, 91
  decline 218
  synthesizers *89*, 91
  tape recorders 90–1

Kachulis, Chris 130, 131
Kaleidophon 191
Kaleidoscopic Vibrations (Kingsley–Perry) 168–9
Kapp Records 137
Kember, Pete 215–16
Kid Baltan 49
Kingsley, Gershon 128
  Moogs 168, 169, 203
Kneale, Nigel 82
Kooper, Al 128
Korg 209
Krause, Bernie 159–60, 161, 163, 220, 221
  decline 167–8
  Moogs 160, 161, 162, 163–4, 166–7, 204

Lambert, Verity 86
'L'âme des Poètes' 46
Lansdowne 98
Ledrut, Jean 218–19
Leigh, Roberta 88, 95
Lenin, Vladimir Ilyich 10
Leslie, Desmond 96–7, 218
  punch-up 96
Levin, Bernard 96
Levindis, Dimitri 12
light projects 175, 183
Lincoln-Mercury Startime 133
Listen, Move and Dance 182
Logan's Run (Anderson) 159
Lost in Space 42
Lost Weekend, The (Wilder) 35
  theremins 35–6, 37
Lothar and The Hand People 138

Moogs 168
Love, Mike 134
'Lucky Man' (Emerson Lake & Palmer) 201
Ludwig, Scott 148, 149, 150
  Moogs *149*, 149–50
  Sonocon 148–9
Luening, Otto viii–ix
Lumpy Gravy (Zappa) 147–8
'Lunarville 7 – Suite' (Gray) 185–6
Lynn, Vera 16

'Ma Maison' 46
MacPherson, Sandy 21
Maestrovox 21–2
Magnetic Monster (Siodmak) 158
Magnetophon 22
Maltese Falcon, The (Huston) 32
Manzarek, Ray 165–6
Marcheschi, Louis (Cork) 142–3, *144*, 145, 146, 220
Margouleff, Robert 168
Marks, Larry 142
Marly, Florence 68
Mars 39
Martenot, Maurice 11
  Ondes Martenot 11–12, 14
Martin, Constant 19–20
Martin, George 200
  tape loops 176
Martin, Steve 223
Maxwell House 110–11, 229n. 89
McCartney, Paul vii, viii–ix, 175, 176–7
McGuffie, Bill 21
McGuinn, Roger 151
  Moogs 151, 164
McWhinnie, Donald 78
Meek, Joe 97–100, 101
  decline 219
  lawsuit 218–19
  tape recorders 98
Mellé, Gil 147
Melodia 152

Mercury 145
Messiaen, Olivier 14
MGM 59
    funding 59–60
    tape recorders 60–1
Miller Organ Company 93
Million Volt Light and Sound Rave
        177–8
Mills, Dick 79, 86, 177, 178–9
Mills College Tape Music Center
        143, 145, 159–60
'Minatour, The' (Hyman) 201
Minimoogs 209, 223–4
Mixtur-Trautonium 15
MOMA 202–3
Monkees, The 164–5
Monte, Rudy 60–1
Monterey festival
    Moogs 151, 162, 163
    scope 162–3
Moog (Fjellestad) 224
Moog (Hyman) 201
Moog, Bob 43–4, 105, 119–20,
        135, 152–3, 155, 161,
        169–70, 195, 224
    customer interaction 155
    decline 223
    electro-theremin 134
    equipment
        Moogs 154–5, 156
        playing and 154
    technophobia and ix–x
Moog 900 Series
    catalogue 157
    demonstration record 156–7
    scope 156
Moog Melodia 152
'Moog Raga' (Byrds) 164
Moog theremins 44
    disparities 134
    models 152
'Moogies Bloogies' (Newley) 176
Moogs 109, 111, 149–50, 159,
        160, 169, 202, 208

catalogue 153p.
classical and popular appeal
        196, 197, 198, 199
creativity and 205
customer interaction 155
decline 167–8
disparities 151–2, 162, 165–6,
        187–8, 199–200, 201–2,
        223
keyboard 154, 170
limitations 161, 166, 203
models 156–7, 209, 223–4
Ondioline and 128
originality and 204
oscillators 166
playing *149*, 150, 200, 202–3
    limitations 205
prototypes 153–4, 155
scope 135, 154–5, 162, 163–5,
        166–7, 168–9, 195–7,
        198–9, 200–1, 203,
        204–5, 224
stability
    dropping and 161
    leaving on and 231n. 145
summer school 156
uncertainty 198
'More' (Winding) 127–8
Morrison, Jim 166
Moskowitz, Dorothy 140–1
Mothers of Invention, The 148
Motown 221
    Moogs 165
Mr Ondioline
    mechanics 47
    mystery and 47–8
Mr Ondioline (persona) 47
    mystery and 47–8
Mullin, Jack 22–3
Musaire 29–31, *30*
Music for Heavenly Bodies
        (Montero–Tanner) 132
Music Out of the Moon
        (Hoffman) 42

theremins 42
Music for Peace of Mind
(Hoffman) 43
Musical Research 93
musicians union 60–1
musique concrète viii–ix, 23, 76,
96, 178, 188
Elektronische Musik and 26,
123
Musitron 125
scope 126
secrecy 125–6
My Favorite Martian 132
mysticism 5

National Theatre storeroom 217
Nayfack, Nicholas 59
Nelson, Esther 129
New Atlantis (Bacon) 80
New Music 1900/60, The
(Copland) 124
New York 1–2, 3
World's Fair 15
Newley, Anthony 176
Nice, The 202
Nin, Anaïs 52–3, 56
'No Time Like the Right Time'
(Blues Project) 128
Nonesuch 160
*Nonesuch Guide to Electronic
Music, The*
(Beaver–Krause)
booklet 163
Moog 163–4
scope 163
nostalgia 21
Notorious Byrd Brothers, The
(Byrds) 164
Novachord 15, 39
failure 15–16
limitations 15, 152
publicity 15
scope 15, 16, 17–18, 21, 32–3
theremins and 42–3

NWDR 26
Nyby, Christian 39

oast house 81
Oberheim, Tom 139
Ochs, Phil 141–2
decline 142
Durrett 142
Ondes Martenot 11, 95, 109,
185, 218
classical instruments and 14
limitations 14, 21
playing 12, 13
controls 13
keyboard 12, 13
ribbon 12, 13
prototypes 12
scope 12–13, 14, 93, 94
speaker 13–14
theremins and 12
Ondioline 18, 44–5, 47, 48–9,
105, 127–8
amplifier/speaker 18
braid 18
controls 19
failure 19, 219
instruments and 46, 115, 127
keyboard 18
mechanics 18
Moogs and 128
multi-tracking 47
playing 45, 46
instruments and 19
scope 126–7
Oram, Daphne 73, 74–5, 76–7,
78, 79, 80–1, 83, 182–3,
192, 193, 213
decline 184, 213–14
funding 183–4, 214
Oramics x, 118, 184, 213, 214
waveform 75, 83
Oramics x
limitations 118, 184, 213, 214
organs 201

'Oscillations' (Silver Apples) 137
oscillators 77, 123, 135, 187
 disparities 135–6, 137, 190
 instruments and 136–7
 limitations 137–8, 166
 playing 136
 scope 136
 see also Durrett Electronic
  Music Synthesizer;
  electro-theremin
Overland Stage Electric Band,
 The 135

Pandel, Ted 129
 Dermatron 130
Paris 76
PDP-8 174, 193–4
Pearlman, Alan R. 208
Peopleodeon 130
Pepsi Cola 108
Performance (Cammell–Roeg)
 187
 Moogs 187–8
Perfume Set to Music (Hoffman)
 42
 sponsorship 42
 theremins 42–3
Perrey, Jean-Jacques ix, 49, 219
 decline 219
 Moogs 168
 mystery and 47–8
 Ondioline 18, 44–5, 46, 47, 48,
  105, 115, 126–7, 128,
  219
Pet Sounds (Beach Boys) 133–4
Philips Electronics 49
Piaf, Edith 126
Pink Floyd 189–90
 scope 190–1
Pink Floyd (Pink Floyd) 189–90
 scope 190
pioneers
 playing and 210
 technology and 210–11

 see also individual terms
Piper at the Gates of Dawn, The
 (Pink Floyd) 189–90
 scope 190
*Pisces, Aquarius, Capricorn &
 Jones Ltd.* (Monkees)
 165
'Please Go Home' (Stones) 186
Pleasures of the Harbor (Ochs)
 disparities 142
 Durrett 142
 scope 141–2
Poème électronique (Varèse)
 48–9, 142–3
pop and rock 97, 180, 186
 disparities 150, 190–1, 219–20
 Moogs 199–200
 scope 125, 162–3, 166, 210
 synthesizers 114
 see also individual names;
  counter-culture
'Popcorn' (Kingsley) 169, 203
'Powerhouse' 104
Prelude au Sommeil (Perrey) 115
Pretty Things, The 189
Project of Music for Magnetic
 Tape 55, 56
Psychedelic Percussion (Blaine)
 159
psychological films 33, 36–7, 158
 scope 183
 theremins 32, 33–6, 37
puppetry 88, 95, 185, 218
 scope 184, 185
Putney (London) vii, 174, 205–6,
 217
Putney, The
 disparities 206–8
 mechanics 206

Quatermass and the Pit (film)
 181
 scope 181–2
 tape loops 182

Quatermass and the Pit (TV) 82
Queen Elizabeth Hall (London) 193
   computers 193–4

Raaymakers, Dick 49
radio 21, 217
   drama 77, 78
   Ondes Martenot 12, 14
   Ondioline 44, 48
   science fiction 77
   scope 179–80
   tape recorders 22–3
   theremins 29
Radio Frankfurt 22–3
Radio and Television News 44
Radiohead 14
Radiophonic Workshop viii, 79, 85, 87, 176–7, 181, 216
   archive 216
   classical and popular appeal 192–3
   closure 216
   constraint 79, 84, 214–15
   disparities 78, 84–6, 179, 180
   equipment 79–80
   etymology 80
   limitations 86
   scope 80–2, 83–4, 85, 86, 87, 88, 178–80, 216
Ragnarok Electronic Funk (Beaver–Krause) 167
Ramones ix
Raymond Scott Quintette 104
RCA 10, 29–30, *30*
Rebecca (Hitchcock) 32
Record Plant 138
records 42, 52–3, 67–8, 91, 99, 101, 104, 131, 145, 148–9, 159, 189–90, 196, 203–4, 226n. 34
   booklet 163
   Buchlas 170–1
   Clavioline 101

disparities 98, 130, 131, 135, 140–1, 142, 147–8, 160–1, 162, 171, 186–7, 191, 192, 196, 197–8, 220
Durrett 142
electro-theremin 132, 133–4
failure 53
instruments and 99
lawsuit 218–19
limitations 114, 123–4
Moogs 159, 162, 163–4, 165–7, 168–9, 196–7, 198–9, 201–2, 203, 204–5
Novachord 16
Ondioline 46, 47–8, 115, 127–8
oscillators 137, 187
scope 23, 26, 42, 49–50, 99–100, 101, 113, 125, 129–30, 138, 141–3, 145–6, 147, 163, 184–5, 186, 188, 189, 190, 191–2
sequencers 114
tape recorders 176, 177, 187, 188
theremins 42–3, 219
Red House, The (Daves) 36–7
   theremins 37
'Reflections' (Ross and Supremes) 165
Reinhardt, Django 46
relaxation music 115, 220
   Ondioline 115
   scope 43, 113, 114–15
   sequencers 114
Revel, Harry 42
'Revolution 9' (Beatles) 188
Revolver (Beatles) 177
Rhea, Tom 109, 118, 229n. 88
Rhythm Ace 117
Richards, Emil 159

Richards, Keith 186
Rimsky-Korsakov, Nikolai 29
robots 58, 67
   tape recorders 63
   theremins 41
rock *see* pop and rock
rock 'n' roll 124–5 *see also*
   individual names
Rockets in Ursa Major 182–3
Rocketship X-M (Neumann) 38–9
   Novachord 39
   theremins 39
Rockmore, Clara 34
Roland 209
Rolling Stones, The 180, 190
   disparities 186–7
   Moogs 187
   scope 186
Roosevelt, Franklin D. 15
Rose, David 60
Roswell Incident 37–8
Roundhouse Theatre 177–8
Royal Festival Hall (London) 202
Rózsa, Miklós 33, 34, 158
   theremins 33–5, 36
RTF 25
'Runaway' (Shannon) 125
Rundfunkversuchstelle 14
Russolo, Luigi 7

Safe as Milk (Beefheart) 219
Sala, Oskar 15
Same Trade as Mozart, The 200
San Francisco 143, 145
San Francisco Tape Music Center
   143, 145, 169
Saucerful of Secrets, A (Pink
   Floyd) 190
Schaeffer, Pierre viii–ix, 23, 24–5,
   49
   tape recorders 24, 25
Schary, Dore 59
science fiction drama 182–3
science fiction films 38–9, 40,

   57–8, 60, 62–3, 68, 158,
   159, 181, 185, 222
   constraint 69–70
   disparities 65–7, 147
   funding
      scope 59
      uncertainty 59–60
   lawsuit 66
   Novachord 39
   Ondes Martenot 185
   scope 38, 41–2, 57, 61, 65,
      181–2
   tape recorders 59, 60–1, 63–4,
      65, 182
   theremins xi, 39, 40–1, 61, 65
science fiction radio 77
science fiction TV 42, 85, 88, 95,
   96–7, 110, 178–9, 218
   disparities 85–6
   electro-theremin 132
   scope 82, 85, 87–8, 185–6
Science Museum x, 214
Scott, Raymond 69, 103–4,
   105–8, 111–12, *121*, 221
   Clavivox 112–13, 119
   controls 104–5
   decline 118, 119, 120–2, 221
   Electronium 115–18, 119, 221
   secrecy and 118, 119
   sequencers 113, 114
   tape recorders 104
Screen Gems 111
Sear, Walter 134
secrecy 118–19, 125–6
Seduction through Witchcraft
   (Huebner) 67–8
Selmer *20*, 20–1, 225n. 16
Selznick, David O.
   psychoanalysis 33
   theremins 33–5
Sender, Ramon 70, 169
sequencers 111
   scope 113, 114, 171, 209
   see also Electronium

SF Sorrow (Pretty Things) 189
*Sgt. Pepper's Lonely Hearts Club
    Band* (Beatles) 188
Shannon, Del 125, 126
    Musitron 126
Siday, Eric 69, 108–12, 221
    Moogs 109, 155–6, 160
    Ondes Martenot 109
    violin 108
Sideman 113
Silver Apples 135, 137, 190
    disparities 219–20
    oscillators 136–8
    scope 138
Silver Apples (Silver Apples) 137
Silver Apples of the Moon
    (Subotnick) 135
    Buchlas 170–1
    disparities 171
    scope 163
Simeon
    destruction 220
    disparities 136–7
    limitations 137–8
*Sketch of a New Esthetic of
    Music* (Busoni) 6
Smart, Harold 21
Smith, Norman 188–9
Society for the Promotion of New
    Music 193
Solovox
    Clavioline and 19–20
    keyboard 17
    piano and
        amplifier/speaker 17
        disparities 152
        keyboard 17
    scope 16–18, 21–2
'Song of the Second Moon'
    (Electrosonics) 49–50
Sonocon 148–9
Soothing Sounds for Baby (Scott)
    115
    limitations 114

scope 113
sequencers 114
Soul Surfin' (Winding) 127–8
Sound Portraits 52–3, 226n. 34
Sounds of Tomorrow, The 149,
    230n. 130
    break-up 150
    disparities 150
    instruments and 148
    Moogs *149*, 150
    Sonocon 148–9
Space Boy (Marly) 68
Space Hymn (Hand People) 138
'Space Odyssey' (Byrds) 164
Space Patrol 88
space travel 38–9, 57–8, 69–70,
    77, 98, 99–101, 107, 181,
    218
    oscillators 77
    tape recorders 64
    theremins 39, 42
'Spaced' (Beaver–Krause) 167
Spellbound (Hitchcock) 33, 158
    theremins 32, 33–5, 36, 37
Spinetta
    failure 94
    scope 93, 94
Spooky Tooth 203, 204
Sprite 106–7
Stalling, Carl 104
Stanford University 223
*Steamed Spring Vegetable Pie,
    A* 139
Still Point (Oram) 73
Stockhausen, Karlheinz viii–ix, 26
Strange Days (Doors) 165–6
Stratton-Smith, Tony 202
street lighting 1–2
Stripper, The (Rose) 60
Subotnick, Morton 120–1, 169,
    170
summer school 156
Sundown (Hathaway) 34
Switched-On Bach (Carlos) 196

disparities 196, 197–8
  Moogs 196–7, 198–9, 201–2
Symphonic Poem for Solo
    Ondes Musicales and
    Orchestra (Levindis) 12
synthesizers 89, 91
  scope 209–11
  tape recorders and xi, 210
  see also individual terms
Synthi 100 217

Tanner, Dr Paul 131
  electro-theremin 131–5
tape 226n. 32
tape loops 176
  limitations 113–14
  scope 182
tape recorders 22, 25–6, 51–2,
    57, 59, 60, 92, 93, 98,
    104, 123, 179, 187, 188,
    226n. 31
  classical and popular appeal
    24
  disparities 190
  editing xi, 24, 25
  funding 55
  humour 63
  limitations 26, 56–7, 64, 174
  mechanics
    disparities 61–2
    limitations 55, 63
    scope 54–5
  scope 22–3, 24, 53–4, 55–6,
    62, 63–4, 65, 76, 90–1,
    177
  stop-and-start 23–4
  synthesizers and 210
  tape loops 113–14, 176, 182
  union and 60–1
tape splicing 24
  scope 25
  speed and 25
  synthesizers and xi
Taubmann, Martin 31

Taylor, Danny 137
  oscillators 136–7
technophobia ix–x, 4–5
telephones 2, 3, 4
  complexity 2
  subscription 2–3
Telharmonium xi, 1, 3
  classical and popular appeal 3
  failure 6–7
  funding 3
  instruments and 3
    technophobia 4–5
  keyboard 1
  mechanics 2
    limitations 4
  patents 1
  prototypes 3
  scope 3–4, 5
  telephones 2–3, 4
'Telstar' (Tornados) 101, 218–19
  Clavioline 101
  lawsuit 218–19
  scope 101
Telstar 1 100–1
Tempest, The (Shakespeare) 58
That Was the Week That Was 96
Their Satanic Majesties Request
    (Stones)
  disparities 186–7
  oscillators 187
  tape recorders 187
Theremin (Martin) 223
Theremin, Leon 8, 31, 32, 222–3
  decline 222
  theremins 8, 9, 10–11
theremins xi, 8, 29, 30, 32, 33–4,
    42, 43
  antennae 8–9
  decline 10, 32, 134–5
  disparities 7–8, 9
  easy listening 43
  Electronde and 31
  instruments and 11, 35, 36,
    40, 41, 61, 65

mechanics 8
Novachord and 42–3
Ondes Martenot and 12
patent 10
playing 9, 31, 43
    scope 30–2
    skill 9–10, 11
    scope 7, 8, 10–11, 21, 29–30,
        34–6, 37, 39, 40–1, 43,
        219
    see also electro-theremin;
        Moog theremins
Thing from Another World, The
    (Nyby) 39
3M 226n. 32
'Time Beat' (Cathode) 176
Tiomkin, Dimitri 39
Titterton, Ralph 218
Tome V1 (Mellé) 147
'Tomorrow Never Knows'
    (Beatles) 177
Tomorrow's World 200–1
Torchy the Battery Boy 95
Tornados, The 101
Trautonium 14–15
    limitations 21
    Mixtur-Trautonium 15
    playing 14
Trautwein, Friedrich 14
Treblico, Leonard 82
Trenet, Charles 45–6
    Ondioline 46
Trumansburg factory 155
    summer school 156
Turangalîla Symphony (Messiaen)
    14
TV 21, 49, 74, 79, 95, 110, 147,
    182, 184, 200
    adverts 91, 94, 106–7, 130,
        183
    Dermatron 130
    electro-theremin 133
    Moogs 166, 200–1
    Ondioline 127, 128

punch-up 96
science fiction 82, 85–6,
    87–8, 95, 96–7, 110, 132,
    178–9, 185–6, 218
    scope 179–80
    theremins 42, 43
Twain, Mark 4

UCLA 139
UFO 218
UFOs 37–8, 40
    theremins 41
union 60–1
Unit Delta Plus vii, 175, 176–7,
    178
    break-up viii, 176
    classical and popular appeal
        175–6
    computers 175
    disparities 175
United States of America, The
    140, 190
    break-up 141
    classical and popular appeal
        138–9
    disparities 140–1, 219–20
    Durrell 140
    instruments and 140
    United States of America, The
        140–1
University of Toronto Electronic
    Music Studio 154–5
Ussachevsky, Vladimir viii–ix
    Moogs 154

Varèse, Edgard 48–9, 142–3
VCS 3
    disparities 206–8
    mechanics 206
Vickers, Mike 200, 202, 204
Vicks 106
Vidal, Gore 67
Vim 107
Vincent, Gene 81

Visit to a Small Planet, A 67
Vorhaus, David 191

WABC 12
Warnow, Stan 120–1
Watermill Theatre (Newbury) 175
Way-Out Record for Children, The
  (Nelson–Haack) 130
WCKY 108
weather balloon 139
Weavers, The 159
'We'll Meet Again' (Lynn) 16
We're Only In It For the Money
  (Mothers of Invention)
  148
Weiss, Jon 187
Westinghouse Electric Company
  111
White Noise 191
  disparities 191, 192
  scope 191–2
Whiteley, Joseph 11, 29–31, *30*
Wiener, Norbert 54
Wilcox, Fred M. 57
Wilder, Billy 35
Williams, Paul 55
Williams, Tennessee 226n. 34
Williams Mix (Cage) 55–6
Wilson, Brian 133, 134
Winding, Kai C. 127–8
Windmill Theatre (Newbury)
  175–6

With a Little Help from My
  Friends 200
Woman's Hour 179
Wood, Robin 217
World of Sound, The 121
World's Fair (Brussels) 48
  Ondioline 48–9
  scope 82–3
World's Fair (New York) 15
Wurlitzer 113

Yamaha 209
Yeats, W. B. 135
'Yesterday' (Beatles) vii
  disparities 176–7
Yorkshire TV 200
Young, Arthur 16
Young, LaMonte 139

Zappa, Frank 147–8
Zinovieff, Peter vii, viii, 173–4,
  175, 177, 181, 193, 207,
  217
  computers vii, viii, 174, 193–4,
  205–6
  sequencers 114
  synthesizers 206
  tape recorders 174
Zodiac, The (Garson)
  disparities 160–1, 162
  Moogs 159, 162